LET'S READ

★ *A Linguistic Approach* ★

LET'S READ

A Linguistic Approach

by

Leonard Bloomfield

&

Clarence L. Barnhart

Detroit • WAYNE STATE UNIVERSITY PRESS

eleventh impression, January 1982

ISBN 0-8143-1115-6

LIBRARY OF CONGRESS CATALOG CARD NUMBER 61-9080

*To my mother, Frances Barnhart, who read to me
and taught me to read, and to the memory of
Leonard Bloomfield, who evolved this system by which
countless children can learn to read.*

C.L.B

Contents

ABCDEFGHIJKLMNOPQRSTUVWXYZABCDEFGHIJKLMNOPQRSTUVWXYZABCDEFGHIJKLMNO

THE BLOOMFIELD
SYSTEM

JKLMNOPQRSTUVWXYZABCDEFGHIJKLMNOPQRSTUVWXYZABCDEFGHIJKLMNOPQRSTUVW

INTRODUCTION FOR PARENTS
by Clarence L. Barnhart

L<small>EONARD</small> B<small>LOOMFIELD</small> created this system of teaching reading so that he could teach his boys to read before the boys started school. You, too, can teach your boy or girl to read. All his life your child can profit by the help you give him for a few moments each day. Within a few months he can know his ABC's and over 300 words, which he will spell and read whenever he sees them. By the end of a year he may know how to read three or four thousand words.

You should not, however, teach your child until he wants to read, just as he wants to walk or talk. Much of the process of learning to read can give great satisfaction to your child, because he will see his own progress and take pride in his achievement. If your child is interested in the shape of letters and is anxious to recognize words, he is ready to learn. You may easily satisfy his curiosity when he begins to show an interest in reading by following a carefully worked out program of teaching especially suited to individual instruction.

Under no circumstances should you start to teach your child to read until he has the necessary muscular skills to see the small distinctions between the letters of the alphabet. You can tell he has the necessary muscular coordination when you notice that he can button his clothes or see and pick up a pin on the floor.

Once your child wants to read and has the necessary muscular skills, you need only the desire on your part to teach him and a set of soundly and skillfully constructed lessons. With this equipment you can start your child on the great adventure of learning to read.

The lessons in this book were planned by Leonard Bloomfield, one of the great linguists of our time. Using scientific principles, Leonard Bloomfield devised these reading lessons so that any child who knows how to talk may learn to read in the most efficient way. By following his methods your child will learn to pay attention to differences between similar words and will learn to say the words he needs to know. His school work will become easier for him because of the training you give him.

If you teach your child to read, you will share with him his first great intellectual experience. You will see him safely launched and able to develop his capacities to their limit.

The task is not a difficult one. You need to spend only ten or fifteen minutes a day teaching. In this book the lessons for the child are printed in big type. You need only to point to each word and ask the child to say it. He should be able to recognize and say each word in the list without hesitation before going on to the next list. You may find it helpful to use a blackboard and chalk, or a pencil (or a crayon) and a sheet of paper. But above all, you will need patience. The time you spend together will give you satisfaction and your child a sense of achievement—and the ability to read.

INTRODUCTION FOR TEACHERS
by Robert C. Pooley

IT IS GENERALLY conceded in the society of Western culture that ability to read is the foundation of our scheme of education. Our heritage of humane letters, of social theory, and of scientific discovery is preserved in manuscript or in print; our daily advances in all the branches of human endeavor are recorded in current journals; and the blueprint of our future, so far as there is one, can be traced, even if faintly, only from an infinite number of written data. It follows, then, that in our society he who runs *must* read, or be left at the starting line. It follows, furthermore, that teaching young children to read is an enterprise of central concern to our entire culture. Anyone who offers to society a method by which this fundamental task may be performed effectively and economically is surely entitled to a respectful hearing and a period of trial in which to substantiate his claims in actual use.

In 1955 *Why Johnny Can't Read* appeared, a book which aroused widespread public interest and a good deal of educational controversy. Its author, Rudolph Flesch, is an Austrian refugee who had previously earned attention and praise for teaching a system by which government agencies might write English which could be generally understood. The reason for the excitement over Dr. Flesch's book was not that he offered a new approach to the teaching of reading; indeed, he advocated a return to materials and methods long since discarded. The reason was that he voiced in concrete terms a vaguely felt but widely experienced dissatisfaction with current instruction in reading in the elementary schools of our country. It was easy to prove, as many educators hastened to do, that many Johnnies did learn to read, and to read very well, at an early age. But there was equally available evidence from teachers in the upper grades, in high schools, and even in colleges that large numbers of students in their classes were unable to read at a level essential to success in their daily assignments. There developed, and are still developing, "reading clinics," staffed by "reading specialists," to attempt to remedy the defects of early instruction. With the known range of human ability to learn, from imbecile to genius, no sane person would expect any method or system of instruction to turn out a uniform product. But if a system of instruction, based upon certain premises and procedures, is completely successful with only a small proportion of the students taught by it, or is only partially successful with a larger number, it is quite rightly subjected to query and investigation, and to the competition of alternate methods and procedures.

It was Dr. Flesch's contention that Johnny failed to learn to read because he was taught by a system which focused attention primarily upon the printed forms of words to the neglect of the sound of words. To remedy this neglect, Dr. Flesch advocated a return to a method known as *phonics*, a system of teaching separate sounds for separate letters as found in the regular spelling of words. Dr. Flesch wrote "Teach the child what each letter stands for and he can read." This system had been in wide use at the turn of the century, but with the intensive research into reading during the first quarter of the twentieth century it was gradually abandoned because of increasingly obvious defects and shortcomings. Nevertheless, it seems apparent today that in throwing out phonics, the educational theorists threw out the baby with the bath water. There *is* an essential and pedagogically sound relationship between the look of words and the sound of words. Learning to read involves more than identifying by eye alone the letter-patterns which make up a printed word. The sounds of words are equally important to the identification of meaning and consequent growth in reading vocabulary. Dr. Flesch was on valid ground in pointing out the significance of sound in the process of deriving meaning from printed symbols. What Dr. Flesch lacked, or at least did not utilize, was a command of the science of linguistics, which would have provided him with an understanding of the relationship between sound and written form. His protest against current methodology was supported by much specific evidence, but his solution was inadequate and did not strike at the heart of the problem.

What Dr. Flesch did not use is, in this book, the center of the project. Bloomfield and Barnhart offer a method of teaching reading whose central thesis is that an inseparable relationship exists between the words as printed and the sounds for which the letters are conventional signs, and that to learn to convert letters to meaning requires from the start a concentration upon letter and sound to bring about as rapidly as possible an automatic association between them. As the discerning reader will at once discover, the basic procedure of the method offered by Bloomfield and Barnhart is to concentrate upon establishing patterns of letters and sounds regardless of meaning, to provide the child with a constantly growing set of sound-letter constants by means of which he converts letters to sounds and almost automatically converts sounds to meaningful words. Despite some attention to word sounds, the now widely-used systems of reading induce the learner to make immediate associations between letters and meaning with the eye alone (on the theory that the meaning supplies the sounds, rather than the sounds the meaning) so that the child gains a rapidly growing "reading vocabulary" but is increasingly dependent upon the method to supply the associations between letters and meaning. The method of Bloomfield and Barnhart is to free the child from such dependence as early as possible.

By teaching him to associate letters and sounds in a vast number of different patterns, at first indifferent to his recognition of meaning, he is advanced step by step in the use of a tool to convert letters to sounds so effectively that in short time he has the equipment to convert any new written word to sounds, and so to meaning, thus freeing himself more and more from any artificial association of written form and meaning.

It should be clear by now that the approach to teaching children to read offered by this book is revolutionary in theory, and largely untried in practice. It is not in any way a minor modification of currently used methods. It will require the understanding and acceptance of principles of linguistic theory as yet known to very few of those who teach, or who direct teaching, in the elementary grades. For a fair trial it will need dedicated and unusually able teachers, ready and willing to be trained in entirely new concepts and procedures, and strong enough to continue under fire of criticism and ridicule.

If the system of reading advocated by Bloomfield and Barnhart in this book should attract widespread attention, or even more, if the method when employed should prove encouragingly successful, it will be severely challenged. Years of research have gone into the development of the present system of reading. Vast sums of money have been spent to produce the current series of reading books, with their teachers' manuals, their guides to students, and their whole apparatus of accompanying materials. Generations of teachers have been trained to use these materials, and will be reluctant to adopt a new methodology.

Nothing in the foregoing remarks should be construed as a claim that the Bloomfield-Barnhart system of reading instruction is proved to be better than any existing system. The point of this introduction is to invite educators to view an exciting and potentially rewarding prospect. Described in this book is a way to teach reading based upon entirely new pedagogical principles, derived from scientific information which has not previously been so directly applied to the teaching of reading. It is a path not yet taken. To the adventurous educator this is the challenge; the path to reading skill offered in this book may be shorter, more direct, and more pleasant to follow than those now in use. The pioneers who explore this path and blaze the trail for others have the prospect of making educational history. They will find as the incentives to exploration:

(1) A system of reading which combines the resources of eye and ear in units of sight and sound as basic elements of learning.

(2) A system in which every new step is not the learning of isolated words, but enlargement of the power to identify words from patterns of letters.

(3) A system in which the translation of letters into sounds and sounds into meaning becomes increasingly automatic.

(4) A system, therefore, which cumulatively builds up the child's independence and competence, providing him with the tools to tackle unknown words by a process of sight-sound-meaning which grows more effective the more it is used.

The authors present to the educational world this challenge and invitation: Here is a possible answer to some of the unanswered problems of current reading instruction. Give it a fair trial under conditions parallel to those offered to students first learning to read by any method, in the hands of teachers who are sincerely interested in teaching children to read, and allow sufficient time for the method to be fully developed. There could be a reward beyond expectations.

This introduction would be incomplete without a word concerning the authors of this book. Their names are honored in linguistic circles and their scholarly works are standard in their fields. But as they may not be known as well to those who teach or who direct teaching in the elementary schools, these biographical data are added.

Leonard Bloomfield, who died in 1949 at the age of 62 years, was at his death Sterling Professor of Linguistics at Yale University. Called to this position from the University of Chicago in 1940, where he had been chairman of the Department of Linguistics, he had taught earlier on the faculties of the University of Wisconsin, the University of Illinois, and Ohio State University. Honored by all who were students of the science of language, Dr. Bloomfield was a recognized authority by reason of his writings, particularly his book *Language*, published in 1933. It was while he was at the University of Chicago that his inquiring mind led him to look into the field of reading, in which he felt the science of linguistics had a fundamental contribution to make. His interest in this project continued to his death. The present writer was invited in the fall of 1948 to lunch with Bloomfield and Barnhart to discuss ways of presenting Dr. Bloomfield's ideas to the educational world.

Clarence L. Barnhart is one of the leading lexicographers of the English language and has been for many years intimately concerned with the education of elementary school children in word learning. Together with the late Dr. E. L. Thorndike he devised, and continues to be editor of, *The Thorndike-Barnhart Beginning Dictionary*, 1945; *The Thorndike-Barnhart Junior Dictionary*, 1952; *The Thorndike-Barnhart High School Dictionary*, 1952; and *The Thorndike-Barnhart Advanced Junior Dictionary*, 1957. Scholars constantly use his many reference works, particularly the *New Century Handbook of English Literature*. The Thorndike-Barnhart dictionaries made notable contributions to elementary education by creating a new phonetic key which made pronunciation of new words simple and clear, by classifying words according to their frequency of use in the vocabularies of children, and by arranging the definitions of words according to frequency in current use rather than in historical order. By this system a child sees first the most common and frequent meaning of a word, and last the least common meaning.

Authoritative scholarship is an assurance to the reader that his earnest attention is not wasted. But the proof of the pudding is in the eating. The adventurous are invited to fall to.

THE STORY OF THE BLOOMFIELD SYSTEM
by Clarence L. Barnhart

Twenty-three years ago Leonard Bloomfield handed me a copy of his reading system from a file drawer in his study to use in training my son to read. Bloomfield told me that he had devised the system because the methods used in the schools were non-scientific in nature and ignored the fundamental principles of the scientific study of language developed during the last 150 years. He felt that a linguistic system of teaching reading would be of great advantage to both teacher and pupil. One of his first letters to me with regard to the reading system is dated November 7, 1937, and says in part:

> Thank you for mimeographed copies of the essay on reading; it was very good of you to have them made. I hope success in teaching your little son will be good enough to repay the labor and expense that you put into this manifolding . . . .
>
> . . . Without hope of publication, I wrote out what I thought and what I had done with my boy. If there is any chance of publication, the present essay could form the basis of the teacher's handbook, and a child's reader, containing material very much like the illustrative sentences now given, would have to be added.
>
> My son went from the one-syllable reading that is in the essay, directly to ordinary readers; probably no change in later readers would be needed, once the pupils had learned what is in the essay. On the other hand, it might turn out that a systematized vocabulary in later reading would speed things up.
>
> If you think the thing has commercial possibilities, perhaps the thing should also be tried out in a school.

Bloomfield's system of teaching reading is a linguistic system. Essentially, a linguistic system of teaching reading separates the problem of the study of word-form from the study of word-meaning. Most children, when they enter school, know at least 5,000 words;[1] many of them know 10,000 words; and in the opinion of some investigators, some know as many as 20,000 or 25,000 words. The child's knowledge of words and their meanings is much more widespread when he enters school that most teachers and parents realize. The child has had five or six years' experience in acquiring meanings, and he uses them readily

---

1. Burleigh H. Shibles, "How Many Words Does a First Grade Child Know?" *The Elementary English Journal*, XLI, No. 1 (January 1959), 42-47.

in many kinds of syntactical patterns. He knows how to speak the English language, but he does not know how to read the forms of words. These forms are usually presented in a hit-or-miss fashion dependent upon the content of the various stories that are presented to him. Bloomfield felt that new words should be presented according to their form; that is, regular forms should be presented first, irregular forms only later. By getting all the associated facts together, the child's power to recognize words in his reading is greatly facilitated. After learning the first list or two, a child should be able to learn a whole list of words almost as rapidly as he learns one word now by means of the word method. In Bloomfield's system the child is engaged in relating the sound of a word to the form of the word in print. He does not need phonics instruction because like words are arranged together so that the pattern of the words is obvious. The child learns to read without a vast array of helps of one kind or another. These helps are not needed if the facts of the language are taken adequately into consideration.

In his essay (see pages 19-42), Professor Bloomfield defines reading so clearly that his definition is worth repeating here:

> In order to read alphabetic writing one must have an ingrained habit of producing the phonemes of one's language when one sees the written marks which conventionally represent these phonemes. A well-trained reader, of course, for the most part reads silently, but we shall do better for the present to ignore this fact, as we know that the child learns first to read aloud.
>
> The accomplished reader of English, then, has an overpracticed and ingrained habit of uttering one phoneme of the English language when he sees the letter *p*, another phoneme when he sees the letter *i*, another when he sees the letter *n*, still another when he sees the letter *m*, still another when he sees the letter *d*, and so on. In this way, he utters the conventionally accepted word when he sees a combination of letters like *pin, nip, pit, tip, tin, nit, dip, din, dim, mid*. What is more, all readers will agree as to the sounds they utter when they see unconventional combinations, such as *pid, nin, pim, mip, nid, nim, mim*. It is this habit which we must set up in the child who is to acquire the art of reading. If we pursue any other course, we are merely delaying him until he acquires this habit in spite of our bad guidance.

Leonard Bloomfield was the first to point out that success with his system of teaching to read depended first upon the child's having an interest in the process of learning and next upon making sure that he knows the letters of the alphabet well so that he will have no difficulty whatsoever in recognizing the small differences that exist between paired words, such as *bad* and *bud*. On March 10, 1938, he wrote to me:

> Don't start your boy on reading until he knows the letters very well—one thing at a time is hard enough.

Another person, Mrs. Bernard G. Mattson, tried the system out at the same time and succeeded in teaching both of her boys to read within a period of one year. She considered the interest factor and laid a firm foundation by insuring thorough mastery of each lesson before the next one was undertaken.

Mrs. Mattson described her methods in a letter to me dated January 7, 1960:

The information that the Bloomfield-Barnhart system of teaching reading is about to be published gives me an intense feeling of pleasure and excitement. While going over the material and introductions I felt all over again the thrill, the inspiration and challenge given me by the method many years ago when you so kindly let me use it in manuscript form to teach our boys to read.

As you know, our firm belief in, and great enthusiasm for, the method have never wavered. Our sons have the distinction of being among the first children to be taught to read by your system, and we are convinced that their growth into wide readers and lovers of books as adults stems in large measure from our friendship with you and hence access to the Bloomfield ideas and your knowledge of how to use them.

Discussion of this book brings back memories of the entirely pleasant experience of teaching the children to read, actually one of the most satisfying experiences of my life. It was so easy, too. Just a few minutes every day, carefully following its logical plan, with a very thorough grounding in the regular words of the first thirty-six lessons, with no frustrations caused by irregular words being brought in, gave them a solid foundation for the later lessons and a lifetime of pleasure in reading. The whole process took only a few months and before we knew it, and before first grade, they were reading practically anything. Although at first glance parts of the book may look complicated, in actual practice I found its method to be quick and easy to use and I believe that parents and teachers will be surprised and delighted at the rate of progress.

There never was a problem of keeping interest at a high level. I added a few words and phrases and later sentences and little stories based on our own family life, always staying carefully within the framework of the system, but stories are not essential. As Dr. Bloomfield says, formal exercises are "not irksome to a child, provided he sees himself gaining in power." And there is the nub of the matter, that "gaining in power." The boys felt such confidence, such a sense of accomplishment, from the steady step-by-step building up of ability to recognize word forms, that the simple lists were a pleasure in themselves.

There are two additional advantages to this system that you don't mention but which I believe will be evident when more children taught by it grow older. One is that a good knowledge of spelling follows naturally along with learning to read this way, and the other that unusual speed and accuracy in reading are attributes in adult life of people who learned to read in this way as children. That is my belief, and our children's experience.

As a teacher's wife, I know that many students reach high school and college without the joy of really knowing how to read. Since not everyone can be privileged to know you personally and be given a chance to use the manuscript, I hope that the book will be published very soon and become available to everyone. It could be one of the best things that ever happened to the English-speaking world.

Dr. Edward L. Thorndike was one of several educators to comment favorably upon the Bloomfield System. In a letter dated March 14, 1945, he wrote:

> I have examined Professor Bloomfield's exercises for teaching reading with interest and profit. It is a fine thing that so eminent a scientist should take up this problem. Fortunately, he is expert in the psychology of language, as well as its history.
>
> In contrast to the old so-called "phonic" methods of teaching reading, Dr. Bloomfield's is a simple, straightforward, economical, and reasonable plan for forming the "SEE-SAY" connections needed for reading. He deliberately omits any special training in forming "SEE—think what it means" connections because he fears that such will cause interference and confusion; and also, probably, because he trusts that these will come as a by-product. They surely will to a considerable extent . . . .

Over a period of twelve years, from 1937 through 1949, Leonard Bloomfield and I offered his system for trial and experiment to the schools of education at three large universities noted for their experimental work in education, submitted it to three large schoolbook publishers and two large tradebook publishers, and offered it to various school systems. Two university presses also considered publication but for various reasons (usually after consulting a psychologist or a teacher in the reading field) were unwilling to go ahead with any experiment.

It is a remarkable fact that a system worked out by one of the great linguists of the twentieth century could get no hearing in educational circles, and that there was only one attempt to try out his ideas of how to teach reading in schools. The Reverend Stanley Stoga, Assistant Superintendent of Schools of the Roman Catholic Archdiocese of Chicago, did try out Bloomfield's system of teaching reading. Sister Mary Fidelia describes the experiment in detail in the following report:

> My first contact with the Bloomfield materials was in 1942. One of our first grade teachers who was visited by Dr. Bloomfield in the company of Rev. Stanley C. Stoga, the Assistant Superintendent of the Chicago Archdiocesan Schools, brought to me a manuscript which Dr. Bloomfield left with her, suggesting that she try the plan with her pupils. The plan, the author claimed, was found successful with individual children.
>
> Examination of the submitted manuscript revealed that the plan was a radical departure from the conventional plans underlying the many basic series on the elementary school market. In his prefatory remarks, Dr. Bloomfield inveighed against the still too common manner of teaching phonics as a method of word-attack.
>
> As I read the manuscript, several problems stood out. First, there were no materials prepared for group teaching in the comparatively large classes of forty or more children; second, Dr. Bloomfield furnished no models of lessons in his manuscript which would suggest to the teacher how she was to go about presenting this linguistic approach to word-attack in reading; and third, it would take a good deal of courage to leave the beaten path of conventional practices to venture unequipped and unguided on the strange seas of linguistic waters. But nothing ventured, nothing gained.

The teacher who ventured to try the Bloomfield approach set about the task of preparing flash cards, charts, and practice exercises to be used as soon as the children would be ready for their use. However, before the plan got under way, Dr. Bloomfield left the University of Chicago for Yale, and Dr. Barnhart became the consultant whose advice we sought when in doubt.

It should be noted at this point that this trial was in the nature of an uncontrolled experiment. According to Dr. Bloomfield, the children were not to be given any books until they mastered by an analogous process the letters of the alphabet to a point of spontaneous association of the correct phoneme with the letter of the alphabet representing it.

Once the children mastered the short vowel sounds in combination with the regular values of consonants, the children read one pre-primer after another. The teacher did notice an absence of rhythm in their reading, but to her great relief the comprehension was very good—something that the experts in reading claim is sacrificed when undue emphasis is placed on word-attack. The disturbing halting reading smoothed out with practice in phrasing, and interest in reading mounted with each day.

At the end of the school year, in this average class of forty children, measured in May on the *Metropolitan Achievement Test Primary I—Battery Form R* and *Stanford Achievement Test Primary Battery—Form J*[2] five children read below the national norm of 1.9 for the first grade. The spread of achievement in reading was from 1.5-3.5. Obviously, the results were satisfying. The fear that the children would gain in word-attack skill at the expense of comprehension—the ultimate goal of reading—was dispelled. The teachers in other schools not using the plan expressed the desire to try the plan in their classes.

The following year eight more first grade teachers used the plan, working under difficulties similar to those of the pioneer teacher—lack of commercially prepared materials for group instruction. In spite of these difficulties the results were comparable to those obtained by the teacher who pioneered in the use of the plan.

To insure continuity of the Bloomfield program, the first class of children exposed to it moved through grades two and three with the same teacher. Observations in each grade confirmed by the results of standardized tests were highly gratifying. There were a few slow readers, but there were no non-readers. At the end of the third grade, the spread of achievement as measured by tests was between 2.9 and 5.9. Six pupils read below the norm (3.9). One of the six (2.9) was a transfer pupil. The results obtained by the pilot group were duplicated by the groups that followed year after year. This empirical study was encouraging, but if only someone would make a controlled study of the Bloomfield plan.

Finally somebody did make a controlled study of the effectiveness of the Bloomfield plan. The opportunity to do so came to the writer when she was doing graduate work at the doctoral level at the Ottawa University in Canada.[3] To determine the relative effectiveness of the content and sequence of the phonemes outlined by Bloomfield in his plan, a comparative study under scientifically controlled conditions was made in which the plan was compared with the sequence of the *Phonics We Use*[4] series.

2. Published by the World Book Company, New York.

3. Sister Mary Fidelia, "Bloomfield's Linguistic Approach to Word-Attack," Ph.D. thesis, University of Ottawa, Ottawa, Ontario.

4. Mary Meighen, Marjorie Pratt, and Mabel Halvorsen, *Phonics We Use* (Chicago: Lyons and Carnahan, 1946).

Perhaps at this point, it should be explained why this particular series was used with the control group in the experiment. As will be recalled, Dr. Bloomfield criticized the "hiss and groan" method of teaching phonics. Since that time there was a progressively revolutionary change in the teaching of phonics. The linguists of today look with approval upon the many refinements in the teaching of phonics as a result of findings in educational laboratories. Carroll and others speculate that Bloomfield's approach seasoned with refinements contributed by psychologists and educational theorists may have considerable merit.[5]

The *Phonics We Use* is a series that presents phonics in a scientific manner. It suggests to the teacher model lessons based on sound psychological principles which correspond to the manner in which the alphabet and corresponding phonemes were presented in the pilot study. The use of this series for the control group reduced the experiment to one variable—the content and sequence in which the letters of the alphabet were introduced. The hypothesis evolved for this study postulated: (1) that there was no significant difference in the results obtained from the application of Bloomfield's content and sequence as outlined in his manuscript and the results secured from the use of the *Phonics We Use* program; and (2) that the Bloomfield approach is not equally effective for children comprising the three instructional categories established on the basis of readiness-status.

The sample involved in the experiment consisted of 1,064 first-grade children in eleven schools of Chicago and neighboring areas selected at random from a list of twenty available schools. The representativeness of the sample was increased by the fact that the neighborhoods of the twenty schools within the system reflected markedly similar socio-economic environmental and cultural patterns.

The experimental design set up for this study was the treatment-by-levels. The two programs representing the word-attack skills—the Bloomfield plan for the experimental group and the *Phonics We Use* for the control group—constituted the treatment. The three instructional categories, Category I, II, and III, established on the basis of the children's measured readiness-status, made up the three levels.

The statistical technique of analysis of variance with its corresponding F test was used in testing the hypothesis. The analysis of variance yielded the following: There were no significant differences found at the 1% level of confidence between the means of the experimental and control group for (1) Total Reading, (2) Paragraph Meaning, and (3) Word Meaning. These findings supported the null hypothesis postulating that there were no significant differences between the Bloomfield plan and the plan of *Phonics We Use*.

These was a significant difference at the 1% level of confidence found between Category I and III of the experimental group using the Bloomfield plan. However, the difference was due mainly to the time element. The children of Category III, because of lack of maturity, had to be exposed to a longer readiness period before they were introduced to the study of the alphabet and corresponding phonemes, and therefore they had only ten weeks of instruction as compared with the twenty weeks of instruction had by the children of Category I.

The generalizations made on the strength of these findings were that the Bloomfield plan, although lacking commercially prepared materials, was as effective at the first grade level as the *Phonics We Use* program on (1) Total Reading, (2) Paragraph Meaning, and (3) Word

5. Henry Lee Smith, *Linguistic Science and Teaching of English* (Cambridge, Mass.: Harvard University Press, 1956), pp. 6,60. John B. Carroll, *The Study of Language* (Cambridge, Mass.: Harvard University Press, 1953), p. 149.

Meaning. The emphasis on word-attack did not in any way sacrifice the final goal of reading—comprehension. Contrary to observations that phonics is not equally effective for all children, the experiment seems to confirm the observation of the teachers that given an adequate amount of time and readiness for word-attack skills, all categories of children are capable of benefiting from instruction in word-attack skills.

Since word-attack skills are cumulatively developed, it appears that a full evaluation of the Bloomfield plan can be obtained only upon the completion of the program in the third or even the fourth grade.

Further, if the linguist's functional approach to word-attack in reading is to be accepted as a means contributing to the improvement of reading instruction, it is necessary that the linguist, the reading specialist, and the educational psychologist unite their efforts in cooperative research and experimentation for the purpose of preparing a program of reading instruction in which the linguist's concept of word-attack will be integrated in the present day "reading for meaning" theory.

This pioneer experimentation, which began in the year 1942, has been continued to the present time.

It shows that the pupils' progress was just as rapid under the Bloomfield System as under traditional systems, even before the exercises and stories were prepared for the present version. Therefore, experiments with the Bloomfield System in the classroom can be safely made.

In its original form the Bloomfield System consisted of seventy-two exercises, each exercise containing a list of words using the same pattern. Sample phrases and sentences showing these words in context were given. In an attempt to make his system more usable, Bloomfield developed a second version in which the lists were separated into more manageable teaching units, and more exercises and stories were given. The word lists in this present version correspond to Bloomfield's second version, except that we have divided the lessons into still more units, we have added words in order to make a more complete list of the words of any particular pattern likely to be encountered by the pupil in the first three years of his school experience, and we have added many two-, three-, and even four-syllable words. We have a total vocabulary of 5,000 words where the original Bloomfield System had a vocabulary of around 2,500 words. Most of these words have been added in Parts IV, V, and VI.

The original Bloomfield System also did not have quite so many two-syllable words (e.g., *about, along, pencil,* etc.). As Bloomfield says in the letter quoted above, his own boy went on without any special instruction from the lists of monosyllables to the reading of ordinary material. However, the circumstances of instruction vary greatly in different parts of the country, and the backgrounds of instruction are so different that we have included the two-syllable words in the lists so that each child will have them at hand and will be able to recognize the words quickly when he encounters them in ordinary reading material.

In 1939 Leonard Bloomfield and I formed a partnership to try to market the Bloomfield System. Chances of near success heartened us from time to time, but in the end we would fail to get any real trial for his system. The system seemed destined to remain in my files. On April 20, 1939, Bloomfield wrote to me:

> To tell you the truth, I don't think we shall ever make more than eight dollars on the thing—but I'll do my best . . . .

Over a period of time Bloomfield worked hard on the readers, adding children's stories, a few of which have been used, with modification, in this book.

When a shortened version of Bloomfield's article on reading was published in *The Elementary English Journal*, we hoped for some attention to his ideas. But as time went on, Bloomfield and I grew more and more discouraged. Here is his letter of April 15, 1948, written after we received a rejection from a publisher for the last time:

> I hope you won't feel bad about the reading system. The Press's adverse letter is merely one of the occasional penalties you, as an optimist, have to pay in amends for living in a more favorable world than the pessimist's.

We made many attempts to obtain some recognition, discussion, and trial of the Bloomfield System. To a certain extent these efforts have succeeded, in that knowledge of the system is widespread. In 1958, an educational foundation gave me the necessary money to write new stories, expand the lists, edit the copy, prepare the Bloomfield System for publication, and see it through the press.

At about the same time, Dr. Harold A. Basilius, the director of Wayne State University Press, became interested in publishing the Bloomfield System as a contribution to the cause of American education. Having been associated with Leonard Bloomfield at Ohio State University, he knew him well and knew that his ideas were a contribution to education and to the problem of teaching reading. With the devoted assistance of Dr. R. A. Goodwin, my adviser on linguistic matters, and of Velma McKay, an experienced textbook writer, and with the editorial help of Robert Barnhart, Pamela Shortall, and Anne-Luise Bartling, I have been able to edit the Bloomfield System for publication. The entire manuscript has been read by Professor George P. Faust, of the University of Kentucky, and Dr. W. R. Lee, a linguist attached to the British Council for Education. Professor Robert C. Pooley, of the University of Wisconsin, has not only read the manuscript but has also contributed the introduction for teachers, outlining the need for experimentation. Natalie Mattson, who was the first parent to use the Bloomfield System, and Dr. Jean Betzner, a former professor of children's literature at Teachers College, Columbia University, have read the lessons and the stories—and I owe much to their friendly criticisms. To all of these co-workers, critics, and advisers I express my deepest thanks.

The Bloomfield System needs trial by teachers of kindergarten and primary grades, and by parents who are concerned with their children's reading ability. I should be very much interested to hear about the results any teacher or parent has in teaching reading by the Bloomfield System. I cannot repeat too often that this is an experimental edition, worked out and designed for widespread experiment throughout the United States. I hope that it will help to solve the reading problem and that it will serve both teachers and parents well. The most useful experiment would be one in which the Bloomfield System was used exclusively in teaching reading, whether in a church kindergarten, or in a public school kindergarten, or in a first grade. It would be helpful if a statistician and a linguist assisted educators in formal experiment.

I am sorry indeed that Leonard Bloomfield is not alive to witness the publication of his system of teaching reading. Our association over a period of fifteen years was a pleasant one, and I obtained from him the inspiration to study linguistics and to apply linguistics to the practical problems of the schoolroom.

TEACHING CHILDREN TO READ*

by Leonard Bloomfield

1. What is Reading?

LITERACY is the most important factor in keeping up our civilization, and teaching children to read is the most important task of our schools. We perform this task clumsily and with a great waste of labor and time. Even at the end of eight years many of our pupils cannot be said to read; yet eight months ought to suffice.

This is not due to a lack of pedagogic methods. The most excellent teaching technique is bound to give poor results so long as the teacher does not know *what to teach.*

It is generally assumed that a teacher, who knows how to read, understands also the linguistic processes that are involved in the act of reading. No one assumes that a cook who prepares a cup of coffee understands the chemical processes which he has called into use. Everybody knows that there is a science of chemistry—that chemical processes have been systematically observed and analyzed—and everyone who deals with chemistry, in the way of teaching or otherwise, makes use of the knowledge that has been gained by generations of scientific study. In quite the same way, though not everyone knows it, human speech has been systematically observed and analyzed. Generations of work have been spent upon this subject, and many useful and interesting facts have been brought to light.[1] No one, not even the cleverest person, could hope, by his unaided efforts, to duplicate these results. Our schools will continue to waste time and energy and to reap meager success unless and until the teacher in the early grades knows the main linguistic facts and principles that play a part in the act of reading.

This essay is planned to present—in a practically useful arrangement—these facts and principles.

2. Speech and Writing

To understand reading, one must understand *the relation of written (or printed) words to speech.*

*Parts of Dr. Bloomfield's essay appeared as an article entitled "Linguistics and Reading," in *The Elementary English Review*, XIX, No. 4 (April 1942), 125-130, and XIX, No. 5 (May 1942), 183-186.
1. This history is very interestingly presented in H. Pedersen's *Linguistic Science in the Nineteenth Century*, translated by J. Spargo (Cambridge, Massachusetts, 1931).

Compared to speech, the use of writing is something artificial and relatively modern. To be sure, writing was used thousands of years ago in Egypt and in Mesopotamia, and the art of writing has never since then been lost. Our own alphabet is probably a descendant of the ancient Egyptian hieroglyphs. However, until recently, the art of writing was confined to a very few nations, and within these nations to a very few persons. It is only within the last two hundred years that literacy has become widespread in a few countries. Most languages have never been represented in writing; it may be that less than half of the people alive today know how to read and write.

Written notations in the English language began to be made only some centuries after the beginning of the Christian Era. For several centuries these notations were confined to words or brief phrases; they were made in the clumsy alphabet known as Runes, and only a few pagan priests or magicians were able to read them. It is only around the year 800 or so that we get connected texts written in English in the ordinary Latin alphabet. Even then the art of reading and writing was confined to the priesthood. Slowly this art spread to wider and wider classes, but anything like general popular literacy has arrived only within the last hundred years. It is well to recall also that in the Middle Ages the few persons who knew how to read and write did most of their reading and writing in Latin rather than in their native language.

To the present-day literate person it seems almost incredible that people could get along without reading and writing, and that even today many savage tribes are in this position, and many civilized nations contain a great proportion of illiterates. What happens to a language if the people who speak it have no books—no dictionaries, grammars, spelling books, and so on? The answer to this question was one of the first and most surprising results of linguistic study: unwritten languages function and develop in the same way as languages that have been reduced to writing. In fact, taking the great mass of human history, the non-use of writing is the normal state of affairs, and the use of writing is a special case and, until very recent times, a most unusual case. The effect of writing on language, where there is no popular literacy, is practically nothing, and where there is popular literacy, as among us, the effect of writing is merely to introduce a few small *irregularities* into the process of linguistic development. This, of course, is the opposite of the popular view, but it is the result of every investigation that has been undertaken and is today firmly accepted by every student of language.

Writing is merely a device for recording speech. A person is much the same and looks the same, whether he has ever had his picture taken or not. Only a vain beauty who sits for many photographs and carefully studies them may end by slightly changing her pose and expression. It is much the same with languages and their written recording.

For our present purpose we need only understand *how speech is recorded by means of written or printed signs.*

Language consists of sounds—musical sounds and noises. These sounds are produced by movements of the speaker's vocal organs (larynx, tongue, and so on). These movements produce sound waves in the air, and these sound waves strike the hearer's eardrums. In this way we signal to one another, and the signals are what we call language.

Suppose we want to signal to someone who cannot be reached by the sound of our voice —to someone far away, or to coming generations. Nowadays we could use the radio or make a phonograph record. These are modern inventions, and writing is only a somewhat less modern invention of much the same kind.

There have been many systems of writing, but all of them seem to consist of three devices or of various mixtures of these three devices: *picture writing*, *word writing*, and *alphabetic writing*.

3. Picture Writing

First, there is *picture writing*, in which you simply draw a picture that represents the story you would tell your reader if you could reach him by the sound of your voice. Some tribes of American Indians were great picture writers.[2] Here is an American Indian's picture message:[3]

At the center are two crossed lines; at one side of these there is a gun and a beaver with thirty little strokes above it; at the other side are sketches of a fisher, an otter, and a buffalo.

This means: "I will trade you a fisher-skin, an otter-skin, and a buffalo-hide for a gun and thirty beaver pelts."

A message like this is effective, provided the writer and reader are in accord as to the meaning of the pictures. They must agree that the crossed lines mean an act of trading, and that the set of strokes means a number, and that the animals are a beaver, an otter, a fisher, and so on. These things are determined by convention: the beaver is always

---

2. The best examples are to be found in G. Mallery's study, published in the 4th and 10th *Annual Reports* of the Bureau of American Ethnology, Smithsonian Institution (Washington, D.C., 1886 and 1893).

3. *Ibid.*, 4th *Annual Report* (1886), p. 220.

drawn in one way, the otter in another, and so on for every animal, so that even a poor draughtsman can show which animal he means.

The important feature of picture writing is that it is not based upon language at all. A reader who knows the conventions by which the pictures are drawn, can read the message even if he does not understand the language which the writer speaks. If the reader knows that the picture of an animal with a big tail means a beaver, he can get this part of the message, even though he does not know how the word for beaver would sound in the writer's language. In fact, he can read the picture correctly, even if he does not know what language the writer speaks. Without going too far into the psychology of the thing, we may say that the reader does not get the speech sounds (the words or sentences) which the writer might use in conversation, but he gets the practical content (the "idea") which in conversation he would have got from hearing those speech sounds.

4. Word Writing

The second main type of writing is *word writing*. In word writing each word is represented by a conventional sign, and these signs are arranged in the same order as the words in speech. Chinese writing is the most perfect system of this kind. There is a conventional character for every word in the language. To write a message you put the character which represents the first word into the upper right hand corner of the paper, below it you write the character for the second word, and so on; when you have reached the bottom of the page you start again at the top, to the left of the first word, and form a second column down to the bottom of the paper, and so on. Each character represents some one Chinese word. As the vocabulary of a literate person runs to about twenty thousand words, this means that in order to read even moderately well, one must know thousands of characters. Learning to read Chinese is a difficult task, and if the Chinese reader does not keep in practice, he is likely to lose his fluency.

It is probable that word writing grew out of picture writing; at any rate, in the system known to us, some of the characters resemble conventionalized pictures. However, the difference between these two kinds of writing is far more important for our purpose than any historical connection. The characters of word writing are attached to words, and not to "ideas." In picture writing you could not distinguish such near symbols as, say, *horse, nag, steed;* but in word writing each one of these words would be represented by a different character. In picture writing very many words cannot be represented at all—words like *and, or, but, if, because, is, was,* and abstract words like *kindness, knowledge, please, care—* but in word writing each such word has a conventional symbol of its own.

We ourselves use word writing in a very limited way in our numerals, 1, 2, 3, 4, 5, 6, 7, 8, 9, 0 and in signs like $, +, —, =, X (in arithmetic, representing the word "times"). The symbol 5, for instance, by an arbitrary convention, represents the word *five*, and the symbol 7 represents the word *seven*. There is no question of spelling or sound involved here; the symbol is arbitrarily assigned to the word. The characteristic feature of word writing, from the point of view of people who are used to alphabetic writing, is that the characters, like our 5 and 7, do not indicate the separate sounds which make up the word, but that each character as a whole indicates a word as a whole. Viewing it practically, from the standpoint of the teacher and pupil, we may say that there is no spelling: the written sign for each of the words (*four, seven,* etc.) has to be learned by itself. You either know that the character 7 represents the word *seven* or you don't know it; there is no way of figuring it out on the basis of sounds or letters, and there is no way of figuring out the value of an unfamiliar character.

Word writing has one great advantage: since a character says nothing about the sound of the word, the same character can be used for writing different languages. For instance, our numeral digits (which, as we have seen, form a small system of word writing) are used by many nations, although the corresponding words have entirely different sounds. The following table shows the words which are represented by the characters 1 to 9 in English, German, French, and Finnish.

CHARACTER	1	2	3	4	5
English	one	two	three	four	five
German	eins	zwei	drei	vier	fünf
French	un	deux	trois	quatre	cinq
Finnish	yksi	kaksi	kolme	neljä	viisi

	6	7	8	9
English	six	seven	eight	nine
German	sechs	sieben	acht	neun
French	six	sept	huit	neuf
Finnish	kuusi	seitsemän	kahdeksan	yhdeksän

The advantage of this is that we can all read each other's numbers. Different regions of China speak different dialects which in part are mutually unintelligible, for the extreme differences are perhaps as great as between English, Dutch, and German. But thanks to a system of conventions like that of our numeral digits, a piece of Chinese writing is readable in all parts of China, regardless of the different-sounding words, just as the digit *4* is readable all over Europe, although the words of the various languages sound very differently.

5. Alphabetic Writing

The third main type of writing is *alphabetic writing*. In alphabetic writing each character represents a *unit speech sound*. The literate Chinese, with his system of word writing, has to memorize thousands of characters—one for every word in his language—whereas, with an alphabetic system, the literate person needs to know only a few dozen characters—one for each unit speech sound of his language. In order to understand the nature of alphabetic writing we need to know only what is meant by the term *unit speech sound*, or, as the linguist calls it, by the term *phoneme*.

The existence of unit speech sounds, or phonemes, is one of the discoveries of the language study of the last hundred years. A short speech—say, a sentence—in any language consists of an unbroken succession of all sorts of sounds. When we hear speech in our own language, the sounds are so familiar and the meaning is so obvious that we do not notice the mere noise effect, but when we hear an entirely strange language, we wonder if there can be any system in such a gibberish of queer noises, and we may question whether it could ever be reduced to alphabetic writing. Systematic study has shown, however, that in every language the meaning of words is attached to certain characteristic features of sound. These features are very stable and their number ranges anywhere from around fifteen to around fifty, differing for different languages. These features are the unit speech sounds or phonemes. Each word consists of a fixed combination of phonemes. Therefore, if we have a written character for each phoneme of a language, the sum total of characters will range anywhere from fifteen to fifty and with these characters we shall be able to write down any word of that language.

The existence of phonemes and the identity of each individual phoneme are by no means obvious: it took several generations of study before linguists became fully aware of this important feature of human speech. It is remarkable that long before scientific students of language had made this discovery, there had arisen a system of alphabetic writing—a system in which each character represented a phoneme. It seems that alphabetic writing has developed out of word writing, and that this remarkable development has taken place only once in the history of mankind—somewhere between 2000 and 1000 B.C. at the eastern end of the Mediterranean, with the Egyptians, the Semitic-speaking peoples (such as the Phoenicians), and the Greeks successively playing the principal role.

All forms of alphabetical writing, then, are offshoots of a single original system. The details of this origin and of the later history, so far as we can get at them, are of great interest but would carry us too far afield. It is important for us to know that alphabetic writing was not invented at one stroke, as a finished system, but that it grew gradually and, one could almost say, by a series of accidents, out of a system of word writing. Neither then nor at any time since was there any body of experts who understood the system of phonemes and regulated the habits of writing.

Accordingly we find many ups and downs in the perfection of the system. The ancient Greeks seem at some times and places to have reached an almost perfect application of

24

the alphabetic principle and then to have lapsed from it: in medieval and modern Greek writing the alphabetic principle is very poorly carried out. A similar story could be told of the ancient Romans. Among modern nations, some have almost perfect alphabetic systems (such as the Spanish, Bohemian, and Finnish systems of writing), but others have relatively imperfect systems (such as the Italian, Dutch, or German), and still others have extremely imperfect and arbitrary systems (such as the modern Greek, and French, and the English).

6. English Writing is Alphabetic.

We can illustrate the nature of alphabetic writing by means of English examples, for, in spite of its many imperfections, our system of writing is in origin and in its main features alphabetic. This is proved by the simple fact that we can write every English word by means of only twenty-six characters, whereas a system of word writing would demand many thousands. As an illustration we may take the written representation of the word *pin*:

p i n

It consists of three characters, and each of these three represents a single phoneme. If anyone told us to use these three characters to represent the word *needle*, we should find the suggestion absurd, because these characters do not *fit the sound* of the word *needle*. That is, each of the three characters *p*, *i*, *n* is used conventionally to represent a unit *sound* of our language. This appears plainly if we compare the written symbol for other words, such as *pig* and *pit*, or *bin* and *din*, or *pan* and *pun*; or if we reverse the order of the letters and read *nip*, or if we place the letter *p* at both ends and read *pip*.

The alphabetic nature of our writing appears most plainly of all, however, when we put together a combination of letters that does not make a word and yet find ourselves clearly guided to the utterance of English speech sounds; thus, nobody will have trouble in reading such nonsense syllables as *nin*, *mip*, *lib*. Alphabetic writing differs entirely from picture writing in that the visible marks do not represent things or stories or "ideas." As a picture of a pin, the marks

p i n

are simply no good at all. Alphabetic writing differs from word writing in that the characters are not assigned, one by one, in an arbitrary, take-it-or-leave-it system, to words, but represent unit speech sounds, so that the way of writing each word bears a close relation to the speech sounds which make up that word.

If our system of writing were perfectly alphabetic, then anyone who knew the value of each letter could read or write any word. In reading, he would simply pronounce the phonemes indicated by the letters, and in writing he would put down the appropriate letter for each phoneme. The fact that we actually can do both of these things in the case of nonsense words, such as *nin* or *mip*, shows that our system of writing is alphabetic.

In order to read alphabetic writing one must have an ingrained habit of producing the phonemes of one's language when one sees the written marks which conventionally represent these phonemes. A well-trained reader, of course, for the most part reads silently, but we shall do better for the present to ignore this fact, as we know that the child learns first to read aloud.

The accomplished reader of English, then, has an overpracticed and ingrained habit of uttering one phoneme of the English language when he sees the letter *p*, another phoneme when he sees the letter *i*, another when he sees the letter *n*, still another when he sees the letter *m*, still another when he sees the letter *d*, and so on. In this way, he utters the conventionally accepted word when he sees a combination of letters like *pin*, *nip*, *pit*, *tip*, *tin*, *nit*, *dip*, *din*, *dim*, *mid*. What is more, all readers will agree as to the sounds they utter when they see unconventional combinations, such as *pid*, *nin*, *pim*, *mip*, *nid*, *nim*, *mim*. It is this habit which we must set up in the child who is to acquire the art of reading. If we pursue any other course, we are merely delaying him until he acquires this habit in spite of our bad guidance.

7. Irregular Spellings

English writing is alphabetic, but not perfectly so. For many words we have a conventional rule of writing which does not agree with the sound of the word. Take, for instance, the two words which are pronounced *nit*. One is actually spelled *nit*, but the other is spelled *knit*, with an extra letter *k* at the beginning, a letter which ordinarily represents one of the phonemes of our language, as in *kin*, *kit*, *kid*.

When we study the history of our language—and this, again, is a branch of the study of linguistics—we learn that up to about two hundred years ago the word *knit* (along with other words like *knee*, *knife*, *knave*) was actually spoken with a "*k*-sound" (that is, with the initial phoneme of words like *kin*, *kit*, *kid*) before the *n*-sound. In fact, we are told that in some places in England the country people still speak in this older way. About two hundred years ago the prevalent manner of speaking English changed: the initial *k*-sound before *n* was dropped. However, the old tradition of writing persisted, all the books one read spelled the word with this letter *k*, and people simply kept on writing it as they had always seen it written. So far as reading is concerned, this extra letter *k* makes no difference at all, for (owing to the above-mentioned change in pronunciation) no English word now begins with sounds *k* plus *n*, and when we see a word written with the initial letters *kn*, we have the habit of not trying to pronounce the *k*.

Now someone may ask whether the spelling of *knit* with *k* does not serve to distinguish this word from *nit* 'the egg of a louse.' Of course it does, and this is exactly where our writing lapses from the alphabetic principle back into the older scheme of word writing. Alphabetic writing, which indicates all the significant speech sounds of each word, is just as clear as actual speech, which means that it is clear enough. Word writing, on the other hand, provides a separate character for each and every word, regardless of its sound, and at the cost of tremendous labor to everyone who learns to read and write. Our spelling the verb *knit* with an extra *k* (and the noun *nit* without this extra *k*) is a step in the direction of word writing. This convention goes a little way toward giving us a special picture for the verb *knit* (as opposed to its homonym, the noun *nit*) and it does this at the cost of a certain amount of labor, since the reader must learn to ignore initial *k* before *n*, and the writer must learn where to place it (as in *knit, knight, knave*) and where not to place it (as in *nit, night, nave*). However, we shall have enough to do later with the irregularities of our spelling; for the present it is far more important to see that in its basic character, in its bones, blood, and marrow, our system of writing is alphabetic—witness merely the fact that we get along with twenty-six characters instead of twenty-six thousand.

8. Phonic Methods

The letters of the alphabet are signs which direct us to produce sounds of our language. A confused and vague appreciation of this fact has given rise to the so-called "phonic" methods of teaching children to read. These methods suffer from several serious faults.

The inventors of these methods confuse writing with speech. They plan the work as though the child were being taught to pronounce—that is, as if the child were being taught to speak. They give advice about phonetics, about clear utterance, and other matters of this sort. This confuses the issue. Alphabetic writing merely directs the reader to produce certain speech sounds. A person who cannot produce these sounds cannot get the message of a piece of alphabetic writing. If a child has not learned to utter the speech sounds of our language, the only sensible course is to postpone reading until he has learned to speak. As a matter of fact, nearly all six-year-old children have long ago learned to speak their native language; they have no need whatever of the drill which is given by phonic methods.

In exceptional cases, children get into school before they have thoroughly learned to speak. A child may replace the *r*-sound by the *w*-sound, saying *wed* instead of *red*, or he may replace the *th*-sound by the *f*-sound, saying *fin* instead of *thin*, or his speech may be altogether indistinct and blurred. Conditions like these may be due to gross anatomical defects, such as a cleft palate; or to a deep-seated deficiency of the nervous system, such as idiocy; or to minor nervous faults, as is the case in stuttering; or to social maladjustment, which will prompt a child to seek advantage in such things as baby talk; or they may be due simply to the fact that he speaks some language other than English, so that English speech sounds are foreign to him. In all such cases, the economical course and the course that is best for the child, is to remove the defect of speech before trying to make the child read. In some cases, to be sure, this cannot be done. The extreme and typical case of this kind is that of deaf-and-dumb children. Such cases demand very elaborate care and training; they must be dealt with in a manner very different from ordinary reading instruction. In short, the problem of teaching children to speak is entirely different from that of teaching children to read. In all normal cases, the child has learned to speak before we are called upon to teach him to read, and our task is merely to give him the habit of uttering the familiar speech sounds at the sight of the printed or written letters. To ignore this distinction, as the phonic methods do, is to befuddle the whole process.

The second error of the phonic methods is that of isolating the speech sounds. The authors of these methods tell us to show the child a letter, for instance t, and to make him react by uttering the t-sound; that is, the English speech sound which occurs at the beginning of a word like *two* or *ten*. This sound is to be uttered either all by itself or else with an obscure vowel sound after it. Now, English-speaking people, children or adults, are not accustomed to making that kind of noise. The phoneme [t] does not occur alone in English utterance; neither does the phoneme [t] followed by an obscure vowel sound. If we insist on making the child perform unaccustomed feats with his vocal organs, we are bound to confuse his response to the printed signs. In any language, most phonemes do not occur by themselves, in isolated utterance, and even most of the successions of phonemes which one could theoretically devise, are never so uttered. English speakers do not separately pronounce the sound of [t] or [p] or of [u] as in *put*, and a succession like [s p], for instance, as in *spin*, does not occur alone, as a separate utterance. Learning to pronounce such things is something in the nature of a stunt, and has nothing to do with learning to read. We must not complicate our task by unusual demands on the child's power of pronouncing. We intend to apply phonetics to our reading instruction; this does not mean that we are going to try to teach phonetics to young children. In this absurdity lies the greatest fault of the so-called phonic methods.

9. The Word Method

In spite of the special methods, such as the "phonic" method, which have been advocated at various times, the actual instruction in our schools consists almost entirely of something much simpler, which we may call the *word method*. The word method teaches the child to utter a word when he sees the printed symbols for this word; it does not pretend to any phonetic breaking-up of the word. The child learns the printed symbols, to be sure, by "spelling" the word—that is, by naming, in proper succession, the letters which make up the written representation of the word, as *see-aye-tee*: *cat*, and so on.

No attempt is made, however, to take advantage of the alphabetic principle. If one examines the primers and first readers which exemplify the various methods that have been advocated, one is struck by the fact that the differences are very slight: the great bulk of the work is word learning. The authors are so saturated with this, the conventional method, that they carry their innovations only a very short way; they evidently lack the linguistic knowledge that would enable them to grade the matter according to relations between sound and spelling. It is safe to say that nearly all of us were taught to read by the word method.

The word method proceeds as though our writing were word writing. Every word has to be learned as an arbitrary unit; this task is simplified only by the fact that all these word characters are made up out of twenty-six constituent units, the letters. In order to read a new word, the child must learn the new word character; he can best do this by memorizing the letters which make up this new word character, but these letters are arbitrarily presented and have nothing to do with the sound of the word.

If this plan could be consistently carried out, our children would be in much the same position as the Chinese child who has to acquire a system of word writing. Like him, they would have to learn thousands of complex symbols, one for each word in the language. Learning to read would be the task of years, and any serious interruption of practice would result in wholesale forgetting. Actually, the child's nervous system is wiser than we are: in spite of our not telling him the values of the letters and in spite of our confusing hodgepodge, the child does acquire, unknowingly, a habit of connecting letters with speech sounds. This appears from the fact that he learns to read in less time than would be required by a genuine system of word writing; it appears also in some of the child's mistakes, such as trying to read *debt* with a *b*-sound or *walk* with an *l*-sound—mistakes which show that the child is operating, however imperfectly, on an alphabetic principle.

The most serious drawback of all the English reading instruction known to me, regardless of the special method that is in each case advocated, is the drawback of the word method. The written forms for words are presented to the child in an order which conceals the alphabetic principle. For instance, if near the beginning of instruction, we present the words *get* and *gem*, we cannot expect the child to develop any fixed or fluent response to the sight of the letter *g*. If we talk to him about the "hard" and "soft" sounds of the letter *g*, we shall only confuse him the more. The irregularities of our spelling—that is, its deviation from the alphabetic principle—demand careful handling if they are not to confuse the child and to delay his acquisition of the alphabetic habit.

Our teaching ought to distinguish, then, between *regular* spellings, which involve only the alphabetic principle, and *irregular* spellings, which depart from this principle, and it ought to classify the irregular spellings according to the various types of deviation from the alphabetic principle. We must train the child to respond vocally to the sight of letters, and this can be done by presenting regular spellings; we must train him, also, to make exceptional vocal responses to irregular spellings, and this can be done by presenting systematically the various types of irregular spelling. For instance, we must train the child to respond by the *k*-sound to the sight of the letter *k* in words like *kiss, kid, kin, kit*, but we must also train him not to try pronouncing a *k*-sound when he sees the written *k* in the words like *knit, knife, knee, knight*.

The material in existing primers and readers is not thus graded, because the authors of these books lacked the linguistic training necessary for such a classification. The knowledge required to make this classification is not very profound. In fact, the teacher who reads over the list in this book will soon grasp the principles that are involved, and in doing so will have acquired all the phonetics needed for ordinary instruction in reading. Although this knowledge is easily gained, persons who lack it are likely to make troublesome mistakes. For instance, the author of a treatise on reading methods asks how we ought to teach children to read the word *of*. He does not know whether we ought to read it with the sound of *f* as in *if* or with the sound of *v* as in *have*; the latter pronunciation he thinks is "careless" and imprecise. This author is to be blamed not so much for his ignorance of phonetics as for his failure to consult a book or a person who could tell him the answer. He is in the position of a writer on chemistry who at this day and age deliberated in print as to whether diamonds were or were not a form of crystallized water. As a matter of fact, a glance into *The New English Dictionary*[4] shows that the word *of* was pronounced with the sound of *f* (as in *if*) up to about the time of Shakespeare. At that time there occurred a change which resulted in two forms of the word: as a preposition (unstressed) it received the sound of *v* (as in *have*) and in this use it is now spelled *of* and pronounced *ov*, but as an adverb (stressed) it kept the old *f*-sound, and in this use it is now spelled *off*. The pronunciation which this author prefers, then, has been out of existence for more than three hundred years.

The author of a textbook or the classroom teacher does not need a profound knowledge of phonetics; he needs only to realize that information on this subject is available and that he need not grope about in the dark.

10. Ideational Methods

Although the various methods that have been advanced are in practice only slight adaptations of the universal method of word reading, it will be worth our while to glance at another method, which has some vogue, namely, the *sentence method* or *ideational reading*. This method attempts to train the child to get the "idea" or content directly from the printed page.

When a literate adult reads, he passes his eyes rapidly over the printed text and,

4. Reprinted as *The Oxford English Dictionary*, 13 vols. (Oxford, England, 1933).

scarcely noticing the individual words or letters, grasps the content of what he has read. This appears plainly in the fact that we do not often notice the misprints on the page we are reading. The literate adult now observes the laborious reading of the child, who stumbles along and spells out the words and in the end fails to grasp the content of what he has read. The adult concludes that the child is going at the thing in a wrong way and should be taught to seize the "ideas" instead of watching the individual letters.

The trouble with the child, however, is simply that he lacks the long practice which enables the adult to read rapidly; the child puzzles out the words so slowly that he has forgotten the beginning of the sentence before he reaches the end; consequently he cannot grasp the content. The adult's reading is so highly practiced and so free from difficulty that he does not realize any transition between his glance at the page and his acceptance of the content. Therefore he makes the mistake of thinking that no such transition takes place—that he gets the "ideas" directly from the printed signs.

This mistake is all the more natural because the adult reads silently; since he does not utter any speech sounds, he concludes that speech sounds play no part in the process of reading and that the printed marks lead directly to "ideas." Nothing could be further from the truth.

The child does his first reading out loud. Then, under the instruction or example of his elders, he economizes by reading in a whisper. Soon he reduces this to scarcely audible movements of speech; later these become entirely inaudible. Many adults who are not very literate move their lips while reading. The fully literate person has succeeded in reducing these speech movements to the point where they are not even visible. That is, he has developed a system of internal substitute movements which serve him, for private purposes, such as thinking and silent reading, in place of audible speech sounds. When the literate adult reads very carefully—as when he is reading poetry or difficult scientific matter or a text in a foreign language—he actually goes through this process of internal speech; his conventional way of reporting this is that he internally pronounces or "hears himself say" the words of the text. The highly-skilled reader has trained himself beyond this: he can actually shunt out some of the internal speech movements and respond to a text without seeing every word. If you ask him to read aloud, he will often replace words or phrases of the printed text by equivalent ones; he has seized only the high spots of the printed text. Now this highly skilled adult has forgotten the earlier stages of his own development and wants the child to jump directly from an illiterate state to that of an overtrained reader.

The marks in a piece of American Indian picture writing represent *things*, or, if you prefer, *ideas*. The characters in a piece of Chinese writing do not represent things (or ideas) but words. The letters in a piece of English writing do not represent things, or even words, but *sounds*. The task of the reader is to get the *sounds* from the written or printed page. When he has done this, he must still, of course, perform a second task: he must understand the meaning of these sounds. This second task, however, is not peculiar to reading, but concerns all use of language; when we are not reading, but hearing spoken words, we have the same task of appreciating the content of what is said. The ideational methods, in short, show us the age-old confusion between the use of writing and the ordinary processes of speech.

It is true, of course, that many children in the upper grades—and even, for that matter, many postgraduate students in the university—fail to seize the content of what they read. It was this unfortunate situation which led to the invention of ideational methods in reading instruction. This, however, meant confusing two entirely different things. A person who can read aloud a text that is before his eyes, but cannot reproduce the content or otherwise show his grasp of it, lacks something other than reading power, and needs to be taught the proper response to language, be it presented in writing or in actual speech. The marks on the page offer only sounds of speech and words, not things or ideas.

So much can be said, however: the child who fails to grasp the content of what he reads is usually a poor reader also in the mechanical sense. He fails to grasp the content because he is too busy with the letters. The cure for this is not to be sought in ideational methods, but in better training at the stage where the letters are being associated with sounds.

The extreme type of ideational method is the so-called "non-oral" method, where children are not required to pronounce words, but to respond directly to the content. They are shown a printed sentence such as *Skip around the room*, and the correct answer is not to say anything, but to perform the indicated act. Nothing could be less in accord with the nature of our system of writing or with the reading process such as, in the end, it must be acquired.

It is not easy for a student of language to speak patiently of such vagaries, in which educationalists indulge at great cost to thousands of helpless children. It is exactly as if these same educationalists should invent their own guesswork system of chemistry and introduce it into our schools.

Even the most elementary understanding of systems of writing suffices to show the fallacy of "ideational" reading. The kind of writing which can be read ideationally is picture writing. There the visible marks directly represent the content and do not presuppose any particular wording. In word writing and in alphabetic writing, the visible marks are tokens for speech forms and not for "ideas." The visible word marks tell the Chinese reader to speak (out loud or internally) such and such words of his language. The visible letters of alphabetic writing tell us to speak (out loud or internally) such and such phonemes of our language. If the Chinese reader or we choose to skip the less important of these directions and to notice only the high spots, we can go all the faster, but we do not accurately reproduce the author's words; as soon as the exact wording is important, as in a poem or a difficult exposition, we do in fact accurately follow the visible signals to speech. In short, the black marks on paper which represent an English word, say,

horse

do not represent the shape or smell or any other characteristics of a horse, or even the "idea" (whatever that may be) of a horse; they merely direct us to utter the speech sounds which make up the English word *horse*. These speech sounds, in turn, are connected for us as a kind of signal, with the animal, and it is only through these speech sounds that the black marks

horse

on the paper have any connection with the animal, or, if you will, with the "idea" of the animal. The adult's instantaneous step from the black marks to the "idea" is the result of long training. To expect to give this facility directly and without intermediate steps to the child is exactly as though we should try to teach the child higher mathematics (which solves complicated problems with power and speed) before we taught him elementary arithmetic. If we insisted on doing this, the child would merely learn elementary arithmetic in spite of us, from our inappropriate examples, and he would not get his higher mathematics until he had, in this irksome way, acquired his elementary arithmetic. Moreover, his mathematics, arithmetic and all, would remain shaky, unless and until, again in spite of us, he had by a vast amount of repetition, gained sureness in the elements which we had neglected to teach him. In practice, the ideational and sentence reading methods are so overwhelmingly diluted with the word method that the children taught in this way are but slightly less sure of themselves than are the pupils of less modern practice.

11. The Content

The circumstances which lead the more intelligent but linguistically untrained schoolman to seek an "ideational" method is the distressing fact that many older students and adults are unable to get the content from a printed text. We have all heard of the devastating results of experiments in which pupils or adults are given a paragraph to read, and then are asked to reproduce the content; a large proportion of the persons tested are unable to make anything like a correct statement of what the author was trying to tell them. The schoolman concludes that these people were not properly taught to read, and therefore seeks to make elementary reading instruction bear more directly on the content. In this, however, he confuses two entirely different things—the ability to respond to visible marks by uttering speech sounds and the ability to respond correctly to speech. The child who is laboring to find out what words or phrases he must utter when he sees certain printed marks cannot be expected at the same time to respond correctly to the meaning of these words or phrases. If he has spelled out the words *Bill hit John*, we need not be surprised that we can trap him with the question "Whom did John hit?" His problem is to say the correct word or phrase when he sees the black marks, and, indeed, this is enough of a problem; it takes a sophisticated but linguistically untrained adult to underestimate its difficulty. The other problem, which the schoolman confuses with ours, is the problem of responding correctly to speech, and it concerns actual speech just as much as reading. When one tests graduate university students by making a simple oral statement and asking them to reproduce it, the result is just as discouraging as that of similar reading tests. This is a problem which our schools have to face, and the beginning will doubtless have to be made in the earliest grades, but the one place where this problem most certainly cannot be solved is in the elementary instruction in reading, where the child has all he can do to pass from the visual symbols to the spoken words.

In fact, an understanding of the latter difficulty will lead us to see our problem in its simplest terms. Aside from their silliness, the stories in a child's first reader are of little use, because the child is too busy with the mechanics of reading to get anything of the content. He gets the content when the teacher reads the story out loud, and later on, when he has mastered all the words in the story, he can get it for himself, but during the actual process of learning to read the words he does not concern himself with the content. This does not mean that we must forego the use of sentences and connected stories, but it does mean that these are not essential to the first steps. We need not fear to use disconnected words and even senseless syllables, and, above all, we must not, for the sake of a story, upset the child's scarcely-formed habits by presenting him with irregularities of spelling for which he is not prepared. Purely formal exercises that would be irksome to an adult are not irksome to a child, provided he sees himself gaining in power. In the early stages of reading, a nonsense syllable like *nin* will give pleasure to the child who finds himself able to read it, whereas at the same stage a word of irregular spelling, such as *gem*, even if introduced in a story, will discourage the child and delay the sureness of his reactions.

There is always something artificial about reducing a problem to simple mechanical terms, but the whole history of science shows that simple mechanical terms are the only terms in which our limited human capacity can solve a problem. The lesser variables have to wait until the main outline has been ascertained, and this is true even when these lesser variables are the very thing that makes our problem worth solving. The authors of books on reading methods devote much space to telling why reading is worth while.

The authors of these books would have done far better to stress the fact that the practical and cultural values of reading can play no part in the elementary stages. The only practical value of mathematics lies in its application in commerce and science, but we do not try to teach economics and physics in connection with first-grade arithmetic. The only practical value of responding correctly to the letters of the alphabet lies in the messages which reach us through the written or printed page, but we cannot expect the child to listen to these messages when he has only begun to respond correctly to the sight of the letters. If we insist upon his listening, we merely delay the fundamental response.

If you want to play the piano with feeling and expression, you must master the keyboard and learn to use your fingers on it. When you have mastered the keyboard and the fingering, you may still fail for other reasons, but certain it is that if you have not the mechanical control, you will not be able to play.

12. Before Reading

The first step, which may be divorced from all subsequent ones, is the recognition of the letters. We say that the child *recognizes* a letter when he can, upon request, make some response to it. One could, for instance, train him to whistle when he saw an A, to clap his hands when he saw a B, to stamp his foot when he saw a C, and so on. The conventional responses to the sight of the letters are their names, *aye*, *bee*, *see*, *dee*, *ee*, *eff*, and so on, down to *zee* (which in England is called *zed*). There is not the slightest reason for using any other responses.

The letters have queer and interesting shapes; their interest is enhanced if they are presented in colors. Begin with the printed capitals in their ordinary simple form. When these have been mastered, take up the small printed letters. The written forms of the letters should not be taught until reading habits are well established; the early introduction of writing is a cause of delay.

The child should be familiar with all the letters, capital and small, of the printed alphabet before reading is begun. Not all of them will be used in the first reading work, but we do not want the reading work, at any stage, to be upset by the appearance of unfamiliar shapes.

Every teacher knows, of course, that the pairs *b* and *d* or *p* and *q* involve a fairly abstract geometrical distinction and have to be carefully presented and practiced. Another feature of the same kind is that of the left-to-right order of our writing and printing. This presents difficulty to some children. The left-to-right order of printed marks corresponds to a sooner-to-later order of spoken sounds and forms. That is, the letters are arranged from left to right in a succession that corresponds to the succession in time of the corresponding phonemes (e.g., *p-i-n* corresponding to the spoken sound of the word *pin*), and the words, also, are arranged from left to right in a succession that corresponds to the succession in time of the spoken words (e.g., *Give me a pin*). This seems simple to us only because of our long practice; in reality it involves considerable abstraction and demands careful teaching. The beginning should be made before reading is begun, in connection with the letters; the letters are presented in alphabetic order and their names read off from left to right. Then other combinations of letters should be presented, including actual words. The child need not even be told that the combinations are words; and he should certainly not be required to recognize or read the words. All he needs to do is read off the names of the successive letters, *from left to right.*

All this belongs to the stage before the child starts to read. Before the child reads we present the letters, capital and lower-case, the numeral digits, and exercises in the left-to-right and top-to-bottom orders. The work should go on until the child can name each letter when it is shown to him and can name in the proper (left-to-right) order a sequence of letters shown to him. The pictures in the before-reading stage show objects which move from left to right.

If the children do not have printed material for the before-reading stage, the teacher must exhibit the letters on the blackboard. In drawing pictures or diagrams to show the left-to-right order, one must be careful to avoid ambiguous subjects. For instance, a railway train is not a good subject. When a train passes us, we see first the locomotive, then the tender, then the baggage car, and so on, but if we draw the train accordingly with the locomotive at the left-hand end, our picture will represent a train which is moving from right to left; the picture is ambiguous. The type of correct picture or diagram is a man shooting an arrow, which in the picture is flying from the left-hand part of the surface toward the right.

When the letters and the left-to-right order have been thoroughly mastered, we are ready to begin reading. In the words to be read during the first stage every letter must represent only and always one single phoneme. The great task of learning to read—one of the major intellectual feats in anyone's life—consists in learning the very abstract equation: *printed letter = speech sound to be spoken.* This equation is all the more difficult because it never occurs in simple form, but only in the complex shape where several letters in left-to-right order serve as the signal for several speech sounds in the corresponding soon-to-later order. If we try to simplify this by presenting single letters as signals for single speech sounds, we only make matters worse, since the isolated speech sounds are foreign to our language. This task is sufficiently difficult; we must not make it even more difficult by introducing irregular spellings before the basic habit is set up, or by asking the child to attend to the meaning of what he reads.

13. Differences of Pronunciation

Before we begin reading we must settle a question which troubles many teachers. How are we to pronounce our words? The sound of English speech differs greatly in different parts of the English-speaking countries. Almost everyone is diffident about the sound of speech—especially the teacher, who is used to reflecting about such matters.

Our first impulse is to follow some authority who will tell us what is proper. If this were possible, our problem would long ago have been settled, and all of us—or, at any rate, all educated people—would be using the same pronunciation. At various times various men have set themselves up as authorities on how English should be pronounced, but none of them has succeeded in getting people to follow his prescriptions. The man who sets himself up as an authority prescribes the style of pronunciation which he happens to use, and the great majority of people, who are used to pronouncing otherwise, object to his prescriptions and in the end ignore them. The reason for this is plain enough. English is spoken differently in different places. It would be very hard to make London teachers talk like Chicagoans. If we decided to make some one local pronunciation the standard for the whole English-speaking world, then all teachers would have to be natives of the favored place, or would have to go through a long and severe training until they acquired the favored pronunciation. Few things are harder to do than changing one's pronunciation in one's native language. There would remain the more difficult task of making the children use this pronunciation. Accordingly, the present-day phonetician who writes about the pronunciation of English does not set himself up as an authority; he tells us whose pronunciation he is describing (usually it is his own) and tries to tell what other people use the same pronunciation; even thus he lists many variant pronunciations; compare, for instance, Daniel Jones, *Outline of English Phonetics* (Third ed., Leipzig, 1932), p. 12. In short, there is no authority, and if there were we should probably find his prescriptions too difficult to follow.

In the theater, our actors are trained to use the type of pronunciation that prevails among the upper classes in southern England. It would be an enormous task, and doubtless in many cases beyond our power, to teach our pupils to pronounce in this fashion. There would be no time left in which to teach reading.

So far as the general style of pronunciation is concerned, then, the teacher of reading need not worry about her own habits. Of course she should speak distinctly and in a style of pronunciation which she herself accepts as polite. Above all, she ought to avoid affectation. Affected and prissy speech is not good for the children and, since one cannot keep up a pose at all times, it leads to inconsistency.

If the teacher comes from a very distant part of the country, there may be noticeable differences between the pronunciation of the teacher and that of the pupils. Even if the teacher does not adapt her pronunciation to theirs, it is well to remember that the most we can ask of our pupils in this respect is that they speak like *the educated people in their own part of the country.*

For instance, if a teacher from New England comes to Chicago, she would be wrong if she tried to train her pupils to speak the so-called "broad" sound of *a* (as in *father, far*) in words like *laugh, grass, aunt*. The attempt would consume a vast amount of time and energy, the pupils would fail to follow consistently, and outside of the classroom they would in any event lapse back into the pronunciation which they hear from everybody else.

The greatest mistake of all, however, is when a teacher, say in Chicago, who does not come from New England and does not naturally use the "broad *a*," tries to affect it in the classroom. She uses it inconsistently, often forgetting to put it into the words to which (in London or New England) it belongs, and sometimes putting it into words where it does not belong (even in London or New England)—words such as *lass, bass,* or *fancy*.

The "broad *a*" has been here mentioned as an example. There are many other differences of pronunciation between different parts of the country. They do no harm, and the teacher need not worry about them. The only kind of practice, in this matter, that will do harm is priggishness and affectation. One sometimes hears teachers use outlandish varieties of pronunciation which no one else, and not even they when they speak plainly and naturally, would ever think of using.

Among the geographical differences in the pronunciation of Standard English there are a very few which we must consider in this book. One of these is the "broad *a*": a word like *class*, for instance, is spoken in England and in eastern New England with the vowel sound of *father, far*, and in most of the United States with the vowel sound of *hat, lass*. We give these words in separate lists; for each of these lists the teacher must decide upon the choice in accordance with the pronunciation that prevails in the part of the country where she is teaching.

The only pronunciations that are not acceptable are those which are not current among educated people in the pupils' locality. In Chicago, for instance, *git* for *get, ketch* for *catch, wrastle* for *wrestle* are widespread, and so, some time back, was *bile* for *boil*, but these forms are not used by educated adult speakers. It would be a mistake to make a fuss when a pupil uses these forms, but the teacher, of course, should use the Standard English forms and should consider only these forms in the reading instruction.

The pupil who uses such forms as *git* or *I seen it* or *I ain't got none* is not making "mistakes in English" or talking "bad English." There is a widespread superstition which attributes the use of forms like these to "carelessness" or some other sort of depravity. The forms just cited, and others like them, are forms of *substandard English* or of local dialects. They are perfectly good English, but they do not belong to the dialect which we call Standard English. Since Standard English is, to all practical purposes, the only type of English that is represented in print and writing, our instruction will naturally ignore all other dialects and consider only the standard forms.

It is another matter, and in the main quite separate from reading instruction, that we want our pupils to learn to speak and write Standard English. So much may be said here, that this can be attained not by instruction in theoretical grammar, such as sentence analysis and the like, but only by a vast amount of drill in the use of the Standard English forms that differ from the pupil's substandard or local dialect. Practice of this kind should cover also the forms which are likely to be confused with the form that is foreign to the pupil. If we merely train a child to substitute *saw* for *seen*, we may find him saying *I have saw it*. We must train him, then, in pairs and sets or phrases:

I saw it.
I've seen it.
I have some.
I've got some.
I have none.
I haven't any.
I haven't got any.

All this, however, is by way of digression, for the teaching of Standard English to pupils who speak some other type is a matter quite different from teaching them to read. There is only this connection, that since the texts are in Standard English, reading helps the pupil to acquire the use of this more favored form of our language.

In sum, then, the teacher should use a polite but natural type of pronunciation and should base the reading instruction upon pronunciations which are current among educated speakers in the pupils' own community. The main thing is to avoid affectation in one's own classroom language; above all, one should never make the mistake of introducing pronunciations that are foreign to the pupils' community (for instance, in the Middle and Far West, *class* with "broad *a*") or outlandish and fantastic forms that are not used anywhere in the English-speaking world (for instance, *lass* with "broad *a*," or *pre-see-us* instead of *preshus* for the word that is written *precious*).

14. First Materials

Our first material must show each letter in only one phonetic value; thus, if we have words with *g* in the value that it has in *get, got, gun*, our first material must not contain words like *gem*, where the same letter has different value; similarly, if we have words like *cat, can, cot*, our first material must not contain words like *cent*. Our first material should contain no words with silent letters (such as *knit* or *gnat*) and none with double letters, either in the value of single sounds (as in *add, bell*) or in special values (as in *see, too*), and none with combinations of letters having a special value (as *th* in *thin* or *ea* in *bean*). The letter *x* cannot be used, because it represents two phonemes (*ks* or *gz*), and the letter *q* cannot be used, because it occurs only in connection with an unusual value of the letter *u* (for *w*).

The best selection of value of letters to be used in the first materials for reading is the following:

VOWEL LETTERS

a as in *cat*	o as in *hot*
e as in *pet*	u as in *cut*
i as in *pin*	

CONSONANT LETTERS

b as in *bit*	n as in *net*
c as in *cat*	p as in *peg*
d as in *dig*	r as in *red*
f as in *fan*	s as in *sat*
g as in *get*	t as in *tan*
h as in *hen*	v as in *van*
j as in *jam*	w as in *wet*
k as in *keg*	y as in *yes*
l as in *let*	z as in *zip*
m as in *man*	

Note that this list contains one duplication: *c* and *k* both designate one and the same English phoneme. This will be a difficulty later, when the child learns to write, but it need not trouble us now, since he has merely to read the words as they are presented to him.

Our first reading material will consist of two-letter and three-letter words in which the letters have the sound values given in the above list. Since the vowel letters *a, e, i, o, u* are the ones which, later on, will present the greatest difficulty, we shall do best to divide this material into five groups, according to the vowel letter contained in each word. Within each of these five groups, two arrangements are possible; we can form groups by final consonants (e.g. *bat*, *cat*, *fat*, etc.) or by initial consonants (e.g. *bad*, *bag*, *bat*, etc.). We begin with the former because it is easier to watch the first letter than the last, and because rhyme is familiar to the child.

The parent or teacher points to the word

c a n

in small printed letters in Lesson 1 on p. 60 in this book, or shows the word either on the blackboard or on a card. The child knows the names of the letters, and is now asked to read off those names in their order: *see, aye, en*. The parent or teacher says, "Now we have spelled the word. Now we are going to *read* it. This word is *can*. Read it: *can*."

The parent or teacher now shows another word with the same vowel and final consonant, but with a different initial, for instance *fan*, and goes through the same procedure.

The aim is now to make the child distinguish between the two words—that is, to get him to read each of the words correctly when it is shown by itself, and, when the two words are shown together, to say the right one when the parent or the teacher points to it, and to point to the right one when the parent or the teacher pronounces it.

We should not, at this stage ask the child to write or print the words: that comes much later.

The early reading lessons should not be very long, for they demand a severe intellectual effort. It may be well to take up only two words in the first lesson.

In the second lesson, after review, add two or three more words of the same group, say *pan, ran, man*.

The drill should continue until the child can read correctly any one of the words when the parent or teacher points to it. Then the words should be shown in various orders, and separately, until the child can easily read all of them. The other words of the group should be added, one by one (*Dan, tan, Nan, van, ban*, and finally, *an*). This may take quite a few lessons: it is all-important to have a firm foundation. Some of the words will be strange to the child. In fact, a familiar word, such as *an*, when presented alone, is likely to convey no meaning. There is no harm in telling the child that "a van is a big covered truck for moving furniture," or that "Nan is a girl's name."

If the child has learned the pattern in the list of actual words, he should be able to read nonsense syllables using the same pattern. Nonsense syllables are included with the words in the tests to accompany Lessons 1-36 (pages 101-116). The nonsense syllables are a test of the child's mastery of the phoneme. Tell the child that the nonsense syllables are parts of real words which he will find in the books that he reads. For example, the child will know *han* in *handle* and *jan* in *January* and *mag* in *magnet* or *magpie*. The acquisition of nonsense syllables is an important part of the task of mastering the reading process. The child will learn the patterns of the language more rapidly if you use the nonsense syllables in teaching. However, the lessons may be taught without teaching the nonsense syllables, if you so desire.

Reading is so familiar to us that we are likely to forget how difficult it is for the beginner. The child has so hard a time forming a connection between visual marks and speech sounds that he cannot attend to the meaning of what he reads. We must help him to establish this connection, and we must not bother him, for the present, with anything else. We can best help him by giving him the most suitable words to read, and these are short words in which the letters have uniform values. We present as many as possible of these, without regard to their meanings. The child will get the meanings only when he has solved the mechanical problem of reading.

When we present a pair of words like *can* and *fan*, a child may have no notion that these words are similar in sound, or that the similar spelling indicates a similar sound. It would be a waste of time to try, as do the advocates of "phonic" methods, to explain this to him. All we do is to present such words together; the resemblance of sound and spelling will do its work without any explanation from us. Only, we must remember that this takes a great deal of time and repetition. Above all, we must not upset the habit by presenting words in which the letters have different values.

When the *an* group has been learned, we may go on to another final-group, such as *bat, fat, hat, mat, Nat, Pat, rat, sat, tat, vat*. In doing this we also present pairs like *bat ban, cat can, fat fan, mat man, Nat Nan, pat pan*.

This brings us into the work of the first reading lessons on page 57.

SPEECH VARIATION AND
THE BLOOMFIELD SYSTEM
by George P. Faust

W<small>E KNOW IN ADVANCE</small> that Leonard Bloomfield's application of the principle of matching letters with sounds will work out better for some localities, social groups, and individuals than for others. After his system of teaching reading has been tried out nationally, some readjustments may have to be made to allow for the variations in standard American speech. For simplicity's sake, the changes should be kept to a minimum.

At first glance the obvious test is the matching principle itself, but in actuality complete consistency on this score is a secondary consideration. Instead, the crucial question is how the presence of a word or set of words affects the build-up of confidence in a child when his normal pronunciation does not match the spelling. Thanks to Bloomfield, we are not concerned here with such outlandish spellings as *one* or such unpredictable patterns as *here*, *there*, and *were*. Our difficulty is only that a spelling which is regular for one child may not be for another, because of differences in pronunciation.

Sometimes a real variation is so slight or so common that most of us are not even conscious of it. Taken by themselves, *at* and *an* clearly rhyme with *bat* and *ban*, but in phrases like *at bat* and *an ad*, very often the vowel changes, as phoneticians know. Or again, *length* and *width* would have to be respelled *lenkth* and *witth* to suit the way many of us pronounce them. Still further, we may very well both say and hear *fith* and *twelth* for *fifth* and *twelfth* without realizing it. As a matter of fact, probably very few of us ordinarily say anything but *sikth* for *sixth*.

It would be possible to spend a good deal of time worrying about pronunciations like these, but we have no occasion to. They are so completely acceptable that we scarcely know they exist, and there is only the remotest chance that any child will ever notice them for himself. Consequently, we can cheerfully go off and forget about them.

The case is somewhat different with *from*, which appears in the same list with *prom* and *drum*. For some Americans, evidently, the spelling of *from* is regular, but for me and others like me, *prom* rhymes with *calm*, and *from* with *drum*. If I were teaching beginners who spoke my dialect, *from* would probably concern me enough to make me do something about it—possibly teach it a lesson or two in advance as an irregular spelling.

Once in a while, a whole string of words may be affected by a single dialectal feature, like the "broad *a*" of some New England speech. Throughout much of the South, for example, *i* and *e* are pronounced exactly alike before *m* and *n*, even in accented syllables. Most often the vowel is the same as the one in *bit*. Of course this dialectal variation is confusing only to outsiders, who are not used to hearing *ten* pronounced like *tin*.

How is the Bloomfield system going to work with the speakers of a dialect like this? No one can know for sure without trying it out, but we can at least make an intelligent guess. If as between *tin* and *ten* there is only one vowel possible in normal pronunciation, the odds are that the variation in spelling will make no difference whatever to the children learning to read. This is a guess, however, and it needs to be tested in the schools. For if it should turn out that the confidence of children is impaired, a considerable rearrangement of the material will be called for.

Other variations in American speech are comparable with the ones already commented on, and so we will go no further. But because we have been exploring the little edges of difference to the neglect of the great areas of identity, let me here emphasize as strongly as possible the size and force of Bloomfield's contribution. We may be left to make a few minor alterations, but the big job has been done.

ABCDEFGHIJKLMNOPQRSTUVWXYZABCDEFGHIJKLMNOPQRSTUVWXYZABCDEFGHIJKLM

LET'S LOOK

JKLMNOPQRSTUVWXYZABCDEFGHIJKLMNOPQRSTUVWXYZABCDEFGHIJKLMNOPQRSTU

This is a test of ability to read from left to right. Have the child answer the questions: (1) Where will the arrow go? (2) Where will the football go? (3) Where will the sled go?

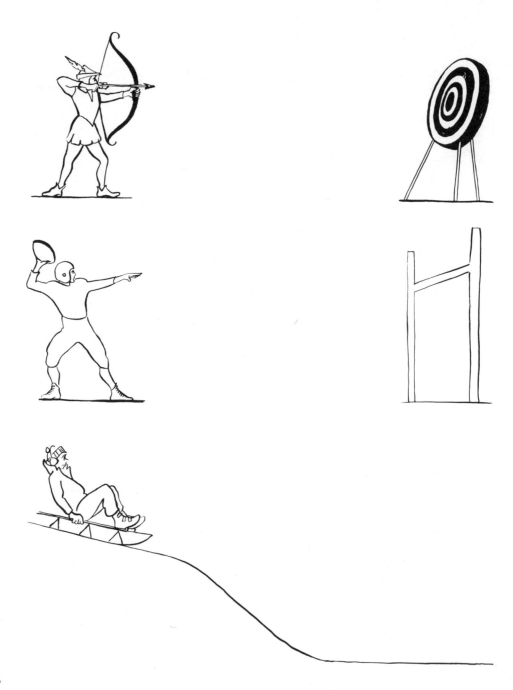

Have the child answer the questions: (1) Where did the arrow go? (2) Where did the football go? (3) Where did the sled go?

Does the child look from left to right?

Have the child answer the questions: (1) What will the dog do? (He chases the cat!)
(2) Will he catch her? (3) How did she get away?

This is a test of the child's ability to see the small differences in the shapes of the letters. Ask the child, "Which shape in each row is different from all other shapes in the row?"

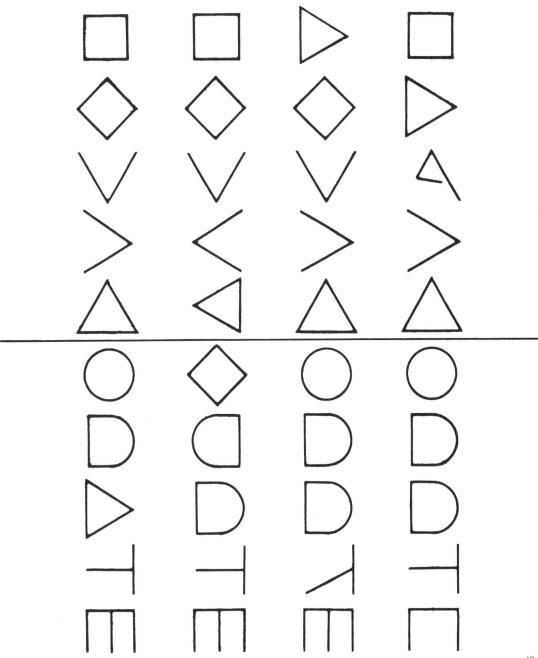

49

Ask the child, "Which two pairs of shapes in each row are alike?"

ABCDEFGHIJKLMNOPQRSTUVWXYZABCDEFGHIJKLMNOPQRSTUVWXYZABCDEFGHIJKLMN

LET'S TEST
OUR ABC's

JKLMNOPQRSTUVWXYZABCDEFGHIJKLMNOPQRSTUVWXYZABCDEFGHIJKLMNOPQRSTUV

This is a test to see if the child knows the letters of the alphabet. Ask him to read the names of the capital letters shown on this page. If he knows them, let him proceed rapidly with the following lessons. If he does not know the alphabet well, read the letters over to him or with him and work with him carefully on the following lessons in this section.

A B C D E F

G H I J K L

M N O P Q R

S T U V W X

Y Z

For every capital letter there is a small one with the same name. Ask the child to say aloud the capital letters and the small letters on this page. If the child can do this without prompting and without hesitation, he probably knows his ABC's.

A a   B b   C c   D d

E e   F f   G g   H h

I i   J j   K k   L l

M m   N n   O o   P p

Q q   R r   S s   T t

U u   V v   W w   X x

        Y y   Z z

LET'S READ
Part I
First Reading

Part I
FIRST READING

THE WORK of Lessons 1-36 is the foundation of the child's reading and perhaps the most important part of his entire formal education.

The first lessons contain words consisting of a vowel letter plus a consonant letter (such as *at*, *in*) and words consisting of a consonant letter plus a vowel letter plus a consonant letter (such as *cat*, *pin*). The letters are used only in the values which we shall call "regular" —the values listed on page 40 in the section entitled *First Materials*.

In addition to these, we introduce the word *a*. In this word, when it is spoken alone, the letter *a* does not have its regular value (as in *hat*), but the "irregular" ("long") sound (as in *cake*). This is true also on the rare occasions when we emphasize the word ("Not my house, but *a* house, any house"). In ordinary connected speech, however, the word *a* is spoken with a low stress and does not unduly contrast or clash with the stressed vowel of *hat*, *cat*, or *man*. Hence, without comment, we teach the child in early lessons to read such phrases as *a cat*, *a pin*.

Each lesson consists of three parts. First we list the words to be studied and read. On the first line we give well-known words which are part of the spoken vocabulary of almost every preschool child. On the second line we give harder words which may or may not be a part of the child's spoken vocabulary but which are useful as nonsense syllables to test the child's relation of letters to phonemes in the lesson. Sometimes we give both groups of words on the same line but separate them by greater space. Secondly, as the child gains in skill in reading individual words, we present phrases or sentences for practice in connected reading. Thirdly, after the phrases and sentences for reading, we give review exercises contrasting words similar to each other except for final consonants (*can*, *cat*), or except for vowels (*big*, *bag*). Both the lists and the sentences are printed for the child in large, clear type. If additional drill is necessary, the teacher or parent can present other phrases and sentences constructed from the same material. He must be extremely careful, however, not to introduce words which have irregular spellings, or words with regular spelling patterns which will be taught in later lessons, since this would only confuse the child and retard the learning process.

The written words in Lessons 1-36 should be practiced until they are overlearned. They should be presented in every possible order and combination. In Lessons 2-8 the written words learned in each lesson are contrasted with the written words learned in the previous lesson. To help the teacher or parent in this, all the words in Lessons 1-36 are given after Lesson 36 in alphabetical order. They should be practiced in groups arranged according to final letters (*bat, hat, cat, rat*), initial letters (*cat, cap, can, cab*), in groups with like consonants but unlike vowels (*hat, hit, hot, hut*), and in irregular orders (*bat, hop, pin, cut*).

No words beginning with *q* or *x* are taught in Lessons 1-36, and in these lessons we also avoid *w* because of the "irregular" value of *wa-* in such combinations as *wan* and *wad*. Initial *w* is taught when we reach the word *wag* in Lesson 5, but the teacher should note carefully that it has to be avoided in the lists in which the "an," the "at," the "ad," the "ap," and the "ag" words are contrasted.

In Lessons 9-16 we introduce the second vowel letter, *i* as in *pin*. As soon as the child has learned to read a word like *big*, we must present pairs like *big* and *bag*. It is contrasts like these which establish the phoneme values of the letters. The child should not be made to read single letters—not even those like *a* and *i*. The connection of letters with sound will be established by similarities and contrasts that appear in words (*big-bag, big-pig, big-bit*) in the lists at the bottom of each page. Hence the words should be presented in all possible orders.

In Lessons 17-24 we give words with *u* as in *rub*. These should be practiced by finals, by initials, and in sets that differ only as to vowel.

In Lessons 25-30, we give words with *e* as in *bet, led*, and so on. These lessons are organized in the same manner as before, but the available contrasts now include those with the same beginning and final consonant but with four different vowels: *bet, but, bit, bat*, for instance.

In Lessons 31-36, we have assigned to the letter *o* as its "regular" value the sound which it represents in words like *hot*. The word *on* has in many types of Standard English this same vowel sound; in communities where this is the case, the word *on* naturally belongs here. In other parts of the country, the letter *o* in the word *on* does not have the "regular" value (as in *hot*); for the speakers in these communities, *on* is a word with "irregular" spelling. In short, for some communities, but not for others, the word *on* is the second word in this series which presents a minor irregularity of spelling. The first was *a*.

Although the *-og* pattern (as in *cog*) is taught in Lesson 35, a number of useful and common words with the spelling *-og* have to be omitted because of variant pronunciations. If pronounced as they are in some parts of the country, *bog, dog, fog, hog*, and *log* (with the same phoneme or vowel sound as in *cog* and *jog*) should be added to and taught in this lesson. However, in other parts of the country these words, or some of them, are pronounced "hawg," "dawg," and so on. For persons who have this pronunciation, the words have to be considered separately in a later lesson (Lesson 166).

The Tests: A series of tests to accompany Lessons 1-36 will be found on pages 101-116. These tests are of special value because they provide practice in the reading of nonsense syllables, which have been purposely omitted from the lessons. By use of the nonsense syllables you will be able to ascertain whether or not the child has actually mastered each lesson.

These tests should be used in the following ways:

1. Progressive Testing. At the end of each lesson, test the child's mastery of it by asking him to read aloud the test words pertaining to that lesson. For instance, at the end of Lesson 1, turn to page 101 and ask the child to read the words in Test 1. When the child has completed Lesson 2, have him read the words in Test 2. Continue the same procedure through Lesson 36, making sure that the child's pronunciation of each nonsense syllable gives the letter its regular value; do not, for example, let him give the letter *s* the sound of *z*.

If the child is worried by the fact that these nonsense syllables are meaningless, you may point out to him that they are part of longer words which he will learn later; that is, *han* is the first part of the word *handle, jan* is part of *January, mag* is part of *magnet* and *magpie.* See your dictionary for other possibilities, but beware of irregular pronunciations (such as *mag* in *magic*, where *g* has the sound of *j*).

2. General Review. The test words and nonsense syllables may be used to good advantage as a general review to follow Lessons 8, 16, 24, 30 and 36. For example, when the child has completed Lesson 8, ask him to read all the words and nonsense syllables in Tests 1-8. If he is able to read these words easily, he is ready to start Lesson 9.

When the child has completed Part I, which ends with Lesson 36, go back to Test 1 and ask him to read two or three words, selected at random, from each test. If he can read these words without any trouble, he is ready to proceed with Part II.

1

can Dan fan man Nan pan ran tan an
ban van

a can a fan a pan a man a van
a tan van a tan fan

Dan ran.   Nan ran.
Van ran.   A man ran.

Nan can fan Dan.
Can Dan fan Nan?
Dan can fan Nan.
Nan, fan Dan.
Dan, fan Nan.

Dan ran a van.
Dan ran a tan van.
A man ran a tan van.

2

bat cat fat hat mat Nat pat rat sat at
tat vat

a bat a cat a rat a hat a mat
At bat. A fat cat. A fat rat.

A fat cat ran. A fat man ran.
Can Pat fan Dan? Pat can fan Dan.
Nan can pat a cat.
A fat rat ran.
A fat cat ran at a fat rat.
Can Nan fan a fat man?
Can a fat man pat a cat?

Nat at bat! Dan at bat!
Can Pat bat?

bat   cat   fat   mat   Nat   pat   rat   vat   at
ban   can   fan   man   Nan   pan   ran   van   an

3

bad dad had lad mad pad sad Tad ad
cad fad gad

a dad a lad a pad an ad

Dan had a tan hat.
Dan had a pad.
Tad had a tan hat.
Pat had a bat.
Nan had a fat cat.
A fat cat ran at a bad rat.

Can Dad bat? Dad can bat.
Can Pat fan Dad? Pat can.

bad   cad   fad   had   mad   pad   sad   Tad   ad
bat   cat   fat   hat   mat   pat   sat   tat   at

4

cap gap lap map nap rap sap tap
pap yap Hap

a cap a gap a lap
a map a rap a tap

Dan had a tan cap.
Hap had a nap. Dad had a nap.
Can a cat nap? A cat can nap.
Dad had a map.
A man at bat had a tan cap.
Tad can bat. Bat, Tad, bat!
Can a cat lap? A cat can lap.
Nat had a cap. Nan had a hat.

cap gap Hap lap map pap sap tap
cad gad had lad mad pad sad Tad

bag gag lag nag rag sag tag wag
fag hag jag

a bag a rag a rag bag
Tad had a bag.
Nan had a rag bag.

Can Pat tag Nan?
Pat can tag Nan.
Can Nan tag Dad?
Nan can tag Dad.

A cat can tag a rat.

Nan can nag Dad.

A rat ran. A cat ran. Wag sat.
Can Wag tag a cat?

gag   hag   lag   nag   rag   sag   tag
gap   Hap   lap   nap   rap   sap   tap

6

dam ham jam Pam ram Sam am
cam yam

a dam   a ham   a yam   a ram

Pat had ham.   Nat had jam.

Sam had a cap.
Dan had a hat.

Sam ran.
Can Sam tag Pam?
Can Pam tag Sam?

Dan had a ram.
Pam had a cat.
Sam had a rat.

ham   jam   ram   Sam
hag   jag   rag   sag

7

cab dab jab nab tab
gab lab

a cab a jab a tab
a dab a lab

Sam had a cab.
Sam ran a cab.

A cat can jab at a rat.
Can a cat nab a rat?
A cat can.

Can Hap tap Dad at tag?

Pam had a fan.
Pam can fan Dad.

Nan had a tan hat.
Pam had a tan bag.

cab dab jab nab tab
cam dam jam Nat tat

8

Al Cal gal Hal pal Sal Val   gas

a gas can   a gas cap

Hal had jam.

Can Hal tag Al?   Hal can.

Can Cal fan Dad?

Tad had a gas can.

Al had a pal, Sam.
Can Sam tag Al? Sam can.

Al had a cap.   Sal had a hat.
Hal had a tan hat.

Cal had a can.
Nan had a pan.

Cal gal Hal pal Sal Al Val gas
cab gab hat pat sat at vat gap

8

a fat ham   a bad gap
a sad man   a tan bag

A tan cat sat.

Can Sam tag Nan?   Sam can.

Dad had a bad map.

Val had a tan cap.

Sam had a fat cat.

Pam at bat.   Bat, Pam, bat!
Can Tad fan Pam?   Tad can!
Can Dad bat?   Dad can bat.

Pat had a pal, Dan.
Dan had a cat.

Wag can tag a cat.

Sam had jam.
Cal had a yam.
Hap had ham.

9

big   dig   fig   jig   pig   wig
gig   rig

a fig   a jig   a wig
a big, fat pig   a big bag

Dan had a big map.
A big van sat at a dam.
Sal had a big pig.
A cat ran.   A rat ran.   A pig ran.
Pal can dig.   Dig, Pal, dig!
Pam had a big fig.
Nan had a wig.

Can Nan jig?   Can a cat jig?
Can a big, fat pig jig?

big   fig   gig   jig   rig   wig
bag   fag   gag   jag   rag   wag

10

bin fin pin tin win in
din kin Min sin

a tin can ham in a pan

Min had a pin.

Can Al bat? Can Al win?

Cal sat in a cab. Min ran in.

A rat sat in a big bin.

Can Nan win at tag?
Can a fat man win?

bin	din	fin	Min	pin	tin	in
ban	Dan	fan	man	pan	tan	an

bin	din	fin	pin	win
big	dig	fig	pig	wig

bid did hid kid lid rid Sid
mid

Did Al bat? Did Al win?

A rat hid in a bin.

Sid hid a cat in a bag.

A bad man hid a pig in a big bag.

Can Sam bid? Did Sam win?

Sal had a tan bag.

A tin pan had a big lid.

A cat hid in a big hat.

bid	did	hid	lid	mid	Sid
bad	dad	had	lad	mad	sad

bid	did	kid	mid	Sid
bin	din	kin	Min	sin

bit fit hit kit lit pit sit it
wit

a bit a fit a hit a kit a pit

Did Sam hit Al? Sam did.

Sid had jam.

Nan had a bit.

Pam had a cat. Did Pam pat it?

A cat bit a rat.

Can a cat sit in a hat?
A cat can sit in a big hat.

bit	fit	hit	pit	sit	it
bat	fat	hat	pat	sat	at

bit	hit	kit	lit	sit
bid	hid	kid	lid	Sid

bib fib rib
jib nib

Did Pat hit a rib?

Nan had jam. Nan had a bib.

Al can dig a pit.

Can Sid tag Dan?

Did Tad fib? Tad did.
Bad Tad!

Sal had a big tan bib.
Did it fit Sal?
Did Nan pin it?
Did a pin jab Sal?
Did Nan pin a bib?
Did Nan pin Sal?

jib	nib	bib	fib
jab	nab	bit	fit

14

dim him Jim rim Tim
Kim vim

A cat sat in a big, dim bin.

A pan had a rim.

Tim hit a rib.

Did Jim hit Dan? Jim did hit Dan.
Bad Jim! Jim did it.

Kim ran. Jim ran.
Tap him, Jim! Tag him, Jim!
Can Jim tag him? Can Jim win?
Jim did tag him. Jim did win.

dim him Jim rim
dam ham jam ram

dim him Kim rim
did hid kid rid

dip hip lip nip rip sip tip zip
Kip pip yip

a dip a hip a lip
a rip a sip a tip

Dan can dip a can in gas.

A fat cat can tip a pan.

A cap had a rip. Did Nan pin it?

Did Tip nip Dad? Did Dad yip?

Dan had a dip. Hal had a sip.

Can a bag zip? Can a rag rip?

lip   nip   rip   sip   tip   yip
lap   nap   rap   sap   tap   yap

dip hip Kip rip tip
dim him Kim rim Tim

16

if   sis   Vic   Lil   Liz

Vic had a rip in a cap.

Liz can nap. Liz had a nap.

Sis can fan Dad. Sis, fan him!

Sal at bat. Hit it, Sal!
If Sal can hit it, Sal can win.
If Pat can fan Sal, Pat can win.

If Nan can tag Jim, Nan can win.
Tag him, Nan!

Hal ran at Sis.
If Hal can tap Sis, Hal can win at tag.

Can Jim bat? Can Jim hit it?
If Jim can hit it, Jim can win.
Did Pat bat? Did Pat hit it?
Did Pat win?

Did Vic hit Sis?
If Vic did it, can Vic fib?
Vic can fib. Vic did.

16

a lip a rib a hip a cap a hat
a ram a cat a kid a rat a pig
a tin can a fat ham a big van

A man had a cat in a big bag.

If Nan can tag Jim, Nan can win.

Tad hit Pam. Did Pam hit him?

Dad had ham in a pan.

Can a pig dig a pit?

A fat man did a jig.

Can Hal bat? Hit it, Hal!
If Hal can hit it, Hal can win.
If Dan can fan Hal, Dan can win.

Sis had a pin.
Tad hid it in a rag bag.
Did it jab Sis? Did Sis yip?
Did Tad fib?

17

bun fun gun nun run sun
dun pun

a cap gun   a sun tan

Can a cat run? Can a rat run?
Can a fat man run?
Can a big, fat pig run?

Sun can tan. Did it tan Liz?
Liz had a big hat. Liz did tan a bit.
Did Min tan? Min had a sun tan.

Can Jim tag Dan?
If Dan can run, Dan can win.
Can Jim tag him?
If Jim can run, Jim can tag him.
Jim had fun. Dan had fun.

bun   dun   fun   pun   sun
bin   din   fin   pin   sin

18

bus   Gus   us

pus

Can Jim run?   Can Jim tag us?
If Jim can tag us, Jim can win.
Run, Jim!   Tag us, Jim!

A fat man sat in a bus.
A fat man had a nap in a bus.
Can a fat man run a bus?
Can a fat man jig in a bus?

Gus hit Tim.   Gus ran.
Bad Gus!   Gus hit him.

Gus had a big rip in a cap.
Sis can pin it.   Sis did pin it.
Sis can jab us.   Sis did.

Gus   pus
gas   pun

cup   pup   up
sup

Can Nan pin up a bib?

Can a pup run?   Can a pup sit up?
Can a pup lap up jam?
A pup can.   Wag did.

Jim had a bad pup.   It bit him.
Jim hit it.   Bad pup!   Bad Jim!

Sis had a cup.   Nan had a cup.
Sal had a big tin pan.

Can Pal sit up?   Can Pal yip?
Sit up, Pal!   Yip, Pal, yip!
Pal can sit up.   Pal can yip.

cup   pup   sup   pup   up
cap   pip   sip   pus   us

20

but cut hut nut rut
gut jut

Dad cut up a ham.

Tim can run, but Al can tag him.

Jim had a pup. Did it nip him?

Pat had a nap, but Dan sat up.

Can a big bus run in a bad rut?

A rat hid a nut in a hut.

A cab ran in a rut. Did it tip?

Gus had a fig, but Sal had a nut.

Did Sam cut up? Did Jim cut up?

Sam ran, but Jim hid.
Jim hid in a hut.

but cut hut nut rut tut
bit cat hit Nat rat tat

21

bug dug hug jug lug mug pug rug tug

Can a pup dig?

A big bug sat on a map. Dad hit it.

A bug hid in a rug.

Can Tim lug a fat pig?

Dan dug a pit.
Did Dan dig a big pit?

Did Sis hug Dad? Did Dad hug Sis?
Did Jim tug at Dad?

Sal had a cup. Nan had a mug.
Sis had a jug.

bug dug hug jug lug pug rug tug
big dig hag jig lag pig rig tag

bug hug jug rug
but hut jut rut

22

cub hub rub sub tub
dub nub

a cub a hub a rub a tub a hub cap

Can a pig sit in a tub?

A bus ran in a rut. It hit a hub cap.

Rip it up! Pin it up!

Rub it!

Rub-a-dub-dub! A cat in a tub!
Rig-a-dig-dig! A pig did a jig!

A fat cub sat in a van.
Did Pal yip at it?
Did Pal nip at it?

cub dub nub rub tub
cab dab nib rib tab

dub hub rub tub
dug hug rug tug

gum   hum   sum   yum
bum   mum   rum

If Pat can hum, Jim can jig.

Nan hid gum in a big tan bag.

Dan can hum. Can a cat hum?

Dad can win a big sum.

Pam can gab, but Dad can sit mum.

If Tad can hum, Sis can tap.
Hum, Tad, hum! But Tad sat mum.

Gus had gum. Dan had jam.
Yum, yum!

hum   rum   sum   yum
him   rim   Sam   yam

hum   rum   sum
hub   rub   sub

24

bud   Jud   mud
cud   dud

Did Tim lug mud in a tin can?

A fat pig sat in mud.
A pig had fun in mud.
Can a fat pig run in mud?

Jud had a big cat.
It hid in a bin.
Did it tap Jud?
Did Jud pat it?

Hal had mud in a rug.
Did Sis dab at it?
Did Sis nag Hal?
Get a rag, Sis. Rub it up.

bud   cud   dud   mud   bud   mud
bid   cad   did   mid   bum   mum

24

a cup   a jug   a mug   a pup

A fat man had a nap in a big bus.

Can a pup dig? Tip dug a pit!

A man had a pig in a mud hut.

Tad ran, but Jim sat.

Tim had a tin tug in a tub.

Hal had a ham. Pat cut it up.

If Nan can hum, Sis can jig!

Sal had a sun tan.

Nan cut a big bud.
Nan put it in a jug.
Did Hap tip it?

Hit it, Dan!   Run, Dan!
If Dan can run, Dan can win.

A cat hid in a tub.
A pup hid in a bin.
A bug hid in a rug.

bet get jet let met net pet set wet yet
vet   sunset

Let Dan bat.

Did Al get wet?

Nan had a pet cat.

Get up, Tad!

Let us in, Sis! Sis, let us in!

Let Sid pet a pup.

Jim let Pam tag him.
Jim let Pam win at tag.

Nan met Dad at sunset.
Nan met Dad at a bus.

Did Sam bat yet? Let Sam bat.
Hit it, Sam! Get a hit, Sam!
Sam hit it. Sam can get a run.

bet jet met net pet set vet wet
but jut mat nut pit sit vat wit

26

Ben den hen Ken Len men pen ten
fen wen yen   pigpen

A big, fat pig sat in a pigpen.

A wet hen sat in a tub.

Ben, get us a net.

Len had a pet hen.

Did Dad let Ken get a cap gun?

Dad met Sis at ten.
Did Sis hug him?

Ten men sat in a bus.
Can ten men sit in a big bus?

Ben den fen Ken men pen ten wen
bun dun fun kin   man pin tin win

Ben Len men pen   wen   yen
bet let met pet   wet   yet

bed fed led Ned red Ted Ed
Jed wed

Jed fed a red pig in a pigpen.

Ted had a red cap.

A man led a pig. A man fed a pig.

Ed had a pet pup. Ed fed it.
Ed fed it a bun. Ed fed it ham.
Did it get big? Did it get fat?

Ned had a nap in bed.
"Get up, Ned!"
Ned sat up in bed.
Did Ned get up yet?

bed fed Jed led red Ted Ed
bud fad Jud lid rid Tad ad

bed fed led Ted wed
Ben fen Len ten wen

beg keg leg Meg peg

Tim ran, but Tad had a bad leg.

Ned had a cap on a peg.

A keg can tip. Meg did it!

Did Pal sit up? Did Pal beg?
Did Pal yip?
Did Pal fib? Pal did!
Meg had fed him!

Ed can get a pet.
Can Ed get a pet pup?
Can Ed get a pet rat?
Did Ed get it yet?

Can a pup nip? Can a pup beg?
If a pup can sit up, a pup can beg.

beg	leg	Meg	peg	beg	leg
bug	lug	mug	pug	bed	led

29

Les Wes yes   hem Lem   pep
hep

Lem had a cub in a pen.

Can Sis hem a bib?
Yes, Sis can hem it.

Get up, Les!
Les, get up! Let us in!
Did Les get up? Yes, Les did.
Les had pep. Les had vim.

Dad! Dad! Let us get a cat.
Did Wes get a cat?
Yes, Wes did.

Lem had ham. Lem cut it up.
Pal sat up.
Lem fed Pal ham.

hem hep pep   Les pep
him hip pip   leg peg

30

web   Mel
Deb Jeb Zeb

Dad, can Jeb get a cap gun?
Did Dad let Jeb get it?

A cat can rip a web.

Deb had a red kid bag.
Can Deb zip it?
Yes, Deb can zip it.

Mel had a tan cap.
It had a bad rip.
Can Mel get a red cap?
Yes, Mel can get a red cap.

Zeb, can Wag sit up?
Yes, Wag can sit up.
Sit up, Wag. Beg, Wag.

Deb Jeb web
dub jib Wes

30

a wet rag   a red hat   a fat hen

A fat man had a nap in a bus.

Hal had a cap gun. Hal had fun.

Jim hit Tad.
Did Tad get mad at him?

Pam had a pet cat.
Pam fed it ham.
Did it sit up?
Can a cat beg?

Can Sid run? Can Sid win a bet?
Yes, Sid can win.
Get set, Sid! Run!

A big bug sat in a web
Did it tug at it?
Did it rip it up?
Yes, it did tug at it.
It did rip it up.

Pat let Nan tag him.
Pat let Pam win at tag.

Can ten big, fat men get in a bus?
Nan had a red hat. Ben had a tan cap.

Can a pup tug at a rug?
Yes, a pup can tug at a rug.
Can a pup sit up? Can a pup beg?
Yes, a pup can beg. Up, Tip, up!

Nat had a fat pup, Wag.
Can Nat get him in a tub?
Yes, Nat did get him in a tub.
Did Wag yip? Did Wag nip Nat?
Did Wag run?
Yes, Wag did run, but Nat can nab him.
Nat can lug Wag. Nat can get him
in a tub.

cot dot got hot lot not pot rot
jot sot tot wot   cannot

Ed had gum, but Pam did not.
Ted ran. Ted got hot.
Can a wet rug rot? Yes, it can.

Dad had ham in a pan.
Dad cut it up.
Tip got a bit. Dad got a lot.

Lem had a cot in a hut.
Lem had a nap. Get up, Lem!
But Lem did not get up.
Pal, get Lem up! Nip him, Pal!
Pal did nip Lem. Pal got him up.

cot got hot jot lot not
cut get hat jet let net

pot rot sot wot
pet rat set wet

32

Bob cob job mob rob sob
fob gob hob lob
popgun bobcat cobweb

a bobcat a cobweb ten men in a mob

Nan got cut, but Nan did not sob.

If Bob can get a job, Bob can get
a cat. Bob got a job. Bob got
a cat. Did Bob get a bobcat?

Did a bad man rob Dad? Yes,
a bad man did rob him and run.
But Dad ran. Dad got him.

cob fob gob hob
cab fib gab hub

job lob rob sob
jab lab rib sub

cob gob hob job lob rob sob
cot got hot jot lot rot sot

hop   mop   pop   sop   top
cop   fop   lop

a hop   a mop   a pop   a top
Sam had pop. Yum, yum!
Mum got a mop. Ed got a top.
If Dan can hop, Pat cannot tag him.

Bob had pop in a cup.
Did Bob tip it? Yes, Bob did.
Did Sis hop? Did Sis get a mop?
Did Sis mop it up? Did Sis
get mad at Bob?
Sis did not get mad.
Sis let Bob sip pop.

cop   hop   lop   mop   sop   top
cap   Hap   lap   map   sap   tap

cop   fop   hop   lop   mop   sop
cob   fob   hob   lob   mob   sob

cod God nod pod rod hod sod

a cod a nod a pod a rod

A man in a tug got a big cod.
Ken got a rod. Ken got a cod.
Ken fed Kit cod, but not Pal.
Pal ran at Ken. Pal sat up.
Pal got a bit, but Kit got a lot.

Dad had a nap. Did Dad nod?
Yes, Dad did nod a bit.

"Bob, get us a mop!"
"Yes, Dad." Did Bob hop? Bob ran!
Bob got a mop. Bob got Dad a mop.

cod	God	hod	nod	pod	rod	sod
cad	gad	had	Ned	pad	red	sad

cod	hod	pod	sod
cop	hop	pop	sop

cog jog tog   Mom Tom

Ed had gum, but Deb did not.
Ed got Deb gum.

Did Tom nod? Did Tom nap?
Jog him, Meg. Get him up.
Tom cannot nap yet.
Meg did not jog him.
Meg let Tom nap.
Sam ran in. "Get up, Tom!"
But Tom did not get up.
Pal ran in. Tom got up.

Jim had a cap. Ted did not.
Mom got Ted a red cap.
It did not fit Ted, but it did fit Al.
Jim had a cap. Al had a cap.
Ted did not.

jog tog   Mom Tom
jag tag   Mum Tim

36

Don on con Lon Ron yon

Dad got on a bus.
Don had a nap on a cot.

A man had a bed in a van.
Did it jog? Can a man nap in a van?

A bad pup got mud on a rug.
Lil, get a wet rag.

Ron had a red cap on. Did Ron
get it wet?

Liz got a big red wig.
Liz had it on.
Did it fit? Did it tip?
Yes, it did tip. It did not fit Liz.
Can Lon get it on? Let Lon get it on!
Lon got it on. Lon did a jig.
Lon did a jig in a wig!

con Don Lon Ron yon on
can den Len ran yen an

Tests For Lessons 1 through 36

To determine how well the child has learned the previous section and to give him additional practice, ask him to read the following words. In these lists, nonsense syllables are included as well as real words.

For more detailed instructions on the use of these tests, see page 59.

TEST 1

ban   can   Dan   fan   gan   han   jan   kan   lan   man
Nan   pan   ran   san   tan   van   yan   zan   an

TEST 2

bat   cat   fat   gat   hat   kat   lat   mat   Nat   pat
rat   sat   tat   vat   at

TEST 3

bad   cad   dad   fad   gad   had   lad   mad   nad   pad
rad   sad   Tad   vad   ad

TEST 4

bap   cap   dap   gap   Hap   jap   kap   lap   map   nap
pap   rap   sap   tap   vap   yap   ap

TEST 5

bag   cag   dag   fag   gag   hag   jag   lag   mag   nag
pag   rag   sag   tag   vag   wag   zag   ag

TEST 6

bam cam dam fam gam ham jam kam mam
nam pam ram sam Sam tam vam yam zam am

TEST 7

bab cab dab fab gab hab jab lab mab nab
pab rab sab tab ab

TEST 8A

bal Cal dal fal gal Hal jal kal mal nal
pal ral Sal tal Val Al

TEST 8B

bas cas das fas gas jas kas las mas nas
pas ras sas tas vas

TEST 8C

bac cac dac fac lac mac rac sac tac
vac Wac ac

TEST 8D

baf caf daf gaf haf jaf kaf raf saf taf af

TEST 8E

cav dav gav hav jav mav nav rav sav
tav av

TEST 8F

daz gaz haz jaz laz maz naz paz raz yaz az

big   dig   fig   gig   hig   jig   lig   mig   nig   pig
rig   sig   tig   vig   wig   zig   ig

big   dig   fig   gig   hig   jig   lig   mig   nig   pig
bag   dag   fag   gag   hag   jag   lag   mag   nag   pag

rig   sig   tig   vig   wig   zig   ig
rag   sag   tag   vag   wag   zag   ag

bin   din   fin   hin   jin   kin   lin   min   nin
pin   rin   sin   tin   vin   win   zin   in

bin   din   fin   hin   jin   kin   lin   min   nin
ban   dan   fan   han   jan   kan   lan   man   nan

bid   did   fid   gid   hid   kid   lid   mid   rid
Sid   tid   vid   yid   id

bid   did   fid   gid   hid   lid   mid   pid   rid   sid
bad   dad   fad   gad   had   lad   mad   pad   rad   sad

tid   vid   id
tad   vad   ad

TEST 12

bit dit fit git hit jit kit lit mit nit
pit sit vit wit it

bit fit git hit kit lit mit nit pit sit
bat fat gat hat kat lat mat nat pat sat

vit it
vat at

TEST 13

bib dib fib gib hib jib kib lib nib rib
sib tib ib

bib dib fib jib nib rib sib tib ib
bab dab fab jab nab rab sab tab ab

TEST 14

dim gim him Jim kim lim mim nim pim rim
sim Tim vim wim im

dim gim him Jim kim lim mim nim pim rim
dam gam ham jam kam lam mam nam pam ram

sim Tim vim im
Sam tam vam am

TEST 15

dip   fip   hip   Jip   kip   lip   nip   pip   rip   sip
tip   vip   yip   zip   ip

dip   hip   jip   kip   lip   nip   pip
dap   hap   jap   kap   lap   nap   pap

TEST 16A

dif   fif   gif   jif   lif   nif   pif   rif   tif   if

dif   gif   jif   lif   pif   rif   tif   if
daf   gaf   jaf   laf   paf   raf   taf   af

TEST 16B

bis   dis   fis   lis   ris   sis
tis   vis   Wis

bis   dis   fis   ris   sis   tis   vis
bas   das   fas   ras   sas   tas   vas

TEST 16C

bic   dic   fic   hic   lic   mic   nic   pic   ric   sic
tic   vic   ic

bic   dic   fic   lic   mic   ric   sic   tic   vic
bac   dac   fac   lac   mac   rac   sac   tac   vac

TEST 16D

bil   dil   Gil   hil   kil   Lil   mil   nil   pil
ril   sil   vil   wil   il

nil   pil   ril   sil   vil   il
nal   pal   ral   sal   val   al

TEST 16E

biv   div   giv   liv   niv   piv   riv   tiv   viv

div   giv   liv   niv   riv   tiv
dav   gav   lav   nav   rav   tav

TEST 16F

diz   fiz   giz   liz   miz   siz   tiz   viz   wiz   iz

diz   giz   liz   miz   iz
daz   gaz   laz   maz   az

TEST 17

bun   cun   dun   fun   gun   hun   jun   mun   nun   pun
run   sun   tun   un

bun   dun   fun   hun   jun   mun   nun
bin   din   fin   hin   jin   min   nin

pun   run   sun   tun   un
pin   rin   sin   tin   in

bus   cus   dus   fus   gus   hus   jus   lus   mus   pus
rus   sus   tus   us

bus   cus   dus   fus   gus   jus   mus   pus   rus
bas   cas   das   fas   gas   jas   mas   pas   ras

sus   tus
sas   tas

TEST 19

cup   gup   nup   pup   rup   sup   tup   up

cup   gup   nup   pup   rup   sup   tup   up
cap   gap   nip   pip   rip   sip   tip   ip

TEST 20

but   cut   gut   hut   jut   mut   nut   rut   sut   ut

but   gut   hut   jut   mut   nut   sut   ut
bit   git   hit   jit   mit   nit   sit   it

TEST 21

bug   dug   hug   jug   lug   mug   nug   pug   rug   tug

bug   dug   hug   jug   lug   mug   nug   pug   rug   tug
big   dig   hig   jig   lig   mig   nig   pig   rig   tig

107

bub cub dub hub lub nub pub rub sub tub

bub dub hub lub nub rub sub tub
bib dib hib lib nib rib sib tib

cum dum fum jum kum lum num pum tum um

dum gum hum jum kum lum mum num pum rum
dim gim him Jim Kim lim mim nim pim rim

sum tum um
sim Tim im

bud cud dud fud hud Jud mud pud rud sud ud

bud dud fud hud mud pud rud sud ud
bid did fid hid mid pid rid sid id

buc duc luc ruc suc yuc

buc duc luc ruc suc
bic dic lic ric sic

TEST 24C

buf   duf   muf   puf   ruf   suf

duf   luf   puf   ruf
dif   lif   pif   rif

TEST 24D

bul   cul   dul   ful   gul   hul   lul   mul   nul   pul
sul   tul   vul   ul

bul   dul   ful   gul   hul   lul   mul   nul   pul   sul
bil   dil   fil   gil   hil   lil   mil   nil   pil   sil

tul   vul   ul
til   vil   il

TEST 24E

buz   guz   muz   nuz   puz   wuz   uz

guz   muz   wuz   uz
giz   miz   wiz   iz

TEST 25

bet   det   fet   get   het   jet   ket   let   met   net
pet   ret   set   tet   vet   wet   yet   et

bet   det   fet   get   het   jet   let   met   net   pet
but   dut   fut   gut   hut   jut   lit   mut   nut   pit

ret   set   tet   vet   wet   et
rut   sut   tat   vat   wit   ut

Ben den fen hen jen Ken Len men pen ren
sen ten ven wen yen zen en

ben den fen hen jen ken len men pen ren
bun dun fun hun jun kin lin mun pun run

sen ten ven wen zen en
sun tun van win zin un

bed ded fed ged Jed led med Ned ped red
sed Ted wed zed ed

bed ded fed ged jed led med Ned ped red
bud dud fud gid jud lid mud nud pud rud

sed ted wed ed
sud tid wid ud

beg deg keg leg Meg neg peg reg seg teg eg

beg deg leg meg neg peg reg seg teg eg
bed ded led med Ned ped red sed Ted et

beg deg leg meg neg peg reg seg teg eg
bug dug lug mug nug pug rug sig tug ug

TEST 29A

bes des fes hes jes kes Les mes nes pes
res ses tes ves Wes yes es

bes des fes hes jes Les mes pes res ses
bus dus fus hus jus lus mus pus rus sus

tes es
tus us

TEST 29B

dem fem hem kem mem nem pem rem sem
tem yem em

dem fem hem kem mem nem pem rem sem
dum fum hum kum mum num pum rum sum

tem yem em
tum yum um

TEST 29C

dep hep Kep lep nep pep rep sep tep zep ep

dep hep kep lep nep pep rep sep tep zep ep
dip hip kip lip nup pup rup sup tup zip up

TEST 30A

deb feb heb jeb leb neb peb reb veb web
Zeb eb

deb feb heb jeb leb neb peb reb eb
dub fib hub jub lub nub pub rub ub

TEST 30B

bel del fel hel jel kel lel Mel nel pel
rel sel tel vel wel yel zel el

bel del fel hel jel kel lel mel nel pel
bul dul ful hul jal kil lul mul nul pul

rel sel tel vel wel el
ril sul tul vul wil ul

TEST 30C

bev dev Kev lev mev nev rev sev ev

bev dev lev nev rev
biv div liv niv riv

TEST 30D

bec dec fec hec jec lec mec nec pec rec
sec tec vec ec

bec dec lec rec sec
buc duc luc ruc suc

112

def jef nef ref ef

def ref
duf ruf

TEST 31

bot cot dot got hot jot lot mot not pot
rot sot tot wot ot

bot cot dot got hot jot lot mot not pot
bet cat det get het jet let met net pet

rot sot tot wot ot
ret set tet wet et

TEST 32

bob cob dob fob gob hob job lob mob nob
rob sob wob ob

bob cob dob fob gob hob job lob mob nob
bib cub deb feb gab heb jeb leb mab neb

rob sob wob ob
reb sub web eb

bop cop dop fop hop jop lop mop pop sop
top op

bop cop dop hop jop lop mop pop sop top op
bap cup dep hep jap lep map pep sep tep ep

TEST 34

bod cod dod fod God hod mod nod pod rod
sod tod vod od

bod cod dod fod God hod mod nod pod rod
bed cud ded fed ged had med ned ped red

sod tod vod od
sed ted vid ed

TEST 35A

cog gog jog mog nog pog rog sog tog wog og

gog jog mog nog pog rog sog tog wog og
gig jug Meg neg peg reg seg teg wig eg

bom com dom gom hom jom lom Mom nom pom
rom som Tom vom wom yom om

bom com dom gom hom jom lom mom nom pom
bum cum dem gum hem jum lem mem nem pem

rom som Tom vom wom yom om
rem sem tem vim wim yem em

bon con Don fon gon lon mon non
pon Ron yon on

bon Don fon hon jon lon mon pon Ron yon on
Ben den fen hen jen len men pen ren yen en

bol col dol fol gol hol jol lol mol nol
pol rol sol tol vol ol

bol col dol fol gol hol jol lol mol nol
bel cul del fel gul hel jel lel mel nel

pol rol sol tol vol ol
pel rel sel tel vel el

coc   doc   joc   loc   moc   noc   poc   roc   soc   toc
voc   oc

doc   joc   loc   moc   noc   poc   roc   soc   toc   voc   oc
dec   jec   lec   mec   nec   pec   rec   sec   tec   vec   ec

TEST 36D

bos   cos   dos   fos   gos   hos   jos   los   mos   nos
pos   ros   tos   os

cos   dos   fos   gos   hos   jos   los   mos   nos
cus   des   fes   Gus   hes   jes   Les   mes   nes

pos   ros   tos   os
pes   res   tes   es

TEST 36E

nov   pov   sov   ov

nov   pov   sov   ov
nev   piv   sev   ev

116

Words in Lessons 1-36

a

ad Al am an at

bad bag ban bat
bed beg Ben bet
bib bid big bin bit
Bob
bobcat
bud bug bum bun bus but

cab cad Cal cam can cap cat
cannot
cob cod cog con cop cot
cobweb
cub cud cup cut

dab dad dam Dan
Deb den
did dig dim din dip
Don dot
dub dud dug dun

Ed

fad fag fan fat
fed fen
fib fig fin fit
fob fop
fun

gab gad gag gal gap gas
get
gig
gob God got
gum gun Gus gut

had hag Hal ham Hap hat
hem hen hep
hid him hip hit
hob hod hop hot
hub hug hum hut

if in it

jab jag jam
Jeb Jed jet
jib jig Jim
job jog jot
Jud jug jut

keg Ken
kid Kim kin Kip kit

lab lad lag lap
led leg Lem Len Les let
lid Lil lip lit Liz
lob Lon lop lot
lug

mad man map mat
Meg Mel men met
mid Min
mob Mom mop
mud mug mum

nab nag Nan nap Nat
Ned net
nib nip
nod not
nub nun nut

on

pad pal Pam pan pap pat

peg pen pep pet

pig pin pip pit

pigpen

pod pop pot

popgun

pug pun pup pus

rag ram ran rap rat

red

rib rid rig rim rip

rob rod Ron rot

rub rug rum run rut

sad sag Sal Sam sap sat

set

Sid sin sip sis sit

sob sod sop sot

sub sum sun sup

sunset

tab Tad tag tan tap tat
Ted ten
Tim tin tip
tog Tom top tot
tub tug

up us

Val van vat
vet
Vic vim

wag
web wed wen Wes wet
wig win wit
wot

yam yap
yen yes yet
yip
yon
yum

Zeb
zip

LET'S READ
Part II
Easy Reading

Part II

EASY READING

Guide to Lessons 37 through 71

Lᴇssᴏɴs 37-71 deal with consonant letters in values which we assign to them as "regular."

First, we present words like *split* or *milk*, which contain two or more successive consonant letters, each in the value that we assigned to it as "regular" on p. 40. These appear in Lessons 37-44 and 46-71. In addition we include here five speech forms that are written with the letter *s*, but only in cases where this letter represents the sound that has been assigned to it as its "regular" value (as in *sit, gas, Sis*). These five forms are:

Lesson(s)

The plural suffix of nouns: *caps*. 51, 54
The third-person singular present-tense suffix of verbs: (Dan) *bats*. 51, 54
The possessive suffix: *cat's, it's*. 52
The unstressed form of *is*: *Nat's* (bad) 52
The unstressed form of *us*: *let's* (run) 52

Although these forms are written as *s* or *'s*, they have the sound of *s* (as in *sit*) only when they follow the "regular" sounds of *p, t, k, f, th*, as in *caps, hats, locks, cuffs, Beth's*. We include only forms where this *s* has thus its regular value. Forms like *ribs, pans* (where the letter *s* represents the sound of *z*) will not be presented until we reach Lesson 100.

Secondly, we assign "regular" values to certain combinations of two or three consonant letters; namely:

Lesson(s)

ng as in *sing* 55
nk as in *sink* 56
sh as in *shed, fish*. 57, 58
ch as in *chin, much* 59, 60

Thirdly, we introduce words like *well, egg,* where a consonant letter in its regular value is written double (Lessons 62, 63, 64, 65).

Fourthly, we give here two other spellings which we shall treat as regular:

Finally, besides *a* and *on* of Lessons 1-36, only one irregular word is introduced: the word *the* in Lesson 45. Its spelling is irregular in two respects: the combination *th* has here not the value which we are assigning as regular (as in *thin*), and the letter *e* has here not its regular value (as in *set*).

The teacher or parent will easily see that, except for the one word *the*, we are only supplementing and not contradicting that which has been learned in Lessons 1-36. In Lessons 37-71 and 72-97 we are still working at the foundations. If enough time and drill have been given to Lessons 1-36, Lessons 37-71 will go much faster, but the work should be carried on in the same way and practiced to the point of overlearning—until the child reads the words and phrases without difficulty or hesitation.

37

led	sled	lab	slab	lob	slob	nag	snag
lid	slid	lag	slag	lop	slop	nap	snap
	slim		slam	lot	slot	nip	snip
lip	slip	lap	slap	lug	slug	nub	snub
lit	slit		slat		slum		snug

cab	scab	kid	skid	mug	smug	wag	swag
can	scan		skim		smut		swam
						wig	swig
cat	scat	kin	skin		smit		swim
cot	Scot		skip				swum
	scum	kit	skit				

Sam slid on a big red sled.

Cal at bat! Slam it, Cal! Run, Cal, run!

Did Sal slap Tip? Yes, Sal hit Tip. Bad Sal!

Let us hop, let us skip, let us run!

Pam did a skit in a red wig.

Did Pal snap at Kit? Did Kit slap at Pal?
Scat, Kit, scat! Kit ran. Pal hid.

pan	span	pit	spit	tab	stab	top	stop
pat	spat	pot	spot	tag	stag	tub	stub
	sped		spud	tan	Stan		stud
pin	spin	pun	spun		stem		stun
					step		

Dad got Stan a red top.

Can Stan spin it? Yes, Stan can spin it.

Step up, Stan. Spin it, Stan!

Stan did step up. Stan spun it.

Can Tom swim? Yes, Tom can swim.

Did Tom swim? Yes, Tom swam.

Can a hen swim? Can a cat swim?

Did Bob step on a wet spot?

Did Bob slip? Bob slid!

Did Tip nip Jim? Yes, Tip bit him.

Stop it, Tip!

Can Deb run yet? Can Deb skip?

Yes, Deb can run, but Deb cannot skip.

Did Ed slop mud on a rug?

Yes, Ed got a big spot on a rug.

scab   scan   scat   Scot   scum

skid   skim   skin   skip   skit

slab   slag   slam   slap   slat

sled   slid   slim   slip   slit

slob   slop   slot   slug   slum

smug   smut

snag   snap   snip   snub   snug

span   spat   sped   spin   spit   split

spot   spud   spun

stab   stag   Stan   stem   step   stop

stub   stud   stun

swag   swam   swig   swim   swum

Did Stan get a stag?   Did Stan bag a big stag?

Jim had a big red sled.   Jim sat on it.
It slid.   It sped.   It hit a snag.
A slat split.   Did Jim skin a leg?
Jim did.   Jim got a scab.
Tom got mud on a rug.   A big spot!
Tom got a big spot on a rug.   Sis, get us a mop.
Run, Sis, skip!   Sis ran.   Sis got us a mop.

40

brad	crab	drab	ran Fran	ram pram
rag brag	rag crag	rag drag	red Fred	rig prig
ran bran	ram cram	ram dram	fret	rim prim
rat brat	rib crib	rip drip		rod prod
rig brig	crop	drop	from	prom
rim brim		rub drub		prop
		rug drug		
		rum drum		

Did Dad get a big crop? Did Dad brag?
Let us not brag.

Wag got a crab. Did Wag drag it in?
Nan had a nap in a snug crib.
A drop on a rug! Did it drip from a pen?
Let Fred bat. Hit it, Fred! Slam it!
Run, Fred! Fred ran. Fred slid in.
Fran had a red hat. It had a big brim.
Did Fred sit on it? Get up, Fred!
Did Fran get mad at Fred?
Liz had a bran bun. Liz had a fig.
Did Liz get fat? Did Liz get slim?

```
ram  tram    ram  gram  grab    ram  scram    rap  strap
rap  trap    rid  grid  grin    rap  scrap    rip  strip
rim  trim    rim  grim  grit    rip  scrip         strop
rip  trip    rip  grip  grog    rub  scrub    rum  strum
rod  trod    rub  grub                        rut  strut
rot  trot
```

Sid had a trip on a bus.

Did Fran grab a hot bun from a pan?

A spot on a rug! Nan, let us scrub it!

A man got a big rat in a rat trap.

Fred got a drum from Dad. Did Fred grin?

Let Stan get a grip on it. Stan can drag it.

Brad fed Kit a scrap from a ham.

Did Pal grab it? Did Kit spit at Pal?

Did Kit slap at Pal? Did Pal yip?

Brad fed Pal a scrap. Brad fed Kit a scrap.

Did Liz cut it? Did Fran trim it?

Can Sal snap it? Can Sal zip it up?

Did it fit? It did not fit.

Sal can snap it, but Sal cannot zip it up.

If Sal can get slim, Sal can zip it up.

42

rip   rip   rip   rag   rag   rap
trip grip drip drag brag trap
strip   strap

brad brag bran brat brig brim
crab crag cram crib crop
drab drag dram drip drop
drub drug drum
Fran Fred fret from
grab gram grid grim grin
grip grit grog grub
pram prig prim prod prom prop
tram trap trim trip trod trot

scram scrap scrip scrub
strap strip strop strum strut

Lil had a tan hat. Lil let Fran trim it.
Sam got a stag. Did Sam brag? Did Sam strut?

Fred had a big tan grip. It had a strap.
Did Fred trip? Did Fred drop it? Grab it, Fred!

lab	blab	lad	clad	lip	clip	lag	flag
	blat		clam		clod	lap	flap
			clan		clog		flat
led	bled	lap	clap	lot	clot	lip	flip
	blob		clef		club	lit	flit
lot	blot		Clem				flog
						lop	flop
						led	fled

lad	glad		plan	wig	twig	flip-flop
	glen		plat	win	twin	
	glib		plod	wit	twit	
	glum	lot	plot			
	glut		plum			
		lug	plug			
			plus			

Fred had a bat. Clem had a club.
Jim had a flag. Tad had a drum.
Did Fred win? Did Len clap?
Fran had a twin. Dan had a twin.

44

blab bled blob blot
clad clam clan clap clip
clod clog clot club
flag flap flat fled flip flit flop
glad glib glum glut
plan plat plot plug plum plus
twig twin twit

Did Tad get gas? Yes, Dad let Tad get gas.
Tom, get us a plum.
Brad got a bad cut. It bled a lot.

Dad got Fred a drum. Fred got a drum
from Dad. Did Fred grin? Did Fred drum?
Rub-a-dub-dub! Rub-a-dub-dub!
Did Fran rub? Did Fran scrub? Did Fran mop?
Yes! Fran did a lot, but Fran did not brag.
Fran did not fret.
Can Jim spin a top? Let Jim spin it.
Yes, Jim can spin a top. Jim spun it.
Ten slim men can sit in a bus. Can ten big,
fat men sit in a bus?

the

cat	pig	sled	drum	flag
a cat	a pig	a sled	a drum	a flag
the cat	the pig	the sled	the drum	the flag

Did Ben flop on the bed?
Ted dug up a big clam.
The red hen cannot swim in the tub.
Fred had a big drum.
Fred got the drum from Dad.

Did Bob get cut? Bob got cut
on the lip. The cut bled.

Dan had a cot in the hut. Dan had a nap
on the cot. Get up, Dan! But Dan did not
get up from the cot.

A man had a rat. The man got a cat. The cat
sat in the sun. It did not run. It did not get
the rat. The man got a rat trap. The man set the
rat trap. The rat got in the trap. Snap! The trap
got the rat!

46

an	and		end	bend		bond	intend
ban	band	men	mend	lend		fond	handbag
	hand	pen	pend	rend		pond	
	land	ten	tend	send	win	wind	
	sand	wen	wend	vend	fun	fund	

Jim and Ted swam in the pond.
Can Mom mend the rip in the cap?
Did the flag flap in the wind?
Did Dad send Pat a popgun and a drum?
Tom dug a pit in the sand and hid a can in it.
Dad sat in the sun a lot and got a tan.
Can Ted split a twig?
Hal got a sled and Clem got a drum.
A fat man had a nap in the big bus.

Sam hit Al on the hand and Hal
on the leg.
Pal had a swim in the pond. Did Pal
get wet? Did Pal drip? Yes, Pal did.
And Tom did! Tom did not swim in the pond,
but Pal got him wet.

an	ant	din	dint	Ben	bent	rent	bun	bunt
pan	pant		hint	den	dent	sent		hunt
ran	rant		lint	Len	lent	vent		Lunt
		Min	mint	pen	pent	went	pun	punt
	font	tin	tint	ten	tent		run	runt

Get us gum, Mom. Get us mint gum.

Ten men sat in a big, tan tent.

Hit it, Pat! Did Pat hit it? Did Pat bunt?

Jim lent Ted a sled. Ted sat on the sled and slid. The sled hit a snag. It got a big dent in it. Can Ted mend it? Ted cannot mend it, but Dad can.

Ed Lunt swam in the pond. Ed got wet. Ed sat on the sand and got a tan.

Lend us a hand, Tom! Hunt up a pen! Did Dad send Tom? Yes, Dad sent Tom. Tom went and got Dad a pen.

Jim had a flag. The flag went flip-flop in the wind.

best	rest	bust	fist	dusk	desk	lisp
jest	test	dust	list	husk	disk	wisp
lest	vest	gust	mist	musk	risk	
nest	west	just		rusk		
pest	zest	must		tusk		
		rust				

A big red hen sat on the nest.
Tom must not drop the flag in the dust.
Dad just got in from a trip in the West.
A man must not brag.
Let us stop a bit and rest.

Ed and Al and Jim swam in the pond.
Ed and Al and Jim can swim, but Ed can
swim best. Jim and Al must stop and rest,
but Ed can swim on and on.

Lon, Mel, and Ben had a test.
Ben did the best. Did Ben brag?
Did Ben strut?

Brad let a disk sit in the wet sand.
Did it rust? Did Dad get mad?

belt	gilt	bilk	self	held
felt	hilt	silk	elf	weld
melt	jilt	ilk	itself	gild
pelt	kilt	milk	himself	
welt	lilt	milkman		
	silt			
	tilt		gulf	
	wilt			

help	bulk	elk	gulp	elm	bulb
kelp	hulk		pulp	helm	
yelp	sulk				talc
				film	

Did Dad get the film yet?

Fran had a red hat and a red belt.

Mom had a silk hat, and Dad had a felt hat.

Dan got the milk from the milkman.

Dan had hot milk in a cup.

Clem cut a twig from an elm. Clem cut himself on the hand.

50

bump	camp	gift	act	kept	apt
dump	damp	lift	fact	wept	rapt
hump	lamp	rift	pact		
jump	ramp	sift	tact		hemp
lump	tamp				tempt
pump	vamp				
rump					

romp		deft	tuft	sect	insect
	left		duct		

imp
limp

At dusk Mom lit the lamp on the desk.
Dan sent Mom a gift from camp.
At camp, Dan had a cot in a tent.
Al got hit on the leg.   Did Al limp?

Fred must help us lift the desk.
Help us, Fred!   Lend us a hand!
The sled hit a bump but did not stop.
It just kept on.   Did it jump the bump?

50

Hot milk in a pot,
Hot milk in a jug,
Hot milk in a cup,
Hot milk in a mug.

Tim felt bad. Mom kept Tim in bed.
Tim must not get up. Tim must not run
and jump in the hot sun. Tim must rest in bed.

Dad got Sal a red hat and a red silk belt.
Sal must not drop the red hat. Sal must not
drop it in the mud.

Fred got a bad bump, but Fred did not fret.

Can Bob help Sam? Can Bob lend Sam a hand?

Let us hop, skip, and jump! Let us not sit
and fret and sulk.

Al had a twig from an elm. Al hit Clem.
Clem felt it. Did Clem get mad? Clem did.
Clem ran at Al. Al sped west. Did Clem get him?

Don and Dad went on a hunt. Dad got an elk.
Don got a stag. Did Don and Dad brag?
Did Don and Dad get it on film?

cat	get	mop	tent	nest	limp	help	desk
cats	gets	mops	tents	nests	limps	helps	desks

bats	jets	fits	cots	cuts	caps	dips	cups
hats	lets	hits	dots	huts	naps	lips	pups
pats	pets	sits	pots	nuts	raps	sips	sups

pants	rests	gifts	bulks	camps	imps	bumps	gulfs
dents	fists	facts	sulks	lamps	romps	lumps	
hints	dusts	tempts					

Cats and pups can run and jump.

Ken sits on the damp sand and gets wet.

Dad sent Mom gifts.

The ham tempts Tip. He gets it! Bad Tip!

Sal and Nan had red hats and red silk belts.

Bob lit the lamps in the den.

Ted, help us lift the sled!

Ted helps us lift the sled.

Pam dusts and mops. Pam dusts ten desks.

Ted lifts up the lamps and helps Pam.

Pat	the cat	it
Pat's bat	the cat's leg	its leg

Pat's hot.	It's hot.	Let us run.
Nat's bad.	It's bad.	Let's run.

Pat had a flag and Pat's pal Dan had a drum.

If Pat's sled hits a snag, the sled gets dents in it.

If Nat's bad, Nat cannot swim in the pond.

Sis sits and sulks. Let's not sulk, Sis!
Let's hop, skip, and jump! Let's run!
Let's stop and rest. Yes, let's rest a bit.
It's hot. Let's not sit in the hot sun.
Let's swim in the pond. Jump in, Fred!
Get wet! Fred jumps in and gets wet.

Hal sips milk from a cup. Kit laps milk
from a pan. Tip gulps the milk.

Pam sits in the sun. Pam gets a sun tan.
Fran got a sun lamp. Fran got a sun tan.

Did Pal get the cat's milk? Yes,
if Kit naps, Pal gets Kit's milk.

skim   stun   plum   wept   rust   lamp   runt
skimp   stunt   plump   swept   crust   clamp   grunt

tract   strict cleft   drift   swift   grandstand
smelt   spelt   spilt   skulk   cramp   bandstand
scamp   stamp   tramp   blimp   crimp
prompt clump   frump   slump   stump
trump   brand   grand   stand   strand
blend   spend   trend   blond   scant
spent   print   splint sprint stint
blunt   crept   slept   brisk   frisk
crest   twist   trust

a brisk run   a strict man
Run, Sam! Sprint!
Fran swept the rug.
Dan can print. Nan cannot print yet.
Fred did a stunt, but Fred did not brag.
Did Pal and Kit romp and frisk?

The tents at Pat's camp had ten cots.
Pat and Dan slept on cots in the tents.

stamp   grunt   twist   trust   blunt   print   drift
stamps grunts twists trusts blunts prints drifts

tracts   clefts   tramps   smelts   skulks
cramps   scamps   frumps   blimps   crimps
prompts   clumps   splints slumps   stumps
trumps   frisks   crests   sprints   stints

Can Tom stand on the sled?

Al swam in the pond and got a cramp.

A pup yelps and a pig grunts.

Nan twists the wet rag.

Ned had ten stamps. Ned got the stamps from Bob.

Run, Ted! Ted sprints!

Fred and Tom did stunts. Fred and Tom had fun.

Can Dad trust Bob? Yes, Dad can trust Bob.
Dad trusts Bob. Bob helps Dad.

Sam tramps mud on the rug. Sam, let's
not tramp mud on the rug!

Deb naps in a bed. Wag naps on a rug.
Did Deb let Wag nap in the bed?

The cat crept up on the rat.

Did Pat get the sled in a drift?

Brad had a swift trip in a jet.

Tom spilt milk on the desk. The scamp!

Get the best brand.

Let's not stand in the hot sun.

Fran spent it on gum.

Lend us a hand, Hal! Hal lent us a hand.

Pam had a blond wig.

Run, Sam! Sprint! Run, Ted! Ted sprints.

Dad and Fred sat in the grandstand.

Can Tom stand on the sled? Tom cannot stand on the sled.

Sal mops up the steps and dusts. Sis helps Sal mop and dust. Sis gets Sal a rag.

Hal did stunts. Hal did a grand stunt, but Hal did not brag. A man must not brag.

A rat sat on a mat. A cat crept up. The rat ran. The cat did not get the rat.

Fran just swept the rug. Let's not tramp mud and sand on the rug!

king	bang	bung	clang	cling	clung
ring	fang	dung	slang	fling	flung
sing	gang	hung	twang	sling	slung
wing	hang	lung	sprang	sting	stung
ding	pang	rung		swing	swung
ping	sang				
ting	rang	sung		bring	
zing	tang			spring	sprung
				string	strung

Deb got a ring from Dad.

Sam, bring us the string.

Hang up the caps and stand up the bats.

A pig cannot sing. A pig just grunts.
A pup cannot sing. A pup just yelps.

Nan and Min had a swing. Min sat in the swing
and Nan swung Min. Min swung in the swing, up and
up and up! Min sat in the swing and sang.

Al at bat! Hit it, Al! Al grips the bat.
Al swung at it. Zing! Al hit it! Al flung
the bat and ran.

56

ink	rink	bank	rank	bunk	punk
link	sink	dank	sank	funk	sunk
mink	wink	hank	tank	hunk	
pink		lank	yank	junk	

blink	brink	blank	crank	drunk
clink	drink	clank	drank	flunk
slink		flank	frank	skunk
stink		plank	Frank	slunk
		spank	prank	spunk
		stank	swank	stunk
				trunk

Nan had a red ring, and Min had a pink ring.
Frank got ink on the rug. The scamp!

Kit had a tug in the tub. It got wet. Did
it sink? Yes, Kit's tug sank in the tub.

Tom drank milk from a cup, but Frank
drank milk from a big mug.

A cat drinks milk. Did the cat drink
its milk? Yes, the cat drank its milk.

57

shed	shot	sham	shrub	shrimp
shelf	shop	shag	shrug	shrift
Shep	shod	shad	shred	shotgun
ship	shut	shank	shrink	
shift	shun	shaft	shrank	
shin	shunt	shalt	shrunk	

Frank had a trip on a big ship.

The man at the shop fed Shep scraps.

A hen had a nest on a shelf in the shed.

Frank cannot shut the big trunk.

Dad shot a shotgun, and Hal shot a popgun.

Dad can mend the sled in the shop.

Frank's cap got wet and shrank.

Nan got shrimps from a can.

Bob got a bad bump on the shin.

Jim left the pups in the shed. The pups got shut up in the shed.

58

ash	clash	mesh	dish	gush	brush
bash	flash	flesh	fish	hush	crush
cash	slash	fresh	wish	lush	blush
dash	splash		swish	mush	flush
gash	smash		bosh	rush	plush
hash	brash		gosh	tush	slush
lash	crash		josh		
mash	trash		slosh		catfish
rash	stash				codfish
sash					dishpan
					dishrag

Let's drink fresh milk.

Splash! went a fish. Hush, Tom, hush!

Can a fish swim in a tank? Yes, a fish
can swim in a tank, and a fish can swim in a pond.

Did Sal smash a dish? Yes. Crash! went
the dish.

Stan had mush and milk in a dish. Did Stan
splash it on Dot's pink silk sash? Did Dot fret?
Dot wept!

chin   chap   chug   chop   chipmunk
chip   chat   chum   chest
chink   champ   chump   Chet
chid   Chad   chunk
chit

Let Chad chop a chunk from the stump.
Frank and Frank's chum Tom had a chat.
Did Sal smash a dish and chip a cup?
Tom and Chad must lift the big chest.

Pat kept a pet chipmunk in a pen.
Pat fed it nuts and milk. But the pen had
a chink in it. The chipmunk fled.

Did Ted chop an elm? Ted just cut
a twig from a shrub.

Stan can run the best. Stan can sprint.
Stan is the champ.

Ken got mad and hit Fred on the chin.
Fred hit Ken on the chest.

Dad had ham and a yam. Chad had hash.
Chet had a chop and a spud.

rich	inch	bench	bunch	filch
much	finch	drench	lunch	milch
such	pinch	French	munch	mulch
	winch	trench	punch	gulch
sandwich	clinch	ranch	crunch	belch

Tom and Frank sat on a bench and had a chat.
If ink drips from the pen, blot it up.

Fran got lunch. Fran got us a ham sandwich
and milk. Such a lunch!

Did Sal pinch Nan? Did Sam punch Dan?
Stop it, Sal and Sam!

Tom and Bob must lift the big chest and
set it up on the bench.

Jim can sip milk and munch on a crust.

Nat's dad had a big ranch and a camp
in the West. Nat slept on a bunk in the camp.
Ten men slept in the camp. The men had
a big job on the ranch.

It is such a big chest, but Dad can lift it.
Dad did lift it an inch. Dad did not lift it much.

thin   thrash   thump   Beth   tenth   width

thing   thresh   thrum   Seth   length   fifth

think   thrush   thrust   Smith   strength   twelfth

thank   thrift   depth

thanks

Tom Smith did not bring us a thing!
Sam left on the tenth. Dan went on the twelfth.

Dad got Beth a red silk sash. Did Beth
thank Dad? Did Beth hug Dad? Yes, Beth did!
    A thin man and a plump man sat on a bench
and had a chat.
    Dan and Ted cannot lift Frank's trunk.
It's a big thing! Dan and Ted think Dad can
lift the trunk. And he can! "Thanks, Dad!"
    Thump on the drum, Bob. Thump it, Bob!
Bang it! Such a din!

    Frank thinks it's hot. "Let's swim
in the pond, Seth."
    "Yes, let's jump in and swim."
Frank and Seth splash in the pond.

62

biff	cliff	cuff	ruff	scuff	Jeff
miff	skiff	puff	gruff	stuff	
tiff	sniff	buff	scruff	bluff	
	stiff	huff		fluff	
		muff		snuff	

Pam had a big, tan muff.

Sam huffs and puffs.   Let's stop and rest.

Mom kept such stuff in a big trunk.

Frank had a stiff leg and did not run.

Nat's tan pants had big cuffs.

Fran must get a stiff brush and scrub the mat.
Tip got mud on it.

The plank is an inch in width and a rod in
length.   Dad thinks the men can lift it.

In the spring a thrush had its nest
in a stump.   The thrush sat on the stump and sang.

Mom got gifts from Dad and Nan.   Did Mom
get a mink muff?   Yes, Mom got a mink muff
from Dad and a pink hat.   From Nan Mom got
a tan kid belt and a tan handbag.

63

kiss	Bess	dress	bless	lass	fuss
miss	Jess	press	chess	mass	muss
hiss	Tess	cress		bass	truss
bliss	less	tress		crass	
Swiss	mess	stress			
		undress			

Ken did not let Miss Smith kiss him.
Chet can dress and undress himself.

Bess had a red silk dress and
a pink silk sash.

Biff, bang, crash! Such a mess!
Such a fuss! Stop it, Jess! Hush!

Dad shot at an elk and hit it.
Dad did not miss it.

Dad got a fish, and Tess got a fish.
Dad got a cod, and Tess got a bass.

Did Mom press Dot's dress? Did Mom
press Nat's pants? Did Dot and Nat thank Mom?

Frank got a gift. Frank got a chess set.
Can Frank win at chess?

bill	Jill	rill	bell	dwell	shall
fill	chill	drill	fell	shell	dull
hill	skill	frill	sell	smell	gull
kill	spill	grill	tell	spell	hull
mill	still	trill	well	swell	skull
pill	swill	shrill	yell	doll	lull
sill	dill	thrill	Nell	Moll	mull
till	gill		dell	loll	cull
will			hell		null
ill			ell		

a windmill   a hilltop

Can Bess spell? Yes, Bess can spell.

If Dad gets Nell a doll, Nell will thank him
and hug him and kiss him. Nell will dress and
undress the doll.

Splash! Bill fell in the pond and got wet.
Bill got a chill. Bill must rest in bed
and drink hot milk.

Did Stan hunt on the hilltop? Did Stan kill
a skunk? Did the skunk smell bad? Did Stan? Yes.

156

65

mitt	fizz	Ann	add	egg
butt	buzz	inn	odd	
mutt	fuzz	jinn		ebb
putt	jazz			

Frank Hunt had a mutt, Spot.

Jess had pop. Did the pop fizz?

Did Cliff get a golf club? Can Cliff putt?

Can Beth add ten plus ten?

Jill ran up the hill.

Nell rang the bell, and Ann let us in.

Bob got an egg from the nest in the shed.

Chet had a mitt and Stan had a bat.

At lunch, Dad had an egg, and Jess had hot mush and milk.

Did the big ram butt Tom? Yes, it did. The ram butts Tom if Tom steps in the pen.

Did the bell buzz? The bell did not buzz. The bell rang.

Seth and Hank slept on cots in a tent. Mom and Dad slept at the inn.

which whiff whish whisk whist

whip whiz whim whit

when whet whelp whang whelk

Which bunk did Chet get at camp?

Hit the drum, Dan. Whang it! Bang it!

When did Beth sing?

Which sled did Chad bring?

When Pal trots in, the cat whisks out.

Fred can smell a skunk. Yes, Jill got a whiff!

Can Jeff whip Tom? If Jeff hits Tom, Dad will spank Jeff!

When Fred swam, Dan sat on the bench. Which pond did Fred swim in?

Which doll will Bess get? Which doll will Ann get? When Bess gets a doll, Ann gets a doll.

Can Bill snap a whip? Snap it, Bill! Snap it!

Did Dad bring the trunk? When did Dad bring it? Did Cliff help Dad lift it?

When Chet and Stan get in a scrap, Stan can whip Chet. But Chet can run!

back	black	Dick	brick	blacksmith
hack	clack	kick	prick	pickup
Jack	slack	lick	trick	
Mack	crack	Nick	click	
lack	smack	pick	flick	
pack	snack	sick	slick	
rack	stack	tick	stick	
sack	track	wick	chick	
tack	shack		thick	
	whack			
	thwack			

Pack the trunk and let Jack help lift it.
Mack had black slacks and a black hat.
Let's stop and get a snack.
Did Jack kick at the bricks?

Dick's hat fell in the pond. Dad went
and got a stick. Dad and Dick got Dick's hat
back. But Dick had a wet hat!
Nick sat on a tack. Did Nick jump up?
Did Nick yelp? Such a thing!

deck	buck	cluck	cock	block
neck	duck	pluck	dock	clock
peck	luck	stuck	lock	flock
check	muck	truck	rock	crock
beck	Puck	struck	sock	frock
	suck	chuck	hock	shock
	tuck	shuck	pock	smock
				stock

Tell him Dad will send a check.
Let Bill cut a thick stick.
The clock struck ten.
Jack and Jill went up the hill.
Mack shot a buck. Cliff shot a duck.
A pig grunts. A pup yelps. A hen clucks.

    Nell had a big red hen and ten chicks.
Nell kept the hen and the chicks in the shed.
    Pick up a stick, Jack, and fling it in the
pond. Pal will swim in and bring it back.
Not a rock, Jack! A stick! Pal cannot
bring back a rock. A rock will sink.

batch	etch	itch	switch	botch	Dutch
catch	fetch	ditch	twitch	notch	hutch
hatch	ketch	fitch	flitch	blotch	clutch
latch	retch	hitch	snitch	crotch	crutch
match	vetch	pitch	stitch	Scotch	
patch	sketch	witch		splotch	
snatch	stretch				
thatch					
scratch					

Ann can patch and stitch the dress.

Mack will sketch the ship.

The hen will hatch the egg.

Chuck can catch fish in the pond.

Jack cut a notch in a stick.

Jim, fetch us a bat and a mitt.

Jack will pitch, and Tom will catch.

Dick's at bat. Hit it, Dick! Hit it and run!

Did Pal snitch ham from Kit's dish?

Did Pal snatch it and run? Kit will slap
at Pal, but Kit will not scratch him much.

x

quack	quip	quit	quid	squib
quell	quick	quiz	squid	squish
quest	quilt	quill	squint	squelch
quench				

Chuck let Al quiz him but did not tell.

Nick got a cod, and Cliff got a squid.

A duck quacks. Ducks quack.

Jess, let's stop and rest.

Let's quit! It's hot!

Dan quit, but Tom kept on.

Jim had a chill. Bring Jim a quilt, Bess!

Jack must not squint at the sun.

Pat dips the quill in the ink.

Quick, Tom, fetch us a big stick!

If Tim hits the cat, it will scratch him. Tim must not hit the cat. Tim must not pinch it. Tim must pet the cat. Tim must not snatch at it and clutch it.

Did Hank punch Bill? Did Bill kick Hank on the shin? Quit it, Hank and Bill!

ax	fix	Rex	next	ox	tux
lax	mix	sex	text	box	flux
Max	six	Tex		Cox	crux
tax	jinx	vex		fox	
wax	minx	flex			
	sixth			sandbox	

Can Max and Rex get the big box on the truck?
A red fox sat on a stump.
Dad will fix Max a sandbox and fill it.
Jack, fetch Dad the ax.

Did Dad miss the bus at six?
Yes, but Dad got the next bus.
Sis can patch and mend. Sis will fix
the rip in Dick's pants. Fetch the pants,
Dick, and Sis will mend them. What a big rip!
Sis will stitch it up and mend it. Sis will
fix it up.
Dip up the mud in a tin can and mix
it well. Next get six cups. Drop the mud
in the cups and add ink—just a dash.

Let's catch fish in the pond. Let's sit
on the bench and catch fish.

The hen will hatch the egg. A chick will
peck at the shell.

A fox will snatch a chick and kill it.
Run, hen, run! Run, chicks, run! Quick!

Lift up the box, Jack, and set it up
on the bench. Shut the lid and lock the box
and set it up on the bench. Yes, Miss Tess!

Dick's sled struck a stump and got
a bad bump. The sled got bent, but Dick's dad
will fix it.

Bob, fetch Dad the ax! Run, Bob! Quick!
The ax is in the shed. It's in the shed.

Jim had a chill and felt ill. Mom kept Jim
in bed. Bring Jim a quilt, Bess! Mom will
tuck him in. Bess went and got a thick quilt.

Dick's cap fell in the pond. Quick, Dick,
fetch us a stick! Run! Quick! Dick got a stick.
Dad and Dick got Dick's cap from the pond.
But Dick's cap got wet. Dick had a wet cap.

LET'S READ
Part III
More Easy Reading

Part III

MORE EASY READING

Guide to Lessons 72 through 97

T HE USES of the letters which appear in Lessons 72-97 may still be called regular; we here take up pairs of vowel letters, such as *ee*, *ea*, and combinations of a vowel letter with *y* or *w*, such as *ay*, *ow*. To each such pair or combination we assign a sound as its "regular" value. In some parts of the country these sounds are greatly modified before *r*; therefore we put some of these combinations which are followed by *r* into separate lessons.

In Lessons 72-97 we introduce also a few additional two-syllable words and compounds.

All of them are of the simple kind which can be read as if two one-syllable words were printed without spacing:

oatmeal

railway

about (a bout)

around (a round)

away (a way)

At the end, in Lessons 95, 96, and 97, we take up words with final *e* as a silent letter. This is for us an "irregular" spelling, since we have taken the vowel sound in *pet* as the regular value of *e*. However, the use of final *e* as a silent letter may be called semiregular, since in most instances a final letter *e*, when it is not the only vowel letter in a word (such as *be*, *me*), serves as a silent letter: *give*, *have*. Apart from this, Lessons 72-97 introduce no new irregular words: they make use only of *a*, *the*, and *on* given in Lessons 1-71.

bee	free	beet	sheet	feed	bleed
see	tree	feet	sleet	seed	freed
fee	three	meet	fleet	weed	speed
lee	spree		sweet	need	breed
tee	flee		street	deed	creed
wee	glee		greet	heed	greed
			tweet		tweed

treetop

At lunch Nick had a sweet bun and jam.
See Pal sit up and beg. Hank must feed him.
Tom ran up the street. Tom ran and slid.

A bee sat on Dick's neck. Dick felt it.
When Dick struck at it, the bee stung him.
Nick will meet Dad and Sis at the bus
at three. Nick will greet Dad and Sis.
Al fell from a tree and did not land
on his feet. Al got a bad bump.
Dad had a box three feet in width
and six feet in length. Dad will need help
from Clem. Meet Clem at the bus and tell him.

deep	creep	peek	feel	seen	beef
keep	sheep	seek	heel	keen	seem
peep	sleep	week	peel	teen	deem
seep	steep	leek	keel	green	teeth
weep	sweep	meek	reel	queen	beech
		reek	steel	sheen	leech
		cheek	wheel	screen	speech
		creek			screech

fifteen   sixteen   beechnut   indeed   weekend

Chet had fifteen beechnuts in a dish.
See the three black sheep.
Jack and Jill went up a steep hill.

Creep in the shed and peep at Pat's chicks.
Keep the hen and chicks in the shed.

At lunch, Frank had beef and beets and
a sweet bun.

Liz had a green belt and a green kid bag.
Bab had a pink dress and a pink hat. Did Bab
and Liz feel grand?

deer   cheer   queer   steer
beer   leer   peer   sheer

Dad will kill a fat steer, and Mom will can it.
A bee stung Pam on the cheek. Did Pam screech?
Can a deer run and jump? Yes, it can.

Bess and Ned will see the King and
the Queen. Bess and Ned will cheer.

Tom and Dick, stop it! Tom must not
step on Dick's feet. Dick must not hit and
pinch Tom. If Tom and Dick keep it up,
Miss Tess will keep them in till six. The scamps!

At camp, Stan and Jim will sleep in a tent.
Stan will sleep in a bunk, and Jim will sleep
on a cot. Stan and Jim will get up at six.

When Sid tracks mud on the rug, Sid must
sweep it up.

When Pat got up at bat, did Frank and Fred
cheer and clap?

Let's get a rod and reel. Let's fish
in the creek.

75

eat	cheat	bean	pea	peanut
beat	wheat	dean	sea	
feat	treat	Jean	tea	
heat	bleat	mean	lea	
meat	cleat	wean	flea	
neat		lean		
peat		clean		
seat				

See Pal scratch! Did Pal scratch a flea?
Dean had lean beef and hot tea.
Can Chet beat Dan at chess?
Frank, let's swim in the pond and beat the heat.
Feed Kit the lean meat and Pal the fat meat.
Bring clean sheets and a quilt.
Jack did not cheat at chess.
Jean got a seat on the bus.

A sheep bleats. A duck quacks.
A hen clucks. A pig grunts. A pup yelps.
Vic had a treat. Dad got him peanuts
and pop.

bead	beak	creak	deal	each
lead	leak	sneak	heal	beach
read	peak	speak	meal	peach
	teak	bleak	peal	reach
	weak	freak	real	teach
		squeak	seal	bleach
		streak	veal	breach
			steal	preach
			squeal	

Let's get a hot meal—not just a snack.
Tom did not eat the veal chop.
A rat can sneak a peek at a cat.

Beth and Sid can each eat a peach. Beth
will drink milk, and Sid will drink weak tea.

Can Lil reach Seal Beach on the bus?
Yes, but can Lil get a seat on the bus?

Can Jack read yet? Not yet, but Miss Cox
will teach him.

Will Brad speak at the club? Brad will
read a speech.

beam	cream	heap	leaf	east	leash
seam	dream	leap	sheaf	beast	
team	gleam	cheap		feast	heath
	steam			least	sheath
	scream	sunbeam		yeast	
	stream				

steam heat   east and west   a green leaf

Beth got a cheap dress at the dress shop.
Jean had a bad dream. Did Jean scream?
A deer can run and leap. A deer can leap well.

Bring clean sheets and a quilt. Bring
a clean, thick quilt.

Whip the cream, Beth. Fran and Max can each
peel a peach. Beth and Fran and Max will feast!

Get the leash, Pal. Get the leash and
bring it. Did Pal leap up and get the leash?
Did Pal bring it?

Stitch up the seam, Nell, and see
if the dress fits.

78

ear	hear	year	beard
dear	near	clear	
fear	rear	smear	
gear	tear	spear	

Hear the ducks quack! Hear the pig squeal!
Hear the hen cluck! Hear the chicks peep!

Bess and Jean will eat at six. Bess will
drink tea, and Jean will drink milk. Bess will
eat a peach, and Jean will eat a plum. Bess
and Jean will eat hot mush and cream. Bess
will fix hot tea. Jean will get the cups
from the shelf and bring fresh milk in a jug.

A man sat near us on the bus. The man had
a big black beard.

Did Nan get a smear on the pink dress? Did
Nan weep? Nan felt bad but did not shed a tear.

Jean will sing at the club when it meets
next year. Mom and Dad will hear Jean sing.

If it will just clear up, Nick can fish
in the stream.

boo	moon	teaspoon	boot	loop	cool
coo	noon	moonbeam	hoot	scoop	fool
moo	soon		toot	sloop	pool
too	boon		loot	snoop	tool
woo	loon		moot	stoop	drool
zoo	spoon		shoot	swoop	spool
shoo	croon		scoot	troop	stool
	swoon			droop	

FRED AND THE RAT

Fred got a gift. "A gun! Thanks, Dad!"
"See my gun, Sis? Soon I will shoot it."
At noon Fred shot the gun.
In the next lot sat a rat. Bang! went the gun.
The rat ran. It hid in a boot.

Did Sis scream and jump up on a stool?
"Keep cool, Fred. Stoop and shoot him!"

Did the rat fool Fred? Yes, the rat did.
The rat ran at Fred!

Did Fred scoot? Fred did!

boom	food	goof	booth	boost	spook
doom	mood	woof	tooth		
loom	brood	poof			
zoom		proof	toothbrush		
bloom			toothpick		

SPOT'S PUPS

Spot had ten pups—a big brood. Ed fed the pups milk. Did Ed heat the milk? Yes, Ed did heat it a bit. The pups spilt a lot.

When the pups got teeth, Ed fed the pups beef. Did the pups gulp the food? Yes! Such greed!

Ed got the meat in a can. Ed spent a lot, but each pup had a feast.

Did the ten pups woof and yap? Did the ten big pups jump up on Ed and lick him?

In the end, Ed had a plan. Did Sam, Max, Nick, and Dan need a pup? Did Jean, Fran, and Beth? Yes, indeed! Did Ann and Liz and Sid, too? Each got a free pup. Such luck!

poor boor moor spoor

POOR JEAN

Poor Jean. Jean got a bad chill. Jean must rest and sleep in bed till noon. Poor thing!

At noon Jean will eat lunch. Jean will get hot food—hot mush and cream. Quick, Bess! Bring Jean a spoon.

FLUFF AND KIT

Can Kit lift Fluff? Yes, Kit gets a grip on Fluff's neck. Kit can lift and drag Fluff. Fluff will squeak and squeal, but Kit will get him back in the box in the shed. Poor Fluff!

When Fluff gets big, Kit cannot keep him in the box. Soon Fluff will get big and can loot Shep's food dish and snitch scraps from him.

Poor Shep! Poor pup! Will Shep grab Fluff's neck and drag him back in the shed, back in the big box, and drop him? But Shep cannot lock the shed. Shep cannot keep Fluff in.

gain	brain	Spain	faint	aid
main	chain	sprain	paint	laid
pain	drain	swain	saint	maid
rain	grain	twain	taint	paid
vain	plain		quaint	raid
lain	stain	maintain		braid
fain	train			staid
	strain			

Tom hung the chain in the shed.
Poor Bill had a bad pain from a sprain.
Dad paid Pat's bill at the shop on Main Street.
Bess and Al will meet Dad at the train.
Soon it will rain, and Ned will get wet.
The maid laid Dot's dress on the bed.

Dick must fix the big box and paint it green. Clem will aid him.

Jill got a plain green dress. Mom will stitch braid on it.

Clem kept the sheep on a chain and fed it grain.

fail	ail	aim	wait	waist	faith
hail	bail	claim	bait		
jail	wail		trait		waif
mail	flail				
nail	frail	mailbox			
pail	snail	mailman			
rail	quail				
sail	trail				
tail					

If Sam can get the bait, Sam and Al will fish.
See the pup wag its tail!
Tom laid the nail on the shelf.

A snail cannot run and jump. A snail
just creeps!

The mailman will bring the mail, and Jess
will get the mail from the mailbox.

Bess and Al will meet Dad at the train. Dad
will bring Bess a green hat and a green dress and
a tan belt. Dad will bring Al a flag and a gun
and a drum. Just wait! Just wait and see!

84

air fair hair pair chair stair lair
airship   airsick   hairpin haircut

Jack, get a haircut! Jack, get a haircut soon!
Frank, run and get Dad a chair. Thanks, Frank!

Mom got Pat's socks at a shop on Main Street.
Mom got Max a pair, too.
Tom laid the nail on the stair.

Nell had fair hair, Bess had black hair, and
Ann had red hair. Bess had black hair in a braid.

It's too hot. Let's get cool! Let's jump
in the pool and swim and get cool.

JACK'S TRIP

Jack had a big trip in an airship. A jet?
Yes, Jack went in a jet. Did Jack get airsick?
Jack had a pill, and Jack did not get airsick.

Did Jack see Spain? Yes, Jack did see Spain.

Will Jack send us mail? Yes, the mailman
will bring it.

Will Jack get back soon? Jack will not
get back till spring.

bay	may	bray	clay	plaything
day	May	dray	flay	railway
Fay	nay	fray	play	haystack
gay	pay	gray	slay	away
hay	ray	pray	stay	
jay	say	tray	sway	
lay	way		spray	
			stray	

a day in May   a railway train

Dick's cat ran away.

Dad will meet the train at Green Bay.

Which way did the cat stray?

On a hot day Dan lay in the hay and slept.

Did Ned pay the man?

Bess, bring us six cups on a tray.

    Dad will spray the crops in the spring.

Dad will spray the crops from the air.

    Fay had a pink and gray hat.

Nell had a gay red hat.

85

It's a cool day.

It's a hot day.

It's a grand day.

It's a sad day.

It's a gay day.

May Tom and Frank stay and play till six? Yes, Tom and Frank may stay. Did Dad say Tom and Frank may stay? Did Dad say yes?

Hear the jay up in the tree! Hear the jay screech!

Lift the box and set it up on the shelf. Lift it the way Dan lifts it. Lift it way up and set it down on the bench.

Lay the sheet on the bed. Stretch it and tuck it in.

Did Dick pick up a stray pup? Well, a stray pup did pick up Dick. Did it jump up on Dick and lick him? Did Dick and the pup play? Dick fed the pup milk and meat. It had a feast! Dick fed it each day. Soon the pup got big and plump. Dick must keep it. It will not stray away.

DICK'S CAT

Dick Smith's cat ran away. Which way did
the cat stray? Dick went east and did not
see the cat. Dick went west and did not see
the cat. Dick felt sad. Too bad!

"Dick! Dick!"

"Yes, Dad!"

"Run and fetch an ax from the tool shed."

"Yes, Dad!"

Dick went way back in the tool shed.
Up on the shelf sat the gray cat!

DAN AND THE HAYSTACK

Dan lay in the hay and slept.

"Get up, Dan. Bring in the hay.
The hay must not get damp." But Dan
did not get up. Dan just slept on.

"Quick, Dan! Get up! It may rain."
But Dan still slept.

Soon it did rain. Dan got wet, and
the hay got wet, too. Dan had let the hay
get wet. And Dan did not get paid.

boat	goad	boast	coach	oak	Joan
coat	load	coast	poach	soak	loan
goat	road	roast	roach	cloak	moan
moat	toad	toast		croak	roan
float			foam		groan
shoat	soap	coal	loam	coax	
throat	oats	goal	roam	hoax	loaf
		foal		oath	oaf

sailboat	toadstool	cockroach
steamboat	railroad	oatmeal

Poach an egg, Jean, and fix the oatmeal.
See the goat leap and jump! See the toad hop!
At lunch Joan had roast veal and fresh beets.
The coach met the team on the road.
Dad got Beth a gray coat.
Let Tess toast the fresh loaf.

Stan fell from the big oak tree. Hear
him moan and groan! Did Stan get a sprain?
Stan did not get a sprain. Stan did fool us.

THE SAILBOAT

Dad got Jack a big sailboat.

"Let's see it sail. Let's sail the boat
on the pond."

Jack set the boat in the pond, and away
it went. See the boat sail! When the wind
hits the big sail, the boat just scoots!
See it skim on the pond.

The boat will not tip and it will
not sink. It will just sail on the pond
in the wind.

AT CAMP

Each year Seth's dad and three men hunt deer
at a camp in Green Bay. Seth's dad and the three
men hunt quail and ducks too.

The men sleep on cots in a big tent. At six
the men get up and fix hot tea and hot oatmeal and
toast.

Each year Seth's dad gets a deer, a duck,
a quail, and a bad chill. Seth's dad may stay
sick a week.

SETH'S GOAT

Seth's dad got him a goat. Seth pets the goat, but the goat jumps and butts him. Seth picks himself up and thinks, "The goat did not mean it." Seth pats the goat on its neck, but the goat jumps back and kicks him. Seth hops away and thinks, "The goat did not mean it." Seth steps up and pats the goat on its back, and the goat jumps and stamps on Seth's feet. Seth skips away and thinks, "The goat did mean it. A goat butts and kicks and stamps. A goat just cannot play!"

THE SEAL

Did Jean see the seal at the beach? The seal did tricks.

Did the man train the seal? Yes, the man fed the seal a fish when the seal did a trick.

Did the man fling the fish at the seal? Yes, but the fish did not land on the sand. The seal can snatch the fish from the air!

A seal can catch fish well!

oar   boar   board   aboard   roar   soar   hoard

a nail in a board   an oar and a sail
a blackboard   a billboard   a steamboat   a sailboat

Hand Jean an oar.
See the jet soar in the air.
Jeff will spend it, but Jill will hoard it.

Just hear the wind roar! See the treetops
sway in the wind! Soon it will rain.

Help us lift the board up! Help us get
the big board up on the shelf in the shed!
Tom will help Frank and Al. Tom will help
get the big board up on the shelf in the shed.

Joan can read well. Joan can read
from the blackboard. Joan can read the print
on a billboard, too. Did Mom teach Joan?

Clem had ten shoats. Clem had a boar, too.
Each day Clem fed the shoats and the boar.
The shoats and the boar got fat. Did Clem
sell the shoats? Did Clem sell the boar?

88

out	scout	ouch	bound	count	outfit
bout	shout	couch	found	fount	about
lout	snout	pouch	hound	mount	around
rout	spout	crouch	mound		playground
tout	stout	grouch	pound	loud	background
mouth	trout	slouch	round	cloud	
south	sprout		sound	proud	
		foul	wound	shroud	
			ground		

Joan must get ground round—about a pound.
The hound pup bit Hank. Ouch!
Let's not sit on the wet ground.
Dad wound the clock and set it at three.
Let Jim count out loud.

Let's run round and round the playground
and scream and yell and shout!
Jean fed a chipmunk. Jean fed it a nut.
See the chipmunk pick up the nut and stuff it
in its mouth! See the chipmunk's cheek
puff out! The chipmunk had a pouch in its mouth!

our   sour   flour   scour

When Mom shops, will Mom get flour?
Joan must scour the pan.
If Jill keeps the milk cool, it will not sour.
Clean the fish and dip it in flour.

THE RAIN CLOUD

See that big black cloud in the west!
Feel the wind! Soon it will rain. Quick,
let's run! Let's not get our feet wet!
Beth's silk dress must not get wet. Let's not
stay out in the rain. Let's play in the shed.

THE PUP AND THE TOAD

Our hound pup found a toad on the ground.
Our hound pup did not grab at the toad.
Our pup just sat still and let the toad hop.
It just let the toad hop around on the ground.

THE TROUT STREAM

Clem will fish in the stream. Clem may
get a trout. If Clem can get a trout, Mom will
fix it and let him eat it at lunch.

90

bow	brow	owl	down	clown	uptown
cow	plow	cowl	gown	brown	downtown
how	prow	fowl	town	crown	
now	scow	howl		drown	cowshed
sow		jowl		frown	
vow		growl			
		prowl			
		scowl			

Hear the cow moo!
Hear the sheep bleat!
Hear the pig grunt!
Hear the pups yelp!
Hear the hen cluck!
Hear the chicks peep!
Hear the ducks quack!
Hear the owl hoot!
Hear the bee buzz!
Hear the thrush sing!
Hear the hound bay and howl.
Hear the hound bay at the moon.

Let's eat our oatmeal now! Let's drink our milk now! Let's not frown and sulk and grouch around. Let's get out in the fresh air and play.

HELP! HELP!

"Help! Help!" Did Jack hear a shout? Fred fell in the pond, but Jack found him. Fred did not drown. Jack got him out.

THE CLOWN

See the clown run around and hop and skip and jump and leap. Hear the clown shout and sing! Such fun! How the clown can jump around.

BESS MILKS THE COW

Bess gets up at six and milks the cow. Each day at six Bess milks our brown cow. Bess gets the milk in a big pail.

Hear the cow moo!

Bess sets the pail down on the ground. Bess sits down on a stool and milks the cow. Bess milks the cow out in the cowshed.

jaw	claw	awl	dawn	outlaw
law	craw	bawl	fawn	seesaw
paw	draw	brawl	lawn	
raw	flaw	shawl	pawn	
saw	slaw	crawl	brawn	
caw	thaw	scrawl	drawn	
daw	straw	sprawl		
maw	squawk		hawk	

It's cool out on the lawn. Jeff, run and
fetch Mom a shawl. Fetch Mom the brown shawl.

Frank can draw. Frank will draw a big ship.
The ship will sail on the sea. See Frank draw
a big ship at sea!

A cat can run and jump and spring and leap
and creep and crawl. A cat can sneak up and jump
on a rat and catch it. A cat can scratch and claw.
A cat eats raw meat and drinks milk.

Get the gun, Tom! Get the shotgun and shoot
the hawk. The hawk may grab the hen and
the chicks. The hawk may kill and eat the chicks.

92

haul	launch	jaunt	taut
Paul	haunch	taunt	
fault	paunch	vaunt	
		flaunt	

If Dad eats too much, Dad will get a paunch.
Jack's dad had a steam launch.
Jean and Joan went on a jaunt in a boat.
Ned and Dick will haul the bricks on Dick's sled.
Paul found a fawn. Mom will let him keep it.

THE DEER HUNT

Dad got a gift from Mom. Dad got a gun. At dawn next day Dad and Paul got up and went on a deer hunt.

"See that thing in the brush!" Dad and Paul went near it.

"A fawn! Let's keep it. Let's bring it back." The fawn did not run away. It let Dad and Paul catch it.

Paul thinks the fawn is the best pet, but Dad did not intend such a deer hunt.

194

93

boy   Roy   coy   cloy   cowboy
joy   toy   soy   Troy

Dad got Roy a toy train. The train ran on a round track. It ran round and round and round. Toot, toot! Whiz!

JACK'S CAP

Ann saw a bad boy snatch Jack's cap. The bad boy kept the cap and ran away.

Ann and Jack had a hound pup, Skip. The pup saw the bad boy run away. When a pup sees a boy run, a pup thinks it must run too. The pup ran at the boy. The boy ran and Skip ran.

Did Skip catch the boy? Yes indeed, the pup did catch the boy and snatch the cap away from him.

Did the boy just let Skip get the cap? Did the boy kick at the pup? Yes, the boy did kick at Skip, and the pup bit him.

Jack got the cap back. "Thanks, Skip!"

94

oil	soil	coin	joint	moist
boil	toil	join	point	foist
coil	foil			hoist
	spoil			joist

Join in and sing!
Lift the trunk, Jack. Hoist it up.
Let's not get oil on our coats and pants.
Jean will boil an egg and fix toast and tea.

Let's play with the toy train, but let's not spoil it. Let's clean it and oil it.

THE OWL

"See the big owl up in the tree!"
Fran saw the owl and Sal saw the owl,
but Tom and Bill did not see it.

"Point at it, Fran. Point it out,
and Tom and Bill will see it too."

The owl still sat up in the tree.
"Hoot, hoot, hoot!" went the owl.

Now Tom and Bill can hear it.
Tom and Bill can hear it and see it, too.

95

goose	coarse	geese	house	else	apse
loose	hoarse	lease	mouse	rinse	lapse
moose		grease	douse	manse	copse
noose		crease	souse	sense	glimpse
			louse	pulse	
			blouse		
			grouse		

Did our cat catch a mouse?

A fox will steal geese.

Jeff must fix the loose board in the house.

Tess will rinse the cups.

Let's not get oil and grease on Beth's blouse.

Let's play at our house. Let's play tag on the lawn. Let's play fox and geese.

Jim had a cowboy pal, Tex. Jim saw Tex shoot a big moose!

Sis will press the blouse and will press a crease in Nick's slacks.

Fran and Sal saw the owl. Tom and Bill got a glimpse, too.

breeze   freeze   sneeze   squeeze wheeze
gauze
adze   axe

a goose, a duck, a chick, a hawk, an owl

It's cool now. Feel the cool breeze.

Hear Tom sneeze! Tom must not stay out in the cool breeze. Tom will sneeze and get hoarse and wheeze.

If this wind keeps up, the pond will soon freeze. In the spring it will thaw.

Dick got up at dawn. Dick got up at dawn and went out. Dick saw a deer and a fawn. The deer and the fawn saw Dick and ran away from him. Dick saw a hawk. A hawk will kill chicks. Run, chicks, run! Dick got the hen and the chicks in the coop and shut it up. The hawk did not get the chicks. The chicks hid in the straw.

Frank cut himself! Rinse the cut! Tell Mom! Mom will get the gauze and fix the cut.

Let Pam pick up the pup. Pam must not squeeze the pup. The pup will squeal.

97

have	sleeve	leave	solve	groove	bade
give	peeve	weave	twelve		
live			shelve		
			delve		

Each board had a groove in it.
Ann must mend the rent in Beth's sleeve.
Will a cow give milk?

Let's have lunch at twelve. Let's
have ham and beets and toast and jam and milk.

Dad will give Bess a dress, a bag, a sash,
a blouse, and a hat.

If Joan will weave us a rug, we can
have it in our house.

Stan and Jean live in a house on the hill.
Each day Stan and Jean leave the house and
play at Jack's house. Jack and Jean and Stan
have fun. At twelve Stan and Jean get back.
Jean helps Mom get lunch and clean up. Jack
helps, too. At six Stan and Jean meet Dad
at the train.

JACK AND PAUL IN A BOAT

Jack and Paul went out on the pond in a boat.

"Sit still, Jack! The boat will rock."
But Jack did not sit still in the boat.

"Sit still, Jack! The boat will tip!"
But Jack did not sit still. The boat did tip
a bit and Jack fell out. Jack fell in the pond.
Splash!

"Help! Help!"

Paul held out an oar.

"Grab the oar, Jack!"

But Jack did not help himself. Jack did not
grab the oar.

Paul can swim well. In jumps Paul and
gets Jack. Paul held Jack up and got him
back on land.

From the bank, Sis saw how Jack fell in
the pond, and Sis saw Paul haul him out.

"It's Jack's fault. Jack just cannot sit
still. But now Jack will at least sit still
in a boat."

A cat will catch a mouse. A fox will steal
a goose. A hawk will swoop down and snatch up
a chick.

Sam can sprint. But can Sam win?
Run, Sam! Did Fred cheer Sam? Did Fred get
hoarse? Did Sam win?

Al and Dick will haul bricks on Dick's sled.
Lend us a hand, Chet! Help us load the bricks
on the sled. Thanks!

FUN AT OUR HOUSE

"May Beth and Jean stay and have lunch
at our house?"

"Yes, Fran, Beth and Jean may stay."

"Thanks, Mom!"

"Let's have lunch at twelve. Let's
have roast veal and beets and a sweet bun
and milk.

"Let's play fox and geese on the lawn.
Let's play till twelve. At twelve Mom
will give us our lunch."

ABCDEFGHIJKLMNOPQRSTUVWXYZABCDEFGHIJKLMNOPQRSTUVWXYZABCDEFGHIJKLMN

BCDEFGHIJKLMNOPQRSTUVWXYZABCDEFGHI

LET'S READ

Part IV

The Commonest Irregular Words

JKLMNOPQRSTUVWXYZABCDEFGHIJKLMNOPQRSTUVWXYZABCDEFGHIJKLMNOPQRSTUV

Part IV

THE COMMONEST IRREGULAR WORDS

Guide to Lessons 98 through 151

There is a great difference between the work of Lessons 1-97 and almost all the child's later work in reading. Lessons 1-97 have taught him a system in which each letter or each combination of two (in one case, three) letters represents always the same sound or sounds of his language.

If our system of writing were completely phonetic, the rest of our work would consist simply of further practice in these habits. But our system of writing is not completely phonetic: the child has now the difficult task of forming a great many new and special habits for single words or classes of words in which the letters represent sounds other than those which he has so far learned.

The teacher or parent need scarcely be warned against taking up this work before the regular spellings (Lessons 1-97) have been thoroughly mastered. It is a bad mistake to take up words in which the same letter or combination has different values (for instance, *but* and *put* or *get* and *gem*). This is the great fault of some of the methods that are now in vogue. It is only after the child has mastered the basic habit of reading (the same letters mean the same sounds) that we can teach him the special cases in which this principle is violated. In short, Lessons 98-151 should be begun only after Lessons 1-97 present no more difficulty.

There is a big difference in the materials presented in these two parts of our work. In our work hitherto we have been dealing with common values of the letters: any word or even any nonsense syllable (such as *nim*, *nib*, etc.) which contains only letters in these normal values, is suitable for practice. When it comes to teaching irregular and special words, each word will demand a separate effort and separate practice. In this work, then, we shall take up only common words; each item must justify its presence, since it can no longer serve as an example of a general rule.

Some irregular spellings are unique; for instance, the word *of* is probably the only word in which the letter *f* is used for the sound of *v*. Other irregularities occur in a few words; thus, *said*, *again*, *says* are perhaps the only words in which *ai* and *ay* represent the sound of *e* as in *set*. Other irregular spellings run through whole sets of words and may be called "semi-irregular" because they can be more or less accurately described by a rule. Thus, the letter *a* followed by a single consonant letter which in turn is followed by a final *e*, has generally the sound of *ai* (as in *bait*); for instance: *came, game, blame, gave, brave*; an exception is *have*, in which *a* has its regular value (as in *hat*). Suffixal *s* has the sound of *z* after vowel sounds and after the consonant sounds that are regularly represented by the letters *b, d, g, v, m, n, ng, l, r*; for instance: *cows, cabs, hands, legs, stoves, dreams, stones, tongs, hills, stars*. Suffixal *-ed* has the sound of *t* after *p, k, f, s, sh, ch*: *stopped, looked, loafed, kissed, washed, reached*. Of such semi-irregular spellings, Lessons 98-151 take up the suffixes *-s* (*-'s, -es*) and *-d* (*-ed*) and later the suffixes *-er, -le, -en, -y*.

Lessons 98-151 deal with the very commonest types and words of irregular spelling.

Lesson 98 introduces *th* as in *then*. In Lessons 73-97 we took up words in which the pair of letters *th* represented the sound that is initial in *thin*, final in *pith*. This, then, in our work, is the "regular" value of the letters *th*. Any word in which these letters represent this sound could serve for practice, provided that also the other letters in it have their "regular" values, and regardless of whether it was familiar or useful to the child, e.g. *pith, filth, thrill*. In the present lesson we are taking up words in which the letters *th* represent a different sound, the sound which is initial in *then*, final in *smooth*. The child soon learns that the *th* combination sometimes represents this sound. Of course, we do not talk to him about it, or ask him to make any statements; we simply show him that *t-h-e-n* is the word "then," and so on. In the case of any familiar word the pupil knows which of the two sounds to use. If we gave him an unfamiliar word in which *th* represented the initial sound of *then* (e.g. *sheathe, mouthe*), we should be burdening his memory and making him uncertain. Therefore, we confine ourselves to the words in the list in the lesson, words which are in the child's vocabulary.

We have stated this at length because it applies to the materials in most of the remaining lessons in this and the later sections.

Lesson 99 introduces words in which the letter *s* represents the sound which is "regularly" represented by *z* (as in *zest, buzz*). Since the child has been taught that the letter *s* represents the sound that appears in *see, gas, Sis*, each of these new words represents a special task. Hence we limit ourselves to familiar words.

Lessons 100-103: The suffixes and unstressed words which are spelled *-s* (or *-'s* or *-es*) have the sound which we have assigned as the "regular" value of *s* only when the preceding sound is that of *p, t, k, f, th*; these cases (*caps, lets, let's, its, it's, Pat's*) were introduced in Lessons 51, 52, and 54.

After the sounds of *s, z, sh, zh* (as in *rouge*), *ch, j*, these suffixes have the sound of *-ez*; these forms will be taken up in Lessons 104 and 105.

In all remaining positions, our suffixes have the sound of *z*; thus *adds* sounds exactly like *adze*. This case, taken up in the present section, includes, therefore, a well-nigh endless set of plural and possessive nouns (*hands, Ned's*), of third-person singular verbs (*grabs, reads*), and of phrases with the unstressed form of the word *is* (*Ned's in the house*).

Our list is only a selection.

Lessons 104 and 105 take up the cases where the suffixes which are spelled *-s* (*-'s, -es*) have the sound of *-ez* (an unstressed vowel plus *z*). This happens whenever the suffix comes immediately after the sounds *s, z, sh, zh* (as in *rouge*), *ch, j*. Our list contains only a few examples out of the vast number of such forms.

Lessons 106-108 take up the past-tense suffix of verbs, written *-d* (*-ed*). Except for the silent *e*, these spellings are regular. In Lesson 109 we shall take up the cases where the *e* is not silent, and in Lesson 110 the cases where the *e* is silent and the *d* represents the sound of *t*. In all of these lessons our list gives only a sample of the many forms.

The case taken up in Lessons 106, 107, and 108 (*e* silent, *d* in its regular value) occurs after vowel sounds (*played*) and after consonant sounds of *b, g, j, v, th* (as in *then*), *z, zh* (as in *rouge*), *m, n, ng, r, l*.

Lesson 109 takes up the cases where the suffix which is written *-d* (*-ed*) has the sound of *ed* (*e* as in *red*, except that it is unstressed). These spellings might be called regular. This case occurs whenever the suffix is preceded by the sounds of *t* or *d*.

In Lesson 110 the *-d* suffix (*-d, -ed*) has the sound of *t* after the sounds of *p, k, ch, f, th* (as in *thin, pith*), *s, sh*. The list is only a sample.

Lesson 111 introduces only one irregular word, *to*. This word is irregular because in it the letter *o* represents the sound which we have assigned to *oo* (as in *boot*) and not the sound which we have chosen as the regular value of the letter *o* (as in *hot*).

Lessons 112 and 113 take up the irregular words *of* and *was*. In the word *of* the letter *f* is used for the sound of *v* (as in *vat*). In *was*, the letter *s* represents the sound of *z* (as in the words of Lesson 99), and the letter *a* represents, in some parts of the country the vowel sound of *o* as in *hot*, in other parts of the country the vowel sound of *u* as in *buzz*.

Lesson 114 introduces five very common words of one syllable in which final *e* represents the vowel sound of *ee* as in *see*. The same use of the letter *e* appears in the accented form of the word *the* (Lesson 45).

Lesson 115 takes up a few of the very commonest words with irregular spellings; the words *one, says, said, are, were, been*. Every child hears and speaks these words many times a day; none of us needs to be told how to pronounce them. However, it may be of interest to the teacher or parent if we state here in what way the spelling of these words is irregular.

If the word *one* were to be written with letters in the values which we have called regular, it would have to be written "wun."

If the words *says* and *said* were to be so written, they would be spelled "sez" and "sed."

The spelling of the word *been* is regular for the parts of the English-speaking world where this word is spoken with the vowel sound of *seen, keen, mean*. But in most parts of the United States the word is pronounced with the vowel of *pin, kin, sin*; for this type of speech a regular spelling would be "bin."

The word *are* has the vowel sound of *father, car*, a sound for which we have, in our scheme, no "regular" spelling, since we have assigned to the letter *a* the vowel sound of *hat*. In Lessons 160-162 we shall take up the words which contain the *a*-sound of *father, car*.

The word *were* is in some places spoken with the vowel sound of *fair, pair*; for these regions a regular spelling would be "wair." In most of the United States, however, this word has the vowel sound of *sir, fir, fur* (the "vocalic *r*" or "syllabic *r*"). This sound differs greatly in different parts of the country, but, in any case, as we have assigned the letters to sounds, there is no "regular" way of writing this sound. Words with this sound will be taken up in Lessons 190-192.

Of course it would be confusing to the child, or at best a waste of time, to try to explain these things to him. We need only tell the child the word when he sees the spelling. Since the spellings are irregular, the child will have to be told more than once. This, of course, is the difficulty about our irregular spellings; we have to learn to read single words or special groups of words.

Lesson 116 assembles a group of personal pronouns (some in combination with common contracted verbs: *we, we've*). It is necessary only to tell the child the word when he sees the spelling. Heard or spoken, they are familiar.

Lessons 117-121 and Lessons 123-127 take up two- and three-syllable words and Lesson 122 takes up the suffix *-ing*. Lesson 117 presents no new irregularities. We take up here a type of two-syllable word that has been occurring from time to time in earlier lessons: the kind of two-syllable word that is read simply as if two words were written or printed without a space between them: *oatmeal* reads just as if it were *oat meal, away* reads just like *a way*. The only added feature is the stress: when one has recognized the combination, one knows which part has the greater stress.

We give first lists of words in which the first part of the word is stressed (Lessons 117-121). Following this we give a list of forms with the suffix *-ing* (Lesson 122), then lists in which the last part of the word is stressed (Lessons 123-127). In column four of Lesson 124, the stress of the words falls on either the first or the last syllable depending upon the part of speech. For example, *conduct* as a noun is stressed on the first syllable, while the verb *conduct* is stressed on the last. After these forms have been presented we give a list of three- or four-syllable words (Lesson 128).

Lesson 117 consists of compound words made up of two well-known words. Most of these compounds have already been studied and listed. This lesson is largely, then, review.

Lesson 118 contains words stressed on the first syllable, which is sometimes a prefix (*out-* in *outlaw, in-* in *insect, chip-* in *chipmunk*).

Lessons 129-134 contain words of otherwise regular spelling with the suffixes that are spelled *-er* (as in *sister*) or *-or* (as in *doctor*) or *-ar* (as in *poplar*) and *-ert* (as in *Robert*) and *-ard* (as in *custard*). These lessons contain also a few words with *-er* that are otherwise irregular in spelling: *bother, gather, lather, wither, together,* with have *th* as in *then.*

We give here also the abbreviations *Mr.* (*mister*) and *Mrs.* (pronounced *missez*).

Lessons 135-137 take up the suffix that is written usually *-le* (as in *apple*) but sometimes *-el* (as in *camel*), *-al* (as in *metal*), *-il* (as in *devil*), *-ol* (as in *pistol*), *-ul* (as in *awful*).

Lessons 138-142 take up the suffix spelled -*en* (as in *kitten*), -*on* (as in *lemon*), -*an* (as in *American*), -*in* (as in *cabin*), -*ain* (as in *captain*).

Lesson 143 takes up the *n't* contraction (as in *didn't*).

Lesson 144 takes up the *m* ending (as in *atom*).

Lessons 145-151 take up the suffix -*y* (sometimes spelled -*ey* or -*ie*, pronounced -*ee*) and the suffix -*ly* (pronounced -*lee*). In other respects the words in the list are regular, or contain irregularities which have been studied in earlier lessons, such as the word *easy*, which has *s* for *z*.

98

the   this   then   them   with
that   than   without
that's   smooth
breathe

Bess will not drink tea without milk in it.
Did Ann and Joan have a smooth trip on the boat?
Let's eat lunch and then let's play tag.
Breathe in this fresh air.

Jack may play with this train, and Dick may
play with that train. Jack must not snatch Dick's
train and Dick must not grab Jack's train.

Nick and Frank cannot lift the big bench.
Gus and Dan will help them. Gus and Dan will
help them bring it out on the lawn. Gus
will help Nick, and Dan will help Frank. Gus
will help lift Nick's end, and Dan will help
lift Frank's end. Gus will help at this end, and
Dan will help at that end. Then Nick and Frank and
Gus and Dan will get the big bench out on the lawn.
That's it! Thanks! Thanks a lot, Gus and Dan!

99

is   as   'tis   tease   raise   choose   noise

his   has   ours   please   praise   cheese   cause

Did Ed Black cut down the tree with his axe?

The Blacks have a house which is as big as ours.

Jeff Bean is a tease.

Joan Black can fix the best cheese sandwich!

Will Pat's dad raise chicks this spring?

A mouse eats cheese.

Please, Dad, give us a toy train.

If Tom can read well, Miss Hoyt will praise him.

Dan must brush his hair and clean his teeth.

How can poor Jack eat his oatmeal without a spoon?

    Bess, is the milk hot? Yes, it is hot.
It will boil soon.

    This noon Ann may have an egg on toast or a veal chop.

    "Choose, Ann! An egg on toast or a veal chop?"

    "An egg on toast, please. Let Tom have the veal chop.
Tom must eat a lot. Tom must haul bricks till six."

100

ribs	beds	trees	bags	bells	plums	guns
bibs	lids		legs	sails	drums	pans
	sounds		eggs	heels		spoons
						clowns

ears	paws	cows	days	toys	upstairs
cheers	laws		ways	boys	downstairs
oars					

Set the lids on the pans.

See the clowns run and jump and kick!

Did Jill help Mom with the beds?

Frank and Ed had cap guns.

When Sam is at bat, Deb cheers.

Tom must get up at six and milk the cows.

Jack, bring us three smooth boards, please!

Paul, please take the toys upstairs.

Did Paul play with the toys downstairs?

Sam will spend ten days at camp.

Please pick up Pat's bags at the train.

On clear days Al sails his boat in the bay.

leaves   elves   ourselves

sleeves   loaves   shelves   themselves

See the green leaves and the buds on this tree!

Sam got oil and grease on his sleeves and on his vest and on his pants. Such a boy!

JACK AND SIS HELP

If Jack will bring the things in, Sis will set them on the shelves. Sis can hand Jack the cans. If Jack will stand on a chair, Jack can reach the shelves.

Hand Jack the jam, Sis, and the yams in cans. Hand up the string beans, too, and the green peas. Now that big box with oatmeal in it.

Sis must not set the cat's food and the pup's food way up on the top shelf. Such a rush at noon when Pal and Kit get fed! Such a fuss! Pal will howl and Kit will yowl.

Sis will say, "If that cat and that pup must eat in such a rush, let them just get the lunch themselves!"

102

Jill's hat	the boy's hat
Dad's coat	the man's coat
Ben's hand	Tom's toys

Ben Hoyt lives on a big ranch out west.
Ben and his dad raise sheep. Ben gets up at six
and helps his dad tend the sheep. Ben and
his dad feed the sheep hay and grain.

Tim Gray's dad plants wheat. In the spring
Tim helps his dad plow. In the fall Tim's dad
sells the wheat.

Bill Brown's dad keeps pigs. Bill helps his
dad feed the pigs. Bill and his dad fetch the pigs'
food in pails. Bill feeds the pigs. The pigs eat
a lot and get fat. When the pigs get big and fat,
Bill's dad sells them.

The Smiths live near the Browns, but Ann Smith's
dad has a job in town. Ann and Ann's mom keep
twelve hens. Ann feeds the hens, and the hens lay
big brown eggs. The Smiths can eat the eggs and
can sell them, too.

103

Ann's in the house.
Our dad's a big man.

LUNCH AT ANN'S HOUSE

Joan and Fran will eat lunch at Ann's house
this noon. For lunch Joan and Fran and Ann
will have meat loaf and string beans and fresh
figs with cream.

Ann can fix the best meat loaf! Ann will
get ground beef and veal. Ann will beat an
egg and mix it with the raw meat. Then Ann will
chop up a leek and add it.

When Joan and Fran and Ann have had lunch,
will Joan and Fran and Ann play tag? Joan and
Fran can play, but Ann cannot. Ann must clean
up the lunch things. Next week when Ann's at
Joan's house, Ann will play, and Joan will fix
the lunch and clean up.

Ann must feed the hens and chicks, too. Fran
and Joan will help with that. Ann will let them
pick up the chicks and play with them.

104

miss	kiss	bus	box	tax
misses	kisses	buses	boxes	taxes

rinse	house	raise	praise	buzz
rinses	houses	raises	praises	buzzes

peach	reach	inch	bunch	dish	wish
peaches	reaches	inches	bunches	dishes	wishes

On our team, Frank Gray pitches and Sam Smith catches. Frank pitches well and Sam catches well.

Now and then Ann rinses the dishes. Now and then Ann smashes a dish. Ann drops the dish, and the dish bangs down. The sink is wet and the dishes slip. It is not poor Ann's fault if the dishes slip in the wet sink. Crash, bang, smash!

Fred Barnes keeps bees. When a bee buzzes around Fred's ears, Fred just stands still. If Fred stands still, the bee will not sting him. Fred's chum Al hits at the bee. But if Al misses the bee, it stings him.

105

Gus	Bess	Jess	Max	Rex
Gus's	Bess's	Jess's	Max's	Rex's

Gus's dad has a steam launch. Gus helps his dad clean up the launch and paint it and grease it and oil it. Gus hands his dad the oil can and the pail with grease in it and the tools. When Gus's dad needs a tool, Gus brings it.

Gus gets oil and grease and mud on his coat and on his pants and on his socks and on his cap. Such spots! Such a mess!

When Gus gets back in the house, it's just too bad! Gus gets mud and sand on the rugs. Gus tracks mud on the stairs. Then Gus sits down on his bed and gets mud and oil and grease on the bed.

Gus's mom will groan and say, "Well, the boat's clean now. But Gus must get clean, too. Jump in the tub, boy!"

Then Gus must get in the tub and scrub himself well with soap and a scrub brush. When Mom tells Gus that, Mom means it!

218

106

boil	cool	sail	clean	cheer	play
boiled	cooled	sailed	cleaned	cheered	played

smell	spell	kill	buzz
smelled	spelled	killed	buzzed

LIZ'S DOLL

Dad got Liz a doll. Liz played and played
with the doll.

"Hop in bed, Liz!"

But Liz just played with that doll.

"Stop it, Liz! Get in bed."

It seemed as if Liz did not hear.

"Liz, lay the doll away in its box.
Quick, Liz!"

Liz got mad and banged the doll down
in the box. Then Liz shut the lid down
on the doll. The lid hit the doll. Crack!

"Too bad, Liz! Too bad about the poor
doll. Dad will mend it. But not now.
Now Liz must stay in bed and sleep."

107

live   please   tease   breathe
lived   pleased   teased   breathed

A fat boy, Jeff Bean, lived in a big gray house on Elm Street. Jeff had a big pup, Shep.

Jeff teased that poor pup each day. When Jeff held out food, Shep sat up. But Jeff just let Shep sit up and did not give him a bit. Jeff teased Shep that way.

When Shep sat on the steps and howled, Jeff did not let him in. Jeff just let Shep scratch and howl and stay out. Jeff teased Shep that way, too.

Then Jeff had a dream—a bad dream.

In the dream, Jeff sat out on the steps in the rain. In the house sat Shep. Shep leaned back in a chair and spooned up a cream puff. The best cream puff! Jeff howled, but Shep did not heed him.

Did Jeff still tease that poor pup? Did the dream help Shep?

Well, not much. Now when Shep begs, Jeff gives him cream puffs. Shep cannot stand them.

108

grab	nab	rub	stub
grabbed	nabbed	rubbed	stubbed

drag	beg	slam	drum	snag
dragged	begged	slammed	drummed	snagged

Frank dragged his sled up a steep hill. Frank
dragged it and dragged it. Then Frank lay down on
the sled and slid down the hill. Whiz! How it
went! How it sped! Frank slid down the hill on
his sled. Zip! Down went Frank!

Nan and Sal got lunch. Nan got up on a chair
and got things down from the shelves. Nan got down
the jam and the cups and the spoons and the dishes.
Sal boiled the eggs. The boys did not help. The
boys just ran around and played until noon.
Then Nan and Sal and the boys sat down and had lunch.

Bob got a gift from Dad. Bob grabbed it.
A drum! Bob drummed and drummed in the house till
Sis got mad and nabbed him. "Out! Scoot! Run!
Bob needs fresh air. Play out on the steps, Bob!"

109

land	mend	crowd	weed	nod	pad
landed	mended	crowded	weeded	nodded	padded

lift	hunt	pet	pat	spot
lifted	hunted	petted	patted	spotted

When the train is crowded, Dad must stand.
The jet landed near Green Bay.

Bess went out in the brush. Bess got snagged.
When Bess got back, Mom mended the rip in Bess's dress.

Dan's dad hunted ducks. Dan's dad shot six
ducks. When Dan is big, Dan will have a gun and
hunt ducks too.

Gus Cobb tended and weeded the beans and peas.
Gus got a big crop. Now the Cobbs can eat beans
and peas, and Gus can sell beans and peas, too.
Gus sells them in town.

Brad had a big gray cat. Brad lifted it up
and petted it. Then the cat saw a bug! In a flash
the cat sailed out of Brad's hands and landed on
the bug. That ended the bug!

110

| slip | rap | tramp | bump | jump | camp |
| slipped | rapped | tramped | bumped | jumped | camped |

| pack | thank | milk | wink | sneak | soak |
| packed | thanked | milked | winked | sneaked | soaked |

| pinch | scratch | brush | wish | fix |
| pinched | scratched | brushed | wished | fixed |

| rinse | fuss | kiss | miss | loaf | tip |
| rinsed | fussed | kissed | missed | loafed | tipped |

Fred saw the big peaches up in the peach
tree. Fred got up in the tree, leaned way out,
and grabbed at a big peach. But Fred missed
the peach and fell. Fred landed on the ground
on his back with a yell. Dan ran up and
helped him up on his feet.

Fred brushed himself and rubbed his back.
"Thanks, Dan. Let's not get our peaches from a tree.
Let's get them from a dish. With cream on them!"

110

HOW BESS HELPS

At six Bess got up and went out in the shed
and milked the cows. Then Bess went back in
the house and fixed oatmeal and boiled three eggs.
When Dad got downstairs, Dad and Bess sat down and
had hot oatmeal with milk, tea, toast, and eggs.

Dad thanked Bess. Then Dad went out and
tended the sheep and the pigs.

Bess swept the rugs and mopped up the stairs
and dusted the shelves. Next Bess got Tim up
from bed and helped him get dressed and brushed
his hair.

Then Bess fed Tim. Tim spilled milk on the
rugs and spilled oatmeal on himself. Tim tipped
the things on the shelves and got mud on the
stairs. Tim went out and yelled at the sheep
and the pigs. When Bess got Tim back in the
house, he kicked the filled milk pails.

Did Bess get mad at Tim? Yes, Bess did.
Bess cleaned Tim up and tucked him back in bed.
Bess kept him in bed till noon.

111

to	Sis sent Tim to bed.
	Tim had to stay in bed.
into	Jim went into the house.
onto	Hang onto that bat!

THE TOY PUP

Jean lived on Green Street. Jim lived in the next house. Jim had a pup, Pal.

"Let's get a pup, too, Dad," Jean begged.

Dad did get Jean a pup—a black pup with a stub tail. Dad got Jean a toy pup.

Jean hugged the pup and hugged Dad. "Thanks, Dad. Next to a real pup, this is the best."

Jean played with the toy pup and petted it. When Jean got into bed, Jean still hung onto it.

The next day when Jean and Jim went out to play, Jean left the pup on the back steps. When Pal went up onto the steps, Pal saw the pup. He yipped. The toy pup just sat.

Pal ran up to the toy pup and sniffed at it. The toy pup did not sniff back.

Pal nipped at the toy and jumped back. Then Pal rushed at the toy and grabbed it. Pal picked it up in his mouth and ran.

111

Jim saw Pal with the toy pup in his mouth and yelled, "Drop it, Pal!" But Pal did not drop it. Pal just ran. Jim ran too. Round and round the house ran Jim and Pal.

When Jean saw Pal running away with the toy, Jean screamed and ran too. Jim shouted, Jean screamed, and Pal just ran.

Then Pal stopped, dropped the toy, and lay down with his chin on his paws. Pal seemed to feel bad, and Jim felt bad too.

Jean frowned as she picked up the toy pup. Then she grinned. "Well, Pal, the pup is not spoiled. But I think Jim must get Pal a toy. Then Pal will not need to steal toys and run away with them. How about that, Pal?"

With a glad yip Pal jumped up and licked Jean's hand as much as to say, "Yes indeed! Let's get it quick!"

112

of   a box of toys
the end of the road

Please heat a pan of milk.
Dad will have a cup of tea.
Please get me a sack of flour.
Ann will eat a dish of oatmeal with milk.
Let's drink the rest of the milk.
Please, Dad, let us have a sack of peanuts.

Bang, bang, bang! Thump, thump, thump!
That's the sound of the drum.

Don shot a big deer. Don cut it up.
The Smiths got a bit of it. The Browns got
a bit of it. The Deans got a bit of it.
Don got a bit of it, too!

Tess went to Main Street to shop. Tess got
a pound of cheese, a pound of boiled ham, three
pounds of flour, a box of oatmeal, milk, cream,
and eggs. Such a load to bring into the house!
Tess had to get Jim to help lug the things into
the house.

was   Fred was in the pool.
           Dan was on the bank.

DAN'S FISH

The tenth of May was a cool spring day.
That was the day when Fred went out to the pond
to catch fish.

In the pond was a board. Fred went out
on the board, way out into the pond. Then
a fish bit! Fred slipped on the wet board
and fell into the pond.

"Help! Help!" Fred yelled.

Dan ran to help Fred. Dan crawled out to
the end of the board.

"Hang on, Fred!" Dan grabbed Fred's hands
and hauled him out of the pond.

Dan fished out Fred's hat, too.

Wet as a fish, Fred went back to the
house. Sis met him on the steps.

"Fred! It is too cool to swim!"

Fred did not say a thing. Fred just sneezed.

Fred had such a chill that Sis sent him to bed
and kept him in bed with just hot milk to drink.
At noon next day Sis let him get dressed to eat lunch.

113

When Fred sat down, he found that Sis had
fixed him a poached egg and a bit of toast,
but Sis and Dad had veal chops and string beans.
Fred gulped down the toast and eggs in a rush,
then begged, "A veal chop, please."

Fred had a veal chop and string beans—lots
of them—and three cups of cool milk. Then Fred
had a big dish of peaches and cream.

Fred's dad was glad to see Fred eat. Dad slapped
Fred on the back and winked at Sis.

"Fred is well now, Sis. If a boy can eat
as much as that, the boy is not sick. Fred may
stay up now.

"But, Fred, stay away from that pond."

Sis grinned. "Fred may as well stay away
from that pond. He cannot fish a thing out of it."

Dad grinned too. "Yes, but Dan can. Dan fished
Fred out of that pond. Fred was Dan's fish!"

114

he   she   we   me   be

HOW TO CATCH A SAILBOAT

Frank had a big toy sailboat. He and Bess
went down to the pond, and Frank let it sail.
Frank had the boat on a string. He held the end
of the string and let the boat sail out on the pond.
When the string was taut, the boat stopped.

Then Frank dropped the string. How the boat
did sail in the wind! It just scooted away.

Bess screamed, "The boat got away! It is way
out on the pond. How can we get it back?"

"Let's get a stick and see if we can reach it."

When Frank had found a stick, the boat was way
out on the pond, and the stick did not reach it.
Bess and Frank had to wait till the boat got to
the bank. Then Frank ran around the pond to get it.
But just when he got near the boat, a gust of wind
sent it out on the pond, away from the bank.

Bess ran back and got the stick, but she did
not reach the boat with it.

"The wind is from the east, Bess. If we wait
at the west end of the pond, the boat will soon
sail up to us."

Then Bess and Frank went to the west end of
the pond and sat down and waited. Soon the wind
sent the boat that way. The boat sailed up to them,
and when it reached the bank, it stopped.

Bess reached down and helped Frank lift the
boat out of the pond. She was glad Frank still
had his sailboat.

"If a sailboat gets away from us, we need
not fret. We must just see which way the wind is,
and then grab the boat when it lands. That is the
way to catch a sailboat."

one	One of the boys fell down.
says	Jim says he can read.
said	Dad said he was glad.
are	We are not in bed.
were	We were glad to see him.
been	He has been away.

CHAMP AND THE DOLL

Champ is a spotted pup with big ears that flop when he runs.

Champ is Nan's pup. When Nan says, "Sit down," Champ sits down and waits.

When Champ yelps, he means to say, "Please give me a drink of milk." Then Nan gives him milk.

When Champ yelps as loud as he can, he means, "Please give me a big dish of chopped raw meat." Then Nan feeds him.

When Champ gives Nan a tap with his paw, he says, "Let's have a run and play tag." Then Nan and Champ play a bit.

One day when Nan's dad got back from town, Dad had a big box. In the box was a doll. The doll had black hair. Its cheeks were pink, and its mouth was red. It had a pink dress with a brown belt.

"Thanks, Dad!" said Nan.

Then Champ saw the doll. He jumped at it.

Dad said, "We must not let Champ play with the doll. If Champ gets at it, he will spoil it. That's the way pups are. Champ is just a pup. He must not play with the doll."

Nan said, "Sit down, Champ!" and Champ sat down and waited.

Nan fed the doll and had it drink milk, and she dressed it and brushed its hair. Then she undressed it and put it to bed in its doll bed.

"Sleep well!" she said and went up to bed.

As soon as Nan went away, Champ must have said to himself, "Let's see this thing, this big thing. Will it play tag with me? If it will not play tag, it may be a thing to eat. Let's see."

Champ sneaked up to the doll's bed and sniffed at the doll. Then he tapped it with one paw. Then he jumped up on the doll's bed.

The doll did not get up. It did not speak, and it did not pet Champ. It just lay still.

"Well," said Champ to himself, "let's see if we can eat it."

Champ jumped at the doll and grabbed it with his teeth. He bit one leg of the doll. Then he dropped the doll. It fell with a bang.

Champ jumped back and said to himself, "This is not the sound of a thing one eats. This thing went bang when it fell."

Champ went away. He went to his bed and slept.

The next day when Nan went to get the doll, she found that it had a crack in one leg.

"Dad, Dad," said Nan, "the doll's leg is cracked!"

"Let's see it," said Nan's dad.

Nan handed him the doll. He held it up in his hand and saw one leg was cracked.

"Yes," said Nan's dad, "one leg has a crack in it. Maybe Champ has been at it. He may have yanked it down from the bed. The leg seems as if Champ bit it. Well, let's see if we can patch it up."

Then Dad and Nan went out to the shed. Dad's paints and tools were in the shed. He sat down and laid the doll on the bench. He plugged the crack in the doll's leg with a bit of wax, and then he painted the wax with flesh-pink paint.

Soon Nan saw that the doll's leg was just as if Champ had not cracked it.

"Thanks, Dad, thanks!" said Nan. "Now let's spank that bad Champ!"

"Nan, Nan dear," said Nan's dad, "we must not be mean to that poor pup. He did not see that it was a doll. When a pup sees a thing, he thinks he must snap at it and yank it around with his teeth. He cannot help that.

"Let's set the doll's bed up on the shelf. Then Champ cannot reach it. And now let's pet Champ and teach him not to grab the doll."

116

	you	they	
my	your	their	her
mine	yours	theirs	hers

I	he	she	you	we	they
I'm	he's	she's	you're	we're	they're
I've			you've	we've	they've
I'd	he'd	she'd	you'd	we'd	they'd
I'll	he'll	she'll	you'll	we'll	they'll

myself		herself	yourself
			yourselves

FRANK'S PAINT JOB

One day in May Dad said, "We'll soon have hot days. Let's set the bench out on the lawn, near the big elm tree. Then we can sit out on the lawn on hot days.

"Frank, will you please clean the bench. It is out in the shed back of the house. Please clean it well and give it a coat of paint."

"Yes, Dad," said Frank. "I'll be glad to."

Frank went out to the shed. He was proud that Dad had picked him for this job.

"This will be a big job," said Frank. "How can I clean this big bench myself? When I see the dust and mud and grease on this bench, it seems to me I've got much too big a job on my hands. Maybe Ann and Jess will help me."

Frank went back to the house to get them.

"Please, Ann and Jess," he said, "can you help me with my job?

I have to clean the big bench out in the shed. If you help me, we three can soon get it clean. Please lend me a hand."

"Well, Frank," said Ann, "wait a bit, and we'll be out in the shed to help you."

"Thank you!" said Frank and went back to the shed.

When Jess and Ann went out to the shed, they had a scrub brush, lots of rags, a pail, and soap. They put down the brush and the rags, and the pail and the soap. Then they saw the bench. "See the dust on that bench!" said Ann.

"And the mud and the grease!" said Jess. "I can see that the boys have been around. They have jumped on this bench and set things down on it and spilled things on it. They have got oil and grease and paint on it and tramped mud on it."

"That's the way boys are," said Ann.

Then Ann and Jess helped Frank. They dusted the bench and scrubbed and scoured it. It was a big job. When they got the bench clean, it was noon.

"Thank you, Ann! Thank you, Jess!" said Frank. "You've helped me a lot. Thank you!"

"Now we must get lunch," said Ann. "It's near noon, and Mom and Dad will be back soon. Frank, will you help us get lunch?"

"Yes," said Frank. "I'll be glad to help you."

"Thanks, Frank," said Ann. "But you must not drop the dishes and smash them."

"And you must not spill milk on the rug," said Jess.

"I'll do my best," said Frank.

Then they went back into the house and set down their pail and brush and their soap and their rags. Then Frank helped Ann and

Jess get lunch. He did not smash dishes, and he did not spill milk.

"Now that we've had lunch," said Frank, "I'll have to paint that bench."

"We'll help paint," said Jess. And out they went to the shed.

"This bench needs to be sanded," said Ann. Then they sanded the bench smooth.

"See how the bench stands on the ground," said Frank. "One leg needs to be sawed down a bit."

Frank sawed the leg. "Too much!" said Tess. "Now you must saw the three legs to match it." Frank did just that.

"You sawed the three legs down too much," said Ann. "Now you must saw that one to match." Frank sawed and sawed, and then at the end they painted.

When Dad went out to the shed, he said, "Well, not much is left of that bench. But at least we need not sit on the ground. We have a smooth green board to sit on!"

117

sunset	blacksmith	mailbox	oatmeal	upstairs
gumdrop	peanut	mailman	sailboat	downstairs
milkman	steamship	haircut	billboard	
grandstand	earmuff	hairpin	blackboard	
	handcuff			

catfish	teaspoon	plaything	playground
codfish	toothbrush	railway	cowboy
dishpan	toothpick	haystack	
dishrag			

windmill	paintbrush	railroad
hilltop		toadstool
eggshell		steamboat

Just set the dishes in the dishpan.
We need red paint and a paintbrush.
Ted sat in the grandstand and cheered.
The mailman left the mail in the mailbox.
Bob took a trip on a railroad train.
The milkman left the milk and the cream on the step.
Did the milkman leave cheese, too?
May I have a gumdrop, please?

Bill needs a haircut. If he will not get
a haircut, he will soon have to braid his hair.

118

outfit	sandwich	insect
outlaw	chipmunk	product
seesaw	picnic	discount

Tim lay in the haystack and slept.
Ken went way up to the hilltop.
Sam and Al had seats in the grandstand.
Liz and Sal played at the playground.
When it gets cool, we will get out our earmuffs.
The cowboy shot the outlaw.
Stan got a catfish. Bill got a codfish.
An insect stung Clem.
Beth has a stamp outfit.

When you visit Lil, you must pack
your toothbrush.

The Smiths and the Browns went on a picnic
at Prospect Pond. Jill saw a chipmunk. Did
Jill give the chipmunk a bit of her sandwich?
Did the chipmunk pick up the food with its paws?

Jean and Jill went on the seesaw at the
picnic. They had a lot of fun.

Anna	salad	gallop	canvas	address
Linda	method	hammock	August	
Wilma				instant
extra				different

LINDA'S HAMMOCK

One hot August day Dad got Linda a gift—a canvas hammock. Linda was pleased.

"I'll stretch out in my hammock," said Linda, "and I'll sip cool drinks and maybe read a bit. Let Nick and Sam and Anna gallop around and play tag and get hot. Not me!" And when Nick and Sam and Anna stopped at the house to get Linda to play with them, Linda sent them away.

Linda spent the day in her hammock. At noon she fixed a salad and had lunch in her hammock.

The next day from her hammock Linda saw Sam and Nick as they played tag. She felt left out.

Linda jumped out of her hammock and went to join them. "A hammock is just grand," said Linda, "if one needs a rest. But not for me! Not now!"

120

attic	wicked	coolest	finish	active
comic	rugged	cleanest	foolish	olive
traffic	hundred	dearest	polish	
	hundredth	thickest	punish	
rapid		thinnest	radish	
liquid	Kenneth	biggest	rubbish	
solid		fattest	selfish	
splendid	dentist			

The toy train is up in the attic.

Finish your oatmeal, Sis!

Sal cut up a radish in the salad.

This is the coolest spot in the house.

Fling the rubbish into the trash can.

Bob's pup is the fattest, and Sam's is the thinnest.

Dan got the biggest fish.

Stan planted an olive tree.

Miss Smith, read to us about the wicked witch!

The shrubs are the thickest near the pond.

Kenneth went to the dentist.

This is the coolest day we have had.

habit	blanket	pocket	blackness	mattress	tennis
limit	bonnet	rocket	sadness		promise
merit	bucket	tablet	sickness		Agnes
rabbit	closet	ticket	stillness		
spirit	cricket	toilet	sweetness		
visit	hatchet	trinket	weakness		
	helmet	trumpet			
	jacket	velvet			
	junket				

Sweets are Pam's weakness.
Agnes, will you please bring the soap and a bucket.
Please fetch me a saw and a hatchet.
Bob beats the drum, and Ted plays the trumpet.
Hear the cricket out on the lawn!

On my bed I have a mattress and sheets
and blankets and a quilt.

Kenneth had a red jacket. He hung it in the
closet, and he left his ticket in the pocket.
When Kenneth got on the bus, he found that he
did not have his bus ticket.

122

mixing	being	painting	batting	grabbing	wedding
acting	seeing	staying	cutting	scrubbing	willing
ending	sleeping	playing	getting	digging	feeling
singing	meeting	loafing	letting	swimming	stocking
catching	eating	soaking	sitting	running	duckling
pitching	reading	drawing	giving	shopping	cunning
fishing	reaching	crawling	living	stopping	
thinking	beating		leaving		
drinking	hearing		having		
locking					
blessing					
spelling					
buzzing					

Stan reads well, but he is best at spelling.

Dan and Fred went fishing.

Sal, you've got a run in your stocking. Too bad!

Agnes is staying at May Smith's house till next week.

Tom thinks it's raining. This is not rain; this is sleet.

123

undress	upon	about	account	balloon
unfair	upset	adjust	address	canal
unless		admit	allow	
unpaid	surround	afraid	appear	
until		agree	disappear	
		aloud	attack	
		amount	attend	
		around		
		asleep		

Each day Nan will dress and undress that doll.
Did Chet upset the tray?
We cannot leave until Dad gets back.
Will Fran's dad allow her to attend the wedding?
Each day Miss Smith will read aloud to us.
Dad did not admit that he had been asleep.
I cannot agree to it unless he will help me.

That balloon will get away if you will not hang onto it.

It seemed that the ram wished to attack the boy but was afraid to.

124

o'clock	today	confess	content
	protect	connect	conduct
	cocoon	consent	contest
	collect	complain	increase
	correct		insult

Pal thinks it is his job to protect the house.
Did they collect the tickets yet?
I shall meet you today at twelve o'clock.
Confess now! You hid the hatchet in the shed.

The mailman did not bring a thing from Frank
today. Did you give him the correct address?

Nell found a cocoon. It was attached to
the trunk of a tree. Nell lifted the cocoon
from the tree and left it on her desk.

Dad will attend the meeting if he can get
tickets. He will be leaving at one o'clock today.

The cat seemed content as it lay stretched
out on the rug.

The traffic is bad today. We cannot increase
our speed. We may not get to the train till six.

125

fifteen	himself	indeed	instruct
fifteenth	itself	insist	intend
sixteen			invent
sixteenth			

CHET AND THE BEE

Hank and Chet went swimming on the fifteenth of May. It was cool that day, but they went back on the sixteenth. On the sixteenth of May it was cool indeed!

"I'm freezing," said Chet.

"You insisted upon swimming today," said Hank. "I was willing to give it up."

"Well, I'm willing now," said Chet. "Let's just sit in the sun and fish."

As they sat in the sun on the bank, Chet felt a bee buzzing around his ears. Chet hit at the bee. The bee zoomed at Chet, and Chet jumped into the pond to get away from it.

"You promised not to swim today," complained Hank, as he hauled Chet out. "But you did!"

126

discuss	within	expect	enjoy
disgust	without	explain	employ
dismiss	withdraw	expense	
display		exclaim	
	misspell		

The expense of the train trip will be too much.
Ed's drawing is on display.
Did Dick expect to win?
Dad drinks his tea without milk.
"Dear me!" exclaimed Mom.

If you'll explain how to paint this bench, I'll be glad to help you paint it.

Linda did enjoy her hammock, but she enjoyed playing tag, too.

A man will employ Stan in August. Stan must cut the man's lawn and weed it. The man is too fat to stoop over and weed the lawn. If the man gets thin, Stan will be out of a job.

The coach thinks he must dismiss Al from the team. The coach says wc shall discuss it today.

because	defeat	repair	elect	request
began	defend	repeat	event	respect
begin	defense		neglect	result
begun	destroy		meow	
beneath				
between				

KENNETH AND THE CHIPMUNKS

Each weekend in the spring the Hunts went on a camping trip in the hills.

The Hunts set up a tent. Mom and Agnes slept on cots in the tent. Kenneth and Dad slept on the ground in sleeping bags.

They had their lunch beneath the trees. They had sandwiches and beans and toasted franks and hot tea.

"This is the best food!" Agnes exclaimed. "Let's give a bit of it to the chipmunks." And Agnes flung the end of her sandwich to a chipmunk.

Kenneth, too, began to feed the chipmunks.

The chipmunks sat on their haunches and picked up bits of food with their paws. Then they held the food between their paws and fed themselves. The chipmunks stuffed food into their mouths until their cheeks stuck out.

"They eat just like boys!" said Agnes. "Such greed!"

That weekend the chipmunks stayed around the camp, and Agnes and Kenneth fed them now and then. The chipmunks got less afraid of Agnes and Kenneth and began to get near them.

"They'll soon be eating out of our hands," said Kenneth. But the chipmunks did not get as near as that.

Then on Sunday, when one of the chipmunks got near, Kenneth reached out and grabbed it. The chipmunk nipped at him, but Kenneth held onto it.

"We'll keep him for a pet," said Kenneth. "We'll bring him back to our house, and he'll be our pet chipmunk."

"Let him loose," said Agnes. "Let him live in the ground as he did. Let him stay with the rest of the chipmunks."

But Kenneth did not wish to let the chipmunk loose. He fixed a box for the chipmunk and shut him in it. And when the camping trip was finished, Kenneth took the chipmunk back to the Hunts' house.

Kenneth did not neglect the chipmunk. He fed it each day. But the chipmunk did not eat. One day Agnes set out a feast of nuts and grain, but she could not get him to eat. Food seemed to disgust him.

The plump chipmunk got thin. He seemed sad and weak.

Then Kenneth said, "This weekend we'll set him free. We'll let him loose at the camp."

At the camp Kenneth lifted the lid from the box. The chipmunk did not stay in the box. Out he jumped and ran away.

"I'm glad!" said Kenneth. "Chipmunks are just to enjoy on camping trips. Chipmunks are not pets!"

Africa	Alaska	America
benefit	Atlantic	arithmetic
cabinet	astonish	Thanksgiving
definite	banana	umbrella
delicate	develop	unfinished
difficult	electric	unwilling
holiday	expensive	
opposite	detective	
relative		
Santa Claus		

Pat has not finished his arithmetic yet.
It's raining! Bring an umbrella.
Dan had a sandwich and a banana for lunch.

The films are finished, but Stan will
develop them on the Thanksgiving holiday weekend.
It is expensive to have them developed at the
shop, and Stan is unwilling to wait. Stan
wishes to see the films of his trip to Alaska.
He has films, too, of his bus trip in America
from the Atlantic way out to the west coast.

129

winter	temper	sister	silver	reader	steamer
enter	jumper	blister	helper	leader	deeper
hunter	number	Buster	flower	cleaner	steeper
painter	lumber	Easter	shower	eager	powder
pointer	limber	oyster	power	heater	sooner
counter	member	rooster	tower	speaker	cooler
under	slumber	shelter		scooter	trailer
thunder	banker	whisper	layer	shooter	dealer
yonder	sinker	whiskers	player		
			lawyer		
			Sawyer		

Ted Hunter's dad is a lumber dealer. Ted's sister Wilma is a lawyer.

The Hunters live in a trailer because their house is not yet finished. The painter is painting it now, but he cannot get a helper. If the painter can get a helper, he will finish sooner.

The Hunters expect to get into their house this winter. Till then, the trailer gives them shelter. Ted thinks that living in a trailer is fun.

If you will get under my umbrella, you can keep out of the shower.

Thatcher	flicker	bother	dresser	beaver	ever
pitcher	thicker	gather	miller	giver	never
catcher	snicker	lather	boxer	liver	clever
teacher	sticker	whether		deliver	proper
preacher	cracker	hither		river	stiffer
singer	checkers	wither		sliver	suffer
chapter	locker			shiver	camera

THE EAGER BEAVERS

Bill Thatcher is the pitcher on our team.
Ed Singer is the catcher. Our teacher is the
coach. I am a member of the team, too. We are
the "Eager Beavers."

It seems that our team can never win.
The players on the opposite team snicker and say,
"Stick to checkers." At least we'd be cooler if
we played checkers.

We "Eager Beavers" keep right on playing,
whether we win or not. We may not ever win, but
we have a lot of fun playing.

131

utter	chatter	pepper	robber	banner	hammer
butter	clatter	dipper	rubber	manner	stammer
mutter	matter	copper	ladder	dinner	summer
flutter	scatter	chopper	rudder	thinner	simmer
shutter	platter	stopper	shudder	winner	glimmer
stutter	better	shopper		runner	slimmer
batter	letter	slipper			shimmer
fatter	bitter	upper			bigger
flatter	hitter	supper			
shatter	glitter				

The pans fell from the shelf with a clatter.
Stan will have supper at Fred's house.
You'd better get a bigger platter for the ham.
The spuds will be better with butter and pepper.
If you drop that cup, it will shatter.
"Batter up!" The Eager Beavers are batting.

"Hand me the hammer, please," said Dad.
"I cannot reach it from the top of this ladder."

Ed Singer is the best hitter on our team, but
Bill Thatcher is a better runner.

doctor	collar	Richard	standard	conductor
mayor	dollar	custard	coward	visitor
sailor	beggar	mustard	Edward	September
tailor	poplar	backward	lizard	
author		backwards	wizard	
mirror		upward		
error		upwards		

MUSTARD ON CUSTARD?

"Richard!" exclaimed Ann. "Are you eating mustard on your custard?"

"Yes," said Richard. "I am fond of mustard. It's much better than cream."

"But, Richard," Ann fretted, "mustard is not correct on custard. One eats cream on custard."

"Not me!" said Richard.

"Richard, you'll get sick," said Ann.

"I'll not get sick. I saw the cat eating a lizard. The cat did not get sick."

"But you are not a cat," said Ann.

"Correct!" said Richard. "Cats are not fond of mustard. If I were a cat, I'd be eating cream."

133

Albert   eastern   record
Robert   western
desert   lantern

Richard has a dollar to spend at the Fair.
Albert went on a visit to the western desert.
Let's play records at your house today.
Edwin is a wizard at arithmetic!
Nell has a mirror in her handbag.

Sam's sister is a teacher. She helps Sam with his arithmetic.

Pat ripped his pants and the collar of his jacket. Mom sent the pants and the jacket to the tailor.

Our pup is a coward. He is afraid of the cat. He is afraid of a lizard, too. When our pup is bigger, he may not be such a coward.

Linda dressed up as a witch in a pointed black hat and a black dress. She had a black cat and a broom, too. When Robert saw her, he jumped back and screamed.

remember	sunflower	together	Mr. Smith
semester	gunpowder	however	Mrs. Smith
	customer	whenever	
	understand		
	interest	consider	
	interested	entertain	
	interesting		

HOW THE SAWYERS SPENT THE DAY

One day in summer, Mr. and Mrs. Sawyer, Richard Sawyer, and Sal Sawyer went out to the river to have a picnic.

When the Sawyers got near the river, they set down their lunch boxes under a tree.

Then Mr. Sawyer said, "Let's play catch."

Richard was glad to hear him say that and began to yell, "Yes, Dad, let's play catch!"

"Not me," said Mrs. Sawyer, "I'm a poor pitcher and a bad catcher. I'd better not play. I'd just spoil your fun."

When Mrs. Sawyer said that, Richard sneaked up to Mr. Sawyer and said in a whisper, "But, Dad, Sal is just as bad as Mom. She just cannot understand how to catch and pitch."

However, Sal said to Dad, "I'll stay with Mom, if I may. You and Dick can play better without me."

Richard was glad to hear this.

"Yes, Sis, you stay with Mom," said Mr. Sawyer. "Dick and I will play catch together."

Soon Mr. Sawyer and Dick were playing catch.

"Sal dear, let's run down to the river," said Mrs. Sawyer to Sal.

134

The river bank was a steep bluff. As they ran downhill, Sal began to skid, and Mrs. Sawyer held her hand to keep her from slipping down.

When they got down to the river, they saw reeds and shrubs and weeds and flowers.

Sal stooped down to grab a flower.

"Let's not pick the flowers," said Mrs. Sawyer. "If we pick them, they will soon wither. Let's just enjoy them as they are."

Then Sal saw a big red flower. She stooped to see it better, and then she screamed, "Mom! Mom!"

Mrs. Sawyer rushed to Sal.

"On this flower, Mom!" Sal exclaimed. "A bug! I'm afraid of it."

"Now, Sal! You must not be afraid of a bug. You're much too big to be afraid of such things."

Then Mrs. Sawyer plucked the leaf with the spotted bug on it and let the bug crawl on her hand. Sal saw that one need not be afraid of bugs.

"Now let me have it, please," Sal begged, and she stretched out her hand.

Mrs. Sawyer dropped the bug on Sal's hand. Then they set it back on a leaf and let it crawl away.

"See the river, Sal," said Mrs. Sawyer. "See how it glitters in the sun."

But Sal was not thinking about the river. "Mom, when will we eat?" said Sal.

"Soon, Sal. It must be getting near noon. Let's get back and fix dinner."

When Mrs. Sawyer and Sal got up the hill, they found Mr. Sawyer and Richard sitting under a tree and resting.

"Was it interesting down at the river?" said Mr. Sawyer.

But Richard just said, "Let's eat!"

Richard and Sal helped get the dinner. Sal helped unpack the boxes, and Richard fetched sticks and twigs. They laid out a big blanket and set the dinner things on it, and they had three rugs to sit on. Richard and Sal sat together on one rug.

They had a big dinner. They had ham sandwiches and cheese sandwiches and sandwiches of butter and jam. They had boiled eggs. And then they had custard in cups. Richard and Sal drank milk, and Mr. and Mrs. Sawyer drank hot tea.

"Now let Sal and me clear away the things and put the cups and dishes and spoons back in the boxes," said Mrs. Sawyer to Mr. Sawyer. "You and Dick may gather up the rugs and the blanket and pack them up."

When they had packed the things away, Mrs. Sawyer said, "You boys must see the river. Sal can lead the way. I think I'll stay here under this tree and read."

Sal led Mr. Sawyer and Richard down the hill to the river.

"See that!" said Mr. Sawyer and pointed at the river. "Did you see it? A fish jumped. The fish are jumping. I think they are catching insects when they jump that way.

"Just wait! Soon you'll see one jump."

Then they did see one. A big fish jumped clear up into the air, and then it fell back into the river with a splash.

134

At three o'clock Mr. Sawyer said, "Now we'll have to get back to town. It's too bad, but we must get back soon."

Sal said, "It's too bad we have to leave the trees and the flowers and the river and the fish and that spotted bug. Whenever we are at the river this summer, I must remember to hunt up that bug."

135

ramble	uncle	noodle	sample	nibble	bottle
scramble	candle	needle	temple	bubble	settle
thimble	handle	wheedle	simple	gobble	kettle
grumble	kindle	cackle	dimple	apple	nettle
rumble	bundle	crackle	crumple	ripple	wiggle
mumble	tinkle	tackle	rumple	cripple	snuggle
fumble	twinkle	pickle	ankle	topple	struggle
tumble	sprinkle	tickle	eagle	battle	juggle
stumble		trickle	measles	cattle	dazzle
tremble		fickle		rattle	sizzle
		buckle		tattle	drizzle
				little	puzzle
				brittle	

Just see Pal gobble up that meat!
Get the kettle on, and we'll have tea.
When the butter begins to sizzle, add the eggs.

It is not raining much—just a drizzle.
You will not need an umbrella.

Jean, bring me a needle and my thimble, and
I'll mend your dress.

apple	apples			
cackle	cackles	cackled	cackling	cackler
settle	settles	settled	settling	settler
tickle	tickles	tickled	tickling	tickler
sizzle	sizzles	sizzled	sizzling	sizzler
rattle	rattles	rattled	rattling	rattler
grumble	grumbles	grumbled	grumbling	grumbler
sprinkle	sprinkles	sprinkled	sprinkling	sprinkler
simple	simpler	simplest		

possible	impossible	terrible	probable

A pup is glad to have you tickle him back of his ears. A cat is pleased to be tickled under the chin. A fish must not be tickled or handled.

Uncle Alfred is a grumbler. He grumbles about this, and he grumbles about that. Today he grumbled because it was too hot. Next week he will grumble because it is too cool.

Ted thinks that arithmetic is simple. Ann thinks that spelling is much simpler than arithmetic.

137

metal	camel	devil	awful
petal	panel		cheerful
total	model	pistol	joyful
pedal	level		faithful
royal	travel	Harold	fearful
several	gravel		helpful
animal	barrel		painful
mineral	tunnel		thankful
capital	nickel		powerful
hospital	towel		

Each winter we eat a barrel of apples.
Robert fell on the gravel and cut his leg.
The flowers are withering and the petals are dropping.
The camel is an interesting animal.

Will you please hang up the towel when you are finished with it?

Edward can be helpful when Dad is painting.
Edward hands Dad paintbrushes and rags, and he dabs up the drops of paint which Dad spills.
Mom is thankful that Edward helps Dad in this way.

Paul, will you get a bottle of milk?
Jean, you must not snicker that way!
Dan Miller had a big box of animal crackers.
A man struck a match and lit a candle.
Hear the geese cackle.
Poor Fran stumbled and sprained her ankle.

137

Please bring me a needle and my thimble.
I have to mend this dress.

Little boys grumble when they have to get to
bed. Let them snuggle up to a toy animal, and
they will keep still.

A deer is an animal. An elk is a big animal.
Pups, cats, and rats are animals. Cows, sheep,
goats, and pigs are animals. Chicks, ducks, and
geese are animals. Fish and insects are animals
too.

Richard had a nickel in his toy bank. He wished
to get a model train, but he needed ten dollars.
He thinks it is impossible to get that much, but
Dad says it is possible if Richard will spend
less on pop and gum.

138

kitten	madden	happen	given
mitten	sadden	Ellen	driven
bitten	gladden	Helen	seven
gotten	redden	chicken	seventh
rotten	hidden	weaken	eleven
eaten	sudden	kitchen	linen
			children

Linda has a little black kitten.
Mom has given Sal a pair of green mittens.
Albert will be away till September seventh.
Ken just happened to have his trumpet with him.
Has Robert eaten dinner yet?
Dad has driven into town to visit the dentist.
Has Paul hidden the hatchet?

Mr. and Mrs. Sawyer have given Helen and Jim a wedding gift of linen. The Smiths have given them silver. Helen's twin sister Ellen has given them several kitchen things and an electric clock.

Al has bitten into several of the green apples, but he has found they are sour.

139

button	cannon	lemon	prison	canyon
mutton	common	wagon	prisoner	crayon
cotton	summon	Stetson	poison	
ribbon	lesson	Dobson	reason	
Madison	gallon	Hobson	season	
Harrison				

COWBOY BILL

Bill Madison went on a trip to the Grand Canyon this summer. Mr. and Mrs. Madison and Bill stayed at a ranch near the Grand Canyon. A man from the ranch picked them up at the train in a wagon.

This man, Sam Harrison, was a real cowboy. He had on a ten-gallon hat, boots, and jeans. Bill spent each day with Sam Harrison. He went with Sam when he rounded up cattle. He got Sam to teach him how to sit in the saddle.

Have you seen Bill Madison now that he's back in town? When I saw him, he had on a Stetson hat, jeans, and a pair of cowboy boots. Bill thinks he's a real cowboy now!

140

American   chairman   errand   second
                          husband
                          thousand

MR. THATCHER AND HIS FISHING

Mrs. Thatcher's husband was chairman of the
fund this year. Mr. Thatcher collected six
thousand dollars. This is Mr. Thatcher's second
year as chairman. He thinks that next year
he can collect seven thousand dollars.

When Mr. Thatcher is not out collecting, he
is fishing. He fishes each weekend in summer,
but the fish that he brings back are little things.
Mrs. Thatcher thinks they are too little to eat,
but as Mr. Thatcher is proud of his catch, she
fixes the fish for dinner.

Mr. Thatcher says that the biggest and best
fish just happen to get away. If ever he catches
a big fish, he has it mounted and hung on a board
in his den. The big fish are not to be eaten—
just displayed.

141

cabin	raisin	napkin
robin	Latin	Wisconsin
Robinson	satin	

SIMPLE LIVING

The Robinsons have a cabin in Wisconsin.
Mrs. Robinson and Harold and Anna Robinson spend
the summer in the cabin, as it is cooler than in
town. Mr. Robinson has a job in town and travels
to the cabin just for the weekends. Then he spends
three weeks at the cabin at the end of the summer.

When the Robinsons are at their cabin they
swim and fish and have lots of fun.

Mrs. Robinson and Anna dress in cotton
blouses and jeans. Harold dresses in jeans and
a battered straw hat.

When the Robinsons are at their cabin in
Wisconsin they will not fuss with big lunches.
They may just drink cool milk and eat nuts and
raisins. Then they will not have dishes and
napkins to bother with.

142

captain   fountain   fashion

mountain

It may be cool in the mountains.
Dad saw a robin today.
Let's get a box of raisins.
We had roast mutton at dinner.
Helen got twelve linen napkins as a wedding gift.

Mr. Robinson was the captain of a big ship
that sailed from America to Africa.

Liz must have a dress that is in fashion.
Liz wished to have a black satin dress, but
Mom got her one of pink cotton. It was trimmed
with brown buttons and brown ribbons, and it
had a brown collar.

Lift Bob up to the drinking fountain and
let him get a drink.

Ed is the best player, and he is captain
of the team. We miss him each summer when he
spends six weeks in the mountains. Our team
cannot win when Ed is away.

143

hadn't	didn't	aren't
hasn't	isn't	weren't
haven't	wasn't	needn't

HOW TO KEEP COOL

"Isn't it a hot day?" said Sal to Linda. "How can we get cool?"

"We can sprinkle the lawn," Linda said. "That may cool the air a bit."

Linda and Sal didn't wait. They got out the lawn sprinkler. Linda held the sprinkler, and Sal went to get a lawn chair out of the way.

As soon as Sal had set down the chair, Linda said, "This will get you cool, Sal," and she aimed the sprinkler at Sal.

Sal screamed and grabbed the sprinkler away from Linda. Then Sal aimed the sprinkler at Linda.

"Stop! Stop!" yelled Linda. "I'm cool now."

"Me too," said Sal. "And soon we'll be much cooler. Because Mom will skin us when she sees that we've got our dresses sopping wet!"

144

atom   freedom   blossom   welcome   problem
wisdom   bottom
seldom
kingdom

Mrs. Smith is glad to have Jim visit her, but she is not glad to have him bring Pal with him. Pal romps and jumps, crumples up the rugs, and tips the lamps and chairs. When Pal stops in to visit, he is not welcome.

Bill Madison now sleeps in back of the house in a tent. In the house he has a bed with a mattress and quilts, but Bill still sleeps in a sleeping bag in the tent. He says, "This is the way we cowboys sleep."

When Dad paints, he has a problem. He spills the paint when he brings it up the ladder. Today Kenneth waited at the bottom of the ladder to hand Dad the paint can. When Dad reached out, he missed. Dad had planned to paint the cabinets, but he painted Kenneth.

145

Jimmy	Sally	badly	correctly	pity	fifty
Jenny	Billy	gladly	cowardly	very	sixty
Bobby	Molly	quickly	suddenly	candy	twenty
Betty	Polly	simply	rapidly	jiffy	seventy
Patty	holly	promptly	awfully	plenty	
Peggy	jolly	nearly		daily	
Harry	jelly	really			
Jerry		clearly			
Andy		possibly			
Sandy		probably			
Blacky					
Henry					

Jenny decked the house with holly.
Please get to the train promptly. It will not wait.

Did Harry speak clearly? Yes, Harry did speak
very clearly and rapidly.

Peggy got six boxes of candy as gifts this week.
That was plenty of candy!

Jerry can add very quickly. He is best in
arithmetic.

body	laundry	daddy	puppy	blackberry
lily	pansy	buddy	berry	strawberry
fairy	daisy	piggy	cherry	cranberry
dairy	country	dolly	kitty	gooseberry
		penny		
		bunny		

| penny | daisy | puppy | fairy | cherry |
| pennies | daisies | puppies | fairies | cherries |

The Smiths have a cherry tree. This summer
they canned twenty cans of cherries.

Ed Singer has six puppies. He will give the
puppies to Andy, Patty, Bobby, Jimmy, and Sam.
Each will get one puppy, and Ed will keep one of
the puppies himself.

Sandy has a piggy bank. He drops pennies in
it whenever he can.

Harry went out and picked blackberries. Mom
fixed blackberry jam from the berries. Next winter
Mom and Dad and Harry will have toast and jam.

147

funny	chilly	rusty	rocky	weary
sunny	hilly	dusty	lucky	oily
fussy	silly	ugly	sticky	cloudy
fuzzy	jolly	cranky	noisy	rainy
dizzy		dandy	drowsy	sleepy
muddy	sickly	sandy	breezy	
merry	empty	windy		

THE PICNIC

It was a sunny spring day.

"Just the day to have a picnic," said Betty.

"It's too windy," said Peggy.

"Just breezy," said Jimmy. "It's a dandy day to have a picnic up on top of the hill."

Peggy and Betty fixed sandwiches, and Jimmy packed them in a box. Then they began their trip up the hill. Soon they were weary, and Betty said, "It's silly to get way up to the top. Let's have our picnic here."

"It's too muddy," said Peggy.

"Let's not be fussy," said Jimmy. "LET'S EAT!"

carry	carries	carried		unhappy
marry	marries	married		uneasy
study	studies	studied		
copy	copies	copied		

happy	happier	happiest	happiness	happily
greedy	greedier	greediest	greediness	greedily
easy	easier	easiest	easiness	easily

OUR GREEDY PUP

Our puppy is the greediest puppy that ever lived. It seems that he never can get his fill.

When we feed our puppy, we feed our cat, too. Our pup gulps his food greedily. Then he rushes to the cat's dish and grabs a bit of her food. He carries it away. Then he sits and growls as he eats it. He is afraid the cat will get it back.

We wish he'd copy the manners of our cat. She never gulps her food. When she has finished eating, she cleans her paws and her whiskers. Then she happily settles down to a nap.

149

every	family	history	delivery	factory
everybody	salary	victory	slippery	satisfactory
everything				
everyone				

Everyone wished he were traveling to the coast with Molly.

"Pack me in your bag," begged Betty. "I'll not need much room."

"Me too!" begged Jean.

"Pack your camera and plenty of film," Betty said. "Carry it with you and never be without it. You must not miss a thing."

Molly did just as Betty said. She clicked that camera at everything.

When Molly got back, Betty and Jean said, "Tell us what you saw."

"I didn't see a thing," said Molly. "The main thing I did was snap that camera. But when we get the film developed, then we'll see everything that I saw on my trip."

150

Annie	Brownie	Millie	Willie	alley
Frankie	Winnie	Milly	Willy	valley
				chimney

BILL THATCHER'S JOB

Bill Thatcher was just leaving King's Shop when he met Kenneth Hunt. "I've got a problem," he said. "Next week is Dad's Day. I need twelve dollars to get my dad a gift."

"Twelve dollars!" Kenneth exclaimed. "That's a lot of cash. You'll have to get a job to raise that much."

But Bill was reading the big display letters on King's Shop. The letters said WE HAVE EVERYTHING.

"And that shop *has* everything, too," said Kenneth. "But it is cash and carry. My mom said she'd be that shop's best customer if they'd deliver."

"Wait," said Bill, and he went back in the shop.

Mr. King was standing at the counter.

"You have nearly everything in your shop, Mr. King," Bill said. "You need just one thing."

"Really?" said Mr. King. "Tell me."

"You need a delivery boy. May I have the job?"

Mr. King leaned on the counter. "I've been thinking of getting a delivery boy. I need a boy just this week. You can help me catch up on my deliveries."

Mr. King picked up a big box. "You can deliver this box now."

When Bill left the shop he was carrying the box. "That was quick," said Kenneth. But Bill did not stop to discuss his job with Kenneth.

Bill did the job well. Up and down streets and alleys he rushed,

276

delivering things from King's. Mr. King's customers were glad that their things were being delivered.

At the end of the week Mr. King said "Bill, I really did need a delivery boy. And you are a very satisfactory one. I'm glad that when I got a delivery boy, I got the best one in town!"

And then Mr. King paid Bill. "Thank you, Mr. King," said Bill.

When Mr. King went to wait on a customer, Bill counted his cash. Just ten dollars! And he needed twelve to get that Dad's Day gift.

As soon as Mr. King had finished with his customer, Bill said, "Mr. King, I'm afraid you may sell that fishing reel before I can get it. May I give you ten dollars now and then pick it up when I can raise the rest of the cash?"

"That's the reel you've been wishing to get your dad as a Dad's Day gift, isn't it, Bill?"

"That's the one," said Bill.

"But Dad's Day is this Sunday," said Mr. King.

"I'll tell my dad he has a gift on the way."

"You'll not tell him a thing," said Mr. King. "You'll deliver this reel to your dad yourself. Wait till I get a gift box and ribbon."

"But—but—" Bill stuttered. "I haven't the twelve dollars, Mr. King."

"And you needn't have. You get a discount because you have a job here, Bill. This reel will be less than ten dollars."

151

Sunday maybe
Saturday
yesterday

TESS AND THE KITTEN

One day Tess Roberts found a little kitten out in the alley back of the Roberts' house.

"You funny little kitty," she said to it. "You'll have to stay at our house and be my kitty."

Then she picked up the kitten and went into the house with it and set it down in the kitchen.

"A cat!" said Ellen Jackson. "That means a lot of mess and fuss and bother. A cat is just the thing we need in this kitchen. It was too easy just keeping house and getting the meals and tending to you children. Well, if we must have a cat, let's give it a drink of milk."

Tess got a dish, and Ellen filled it with milk. Then Tess set it down, and the kitten quickly lapped up the milk.

"See, Ellen, it's drunk all the milk," said Tess.

"It's a greedy little thing," said Ellen. "Well, fill up the dish, Tess," and she handed Tess a bottle of milk.

Tess filled the dish with milk, and the kitten drank up this milk, too. It got milk in its whiskers and on its paws and on one ear, but then it sat down and cleaned itself.

Soon Ellen had to leave the kitchen. Tess stayed and sat playing with the kitten. She petted it and patted it and rubbed and scratched its back. The kitten snuggled up to her.

"Maybe it will eat a bit of jelly," Tess said to herself. "Let's see if it will eat jelly."

278

151

Tess got up on a chair and reached up on a shelf and got down a dish of apple jelly. She set the dish down, but the kitten did not seem to see it. Then Tess held the jelly up to the kitten's mouth. The kitten smelled it and sniffed at it, but it did not eat it.

"Kitty," said Tess, "everyone is fond of jelly. You'd better eat it."

She held the dish under the kitten's chin and kept telling it to eat. Suddenly the kitten began to struggle and scratch. Tess dropped it, and it fell into the dish of jelly. It scrambled out and ran under a chair. As it ran, it left a trail of jelly. Then it sat under the chair and began to lick itself clean.

Tess got a damp rag and set about mopping up the spots of jelly.

Just then Ellen got back to the kitchen. With her were Mrs. Roberts and Ann, Tess's big sister. They saw the trail of jelly.

"It isn't the kitten's fault," said Tess. "It's my fault. Please, let me keep the kitten."

Tess's big sister, Ann, began to tease her. "The kitten seems to have better sense than Tess," said Ann. "We had better keep the kitten and let Tess stay out. The house will be cleaner that way."

Tess acted as if she did not hear Ann.

"Please, Mom," she wheedled, "may I keep the cat?"

"That will depend on Ellen," said Mrs. Roberts. "If Ellen is willing to have the cat stay, then you may keep it."

"Please, Ellen, may I?" begged Tess. "May I keep the kitten?"

"Well," said Ellen, "maybe we can keep it, but we must not let foolish things happen, the way they did today. Can you promise that?"

"Yes, yes, Ellen dear! I promise!" said Tess, and jumped up and down with joy.

"Very well," said Ellen, "from now on the kitten is a member of

279

the family, and you, Tess, will be the one to feed it and tend to it."

"Thank you, thank you, Ellen!" said Tess. "I'll feed the kitten every day. I'll feed it milk and meat and cat food. But not a bit of jelly. I'll eat the jelly myself!"

LET'S READ

Part V
The Commonest
Irregular Spellings
of Vowel Sounds

THE COMMONEST IRREGULAR SPELLINGS
OF VOWEL SOUNDS

IN LESSONS 152-199 we take up the commonest irregular spellings of vowel sounds.

Some of these spellings are new ways of representing sounds to which we have assigned regular spellings. For instance, the vowel sound in *cut*, which is regularly represented by the letter *u*, is represented by an *o* in certain words, such as *son, love, mother.* Other spellings that are taken up in Lessons 152-199 represent vowel sounds for which we have no regular letter or combination of letters; for instance, the vowel sounds in *father, pine, book, bird.*

Lessons 152-157 take up the use of the letter *a* to represent the vowel sound of words like *safe, game, bake.* We call this an irregular spelling because we have taught the child when he sees a word with the letter *a* to produce the vowel sound of *hat, bat, mat.* We must now modify this habit and teach him, when he sees certain spellings with the letter *a*, to produce a different sound. This is the sound to which we have assigned the spelling *ai*, as in *bait, wait,* and *ay* as in *day, gay.*

Most of the spellings in this section may nevertheless be called "semi-irregular." In most of the words of this sort, the letter *a* is followed by a single consonant letter, and this, in turn, by a silent *e*, as in *cake, cape, game, safe.* Only the word *have* is spelled this way while having the "regular" sound of *a*, as in *hat.* Some other words of the present section have the letter *a* followed by a single consonant letter which in turn is followed by *-le*, as in *table, cradle.* Others have *a* followed by a single consonant letter with suffixal *y* after it, as *lady, gravy.* In short, we could state some rules about English spelling which would cover these words and make them "regular." To be sure, these rules would be rather complicated. We shall not try to explain such things to the child. We merely take advantage of such uniformity as there is in these spellings.

Our procedure is the same as before. First, the teacher or parent presents the words one by one, in various orders, reading them to the child and letting the child read them back. Our list of words contains a selection of words that exhibit this spelling; the teacher or parent may omit any of these that may seem unimportant or unfamiliar, and may add other words with this spelling of *a* for *ai*. After the child has learned to read these words, the exercises in the book following the lists should be taken up. During all this time, the teacher or parent may write on the blackboard additional sentences which contain these words; we give sample sentences of this kind. He should be extremely careful, however, not to use words having spelling irregularities not yet presented.

The word *a* which we have been using in all the lessons has the sound of *ay* when it is spoken alone or under emphasis.

Of the words which we give here, three show other irregularities of spelling—*bathe* and *lathe* have *th* as in *then*, and *James* has suffixal *es* for *z*. The word *lathe* need not be used, however; it is given here because it may be a familiar word for some children.

Lesson 158 takes up the words *break, great, steak,* in which the spelling *ea* is used for the sound of *ai*. Since there are only a few new words here, the story is rather a review of the words in Lessons 152-158.

Lesson 159 takes up words in which *are (ar)* is used for the sound of *air*, words in which *ear* is used for *air*, and the words *there, where,* in which *ere* is used for this sound. These last two words are important on account of their great frequency. They differ in pronunciation in different parts of the country; especially when they are unstressed, their vowel sound is shortened in some types of pronunciation.

Lessons 160-162 take up words in which the letter *a* represents the vowel sound of words like *father, car, far*. None of our "regular" spellings represent this sound. We could state as a rule that the letter *a* before final *r*, as in *car*, and before *r* followed by another consonant, as in *cart*, represents this sound. This would cover most of the words, but not all; the spelling of *father*, for instance, would still contain an irregular use of the letter *a*, in contrast with *gather, lather*. The word *are* has been introduced in Lesson 115; its spelling is irregular and moreover contrasts with the semi-irregular spelling in *care, fare, share*.

The word *what* given in Lesson 160 is sometimes pronounced "whot," but in some regions it is pronounced "whut," especially when unstressed.

Lesson 163: The words in this lesson are spoken differently in different parts of the country. In most of the United States, *ask, bath, pass,* and so on, contain the vowel sound of *hat, cap, gas*. This is the sound which we have been treating as the regular value of the letter *a*. Therefore, in most parts of the United States the reading of these words presents nothing new; some of them, in fact, could have been given in Lessons 1-36.

In some parts of the English-speaking world, however, these words contain the vowel sound of *father, car, cart*. This is true of parts of New England (especially Boston) and of England and some of her Dominions. For communities which speak this way, Lesson 163 is a continuation of Lessons 160, 161, and 162.

The teacher or parent doubtless knows which pronunciation is current in the community where he or she teaches or lives. In a community where these words are spoken with the "flat *a*" (as in *hat*) no special drill will be needed. In a community where some or all of these words are spoken with the "broad *a*" (as in *father*) the teacher or parent will have to give some drill on the list in Lesson 163.

In no case should the teacher or parent try to change the child's pronunciation of the vowel sound in these words. Teachers and other people have been trying to do that for a long time, with no success. It takes more than the schoolroom to bring about such a change. Anyone who has tried to change his own speech in this regard will realize what a very difficult thing it is. Our children have enough to do learning to read.

As to the teacher's or parent's own pronunciation, the most important thing is to keep it natural and free from affectation.

Lessons 164, 165: In Lesson 164 we take up another irregular use of the letter *a*: the words, like *salt*, in which it is used to represent the sound that is regularly represented by the letters *aw* or *au*, as in *saw, haul*.

Some of these words could be put under a rule: where the letter *a* appears before *ll*, *ld*, and *lt*, it represents the sound of *aw*. Hence we may call this a semi-irregular spelling.

There is also a set of words in which the letter *a* comes after *w* and before *r*, such as *war;* here, too, the vowel sound in most types of pronunciation is the sound of *aw*, except that it is variously modified by the following *r*.

Finally, we give here a set of words in which *a* comes after *w* and has in some parts of the country the sound of *aw* (as in *saw*) and in other parts of the country rather the sound of *o* (as in *hot*).

The best results will be obtained if the teacher or parent follows his or her natural pronunciation and lets the child follow his.

Lesson 166: Words like *dog, long, soft*, which we give here, are spoken in England and some parts of the United States with the vowel sound of *hot, stop, cot*. This is the sound which we have treated as the regular value of the letter *o*. Therefore, in communities where *dog, long, soft*, and so on are spoken with this sound, these words are regular in spelling and require no special drill.

In most parts of the United States, however, some of these words are spoken with the vowel sound of *aw* (as in *saw, law*). There may be places where all of them have this sound. Wherever any of these words are so pronounced, the spelling with *o* for the sound of *aw* constitutes an irregularity. The teacher or parent will probably find, if he or she stops to notice, that children differ as to the words in which they use the sound of *aw*. Families and persons differ in this. These differences are not important, and the teacher or the parent should not try to change the child's habits or his own.

One such word is *on*, which we introduced in Lesson 36.

Lessons 167-170 take up words like *go* and *hope*, in which the letter *o* is used to represent the vowel sound of *oa*, as in *coat*. Most of these spellings are semi-irregular; we could cover them by special rules: final *o* (as in *so*), final *oe* in which the *e* is silent (as in *toe*), *o* before one consonant letter that is followed by final silent *e* (as in *hope*), and *o* before *ld* and *lt* (as in *bold, bolt*) represent the sound of *oa*. Of course, we shall not try to present rules like these to the child, but we can be fairly liberal about including words that are covered by them, since the child will soon get used to the pattern of these spellings.

The words *nose, rose, chose, close, suppose* have *s* for *z* and *those* has also *th* as in *then*.

Lessons 167, 168, 170 contain derivative words *(goes, broken)*, compound words *(over-*

coat, backbone), and most common two- and three-syllable words *(open, sober)* occurring in the most frequent 3500 words in the English language.

Lessons 171, 172: In Lesson 171 we take up words like *snow*, in which *ow* represents the sound of *oa*. We must call the spelling of these words irregular, since we have treated as regular the words like *how*, in which *ow* represents a different sound. The difficulty here is a good example of the problems a child faces when he is learning to read. The marks *sow* represent two different words: one meaning "mother pig" and the other "scatter seed." The two words differ in sound, but our writing does not show which one is meant; we have to distinguish by the context.

We should give only such of these words as are familiar to the child.

In Lesson 172 we include suffixal *-ow* (for *oa*), as in *window*. This offers less difficulty, since suffixal *-ow* usually has this value.

Lessons 173-177: Words spelled with *or* and *ore*, such as *for, corn, core*, may be called semi-irregular, since in this position the letter *o* has its regular value (as in *hot*) with some speakers in only a few words (such as *sorry, horrid*). The spellings *oor* (as in *door*) and *our* (as in *pour*) are quite irregular, since they conflict with such spellings as *poor* and *sour*.

In all these words, the *r* which follows upon the *oa* sound affects the quality of this vowel. The result differs in different parts of the country. In some regions the *r* disappears, so to speak, and exists only in its effect on the vowel sound; in other regions the *r* is plainly sounded but produces various modifications in the vowel. Of course we need not tell the child anything about this. We need only to get him used to reading the combination *or* or *ore* and teach him the most necessary words with the entirely irregular spellings of *oor* and *our*.

Lessons 178-181 take up words in which the letter *i* is used to represent the vowel sound of words like *bite, five, time*. Most of these words may be called semi-irregular in spelling, since we could state the rule that the letter *i* followed by a single consonant letter and then by silent *e*, represents this sound. Then the spelling of *give* and *live* (verb) would have to be called irregular. But we shall not confuse the child with matters like these. Our task is a different one. We have trained the child to utter words with the vowel of *pin, bit, bid* whenever he sees words spelled with the letter *i*. We must now teach him a different and more special habit, the habit of uttering the vowel sound of *bite, five, time* when he sees certain special words.

The word *I* was introduced in Lesson 116.

The words *rise, wise* have *s* for *z*.

Lesson 182 takes up the words in which the letter *y* represents the vowel sound which in the words in Lessons 178-181 is represented by *i*. The spellings here are semi-irregular, for we state it as a rule that in words of one syllable a final *y* represents this sound.

However, we have assigned to the letter *y*, as its regular sound, the consonant sound in *yes*, *yet*, *year*, and we have had a good deal of practice on suffixal *y* with the sound of *-ee*, as in *penny*, *story*. Therefore, we now have to set up in the child an additional and more special habit for the words like *by*.

Of these words we have been using only one, the word *my*.

We have here the additional task of reading forms with *ie*, such as *flies*, beside *fly*. These forms are likewise irregular, since they belong in Lessons 178-181.

Lessons 183-186: Lessons 183, 184, and 185 introduce the spelling of *o* for the sound which we have taken as the regular value of the letter *u*. For instance, the two words *sun* and *son* sound exactly alike but differ in meaning and spelling. For the sound of these words, we have called the spelling *sun* regular. The spelling *son* is irregular because to the letter *o* we have assigned, as its regular sound, the vowel sound of words like *hot* and *hop*.

The word *one*, which we have been using hitherto, belongs here, but, apart from the silent *e* at the end, it has the additional irregularity of not indicating the initial sound of *w*.

The words *other*, *mother*, *brother*, in addition to the irregular vowel sound, have *th* as in *then*.

The word *donkey* is in some places spoken with the vowel of *hot;* in this case the only irregularity in its spelling is the *-ey*, representing the *y*-suffix. In another common pronunciation, the *o* in *donkey* is pronounced "aw."

In Lesson 186 we take up also words like *touch*, in which *ou* is written for the sound of *u* (as in *much*).

Lessons 187-189: The words in Lessons 187 and 188 contain a vowel sound, that of *put* and *book*, for which we have no regular spelling. In Lesson 187 we take up the words in which the letter *u* is used to represent this sound.

Lesson 188 takes up the words in the spelling of which this sound is represented by *oo*. This spelling is irregular, since we have assigned the spelling *oo* to the vowel sound in words like *moon*.

In Lesson 189 we present some words, such as *room*, which fluctuate between the vowel sounds of *book* and *moon*. For persons or districts where these are spoken with the vowel sound of *moon*, the spelling of these words is regular.

Lessons 190-192: The *r*-vowel in words like *bird*, *fur*, *word*, *earn* differs very much in different parts of the English-speaking world. These differences do not concern us; when the child reads words which contain this sound, he will pronounce them according to the habit which prevails in his community.

In the spelling of nearly all such words, the *r*-vowel is represented by one or two vowel letters followed by the letter *r*.

The *r*-suffix, as in *teacher*, *doctor*, which we have been reading for some time, consists of the *r*-vowel. The words which we now introduce have the *r*-vowel in their accented syllables.

We have also had the words *her* and *hers*, which contain this vowel sound. The word *were*, introduced in Lesson 115, contains this vowel sound in this country; in England it sometimes has the sound of -*air*.

Lessons 193-195 take up words like *tune*, in which the letter *u* represents the sound of *oo* (as in *moon*) or the same sound preceded by the sound of *y* (as in *yes*).

This group contains three kinds of words. In some, such as *mule, pure*, the *y*-sound is spoken probably in all types of Standard English. These words are presented in Lesson 193. In the second type, the *y*-sound is not present; these are the words in Lesson 194 in which the *u* appears after *r* (as in *rule*) or after a consonant plus *l* (as in *blue*). In the third type, some districts and some speakers pronounce a *y*-sound, but others do not; these are the words in Lesson 195 in which the *u* comes after *n* (as in *numeral*), *d* (as in *due*), *t* (as in *tune*), *st* (as in *student*).

The word *use* (in Lesson 193) as a verb has *s* for *z;* the noun *use* has the regular sound of *s*.

Lesson 196: The words in Lesson 196, like those in Lessons 193-195, contain the sound of *yoo* or *oo*, but represent this sound by the letters *ew*.

Just as in Lessons 193-195, we have here three kinds of words, some are everywhere spoken with the sounds *yoo*, as, for instance, *few*; others, like *grew*, are everywhere spoken with the sound *oo*; others, finally, like *new*, are spoken in come communities with the sound *yoo* and in others with the sound *oo*.

Lesson 197: We have taken the regular value of the spelling *ea* to be the vowel sound of *meat, cheap, clean*. In Lesson 197 we take up words in which the spelling *ea* represents the vowel sound that is regularly written *e;* words like *bread* (which sounds like *bred*).

The words *feather, weather, leather*, in addition to the irregular vowel spellings, have *th* as in *then*.

Lessons 198, 199: In Lesson 114 we took up words in which final *e* represented the sound that is regularly written *ee* or *ea*, words like *be, he, she, we, me*. We now take up words like *Eve*, in which a non-final *e* represents this sound. The letter *e* is followed in most of them by a single consonant letter plus a silent *e*.

Only a few words appear in our list, because only a few are likely to occur in children's reading. Many words in the grown-up vocabulary are spelled this way: *recede, concede, sere, sphere, revere, scheme*. In fact, this use of the letter *e* amounts to a semi-irregular spelling.

152

ate	bake	came	cave	gale	cane	fade
date	cake	dame	Dave	male	Jane	made
fate	fake	fame	gave	pale	lane	wade
gate	Jake	game	pave	sale	mane	blade
hate	lake	lame	rave	tale	pane	grade
Kate	make	name	save	scale	crane	shade
late	rake	same	wave	stale	plane	spade
mate	sake	tame	brave	whale		trade
rate	take	blame	grave		ape	
crate	wake	flame	shave	base	cape	
grate	flake	frame	slave	case	tape	
plate	brake	shame		vase	drape	
skate	quake		bathe	chase	grape	
state	shake	James	lathe		shape	
	snake			safe	scrape	
gaze						
blaze	haste			babe		
graze	paste					
	taste					
	waste					

152

Let's sit in the shade under the elm.
Kate ate a date, and Jane ate a fig.
Can Jane bake a cake?
James played second base on our team.
Please wake me at seven o'clock.
When you clean the house, brush each drape.
James came late and missed the game.
Poor Dave got the blame.
May I taste that milk shake?
See the flame blaze up in the grate!
Please tell me your name.

You're not a very brave man if you're afraid of a poor little snake.

That poor little snake is a rattler!

Jake, please spade up the flower bed and rake away the weeds.

This winter we'll skate on the lake. When we get back to the house, we'll sit around the grate and eat cake and drink hot tea.

Jake made a trade with Dave. Jake gave Dave his model plane. Dave gave Jake his toy crane.

hate	hates	hated	hating	gate	gates
skate	skates	skated	skating	crate	crates
gaze	gazes	gazed	gazing	lake	lakes
rake	rakes	raked	raking	snake	snakes
brake	brakes	braked	braking	taste	tastes
paste	pastes	pasted	pasting	game	games
name	names	named	naming	flame	flames
blame	blames	blamed	blaming	cape	capes
tape	tapes	taped	taping	lane	lanes
cane	canes	caned	caning	pane	panes
plane	planes	planed	planing	cave	caves
save	saves	saved	saving	Dave	Daves
shave	shaves	shaved	shaving	lathe	lathes
bathe	bathes	bathed	bathing	sale	sales
pale	pales	paled	paling	male	males
scale	scales	scaled	scaling	case	cases
chase	chases	chased	chasing	spade	spades
wade	wades	waded	wading	grade	grades
trade	trades	traded	trading		

153

WIGGLES, THE SNAKE

Dave had a snake named Wiggles.
He kept it in a crate.

Dave is fond of snakes, but Kate
hates snakes.

"Get rid of that awful thing,"
said Kate to Dave.

"It is not an awful thing,"
said Dave.

"Yes, it is," said Kate. "I am
afraid of it. Give it away."

"I will never give away my snake,"
said Dave.

"Sell it then," said Kate. "Sell it
to the Handbag Shop."

But when Dave and Kate went to get
the snake out of the crate, it had
disappeared.

"That snake did not wish to be
a handbag," said Dave. "Wiggles
wished to stay a snake."

154

hater	taster	wader	late	later	latest
grater	waster	trader	tame	tamer	tamest
blazer	shaper	saver	brave	braver	bravest
skater	scraper	shaver	pale	paler	palest
baker		bather	safe	safer	safest
maker					
taker					
shaker					

Grate the cheese with a grater.
In May it's still too cool to bathe in the lake.
The street is not the safest spot to play.
Beth is a string-saver. She saves every bit.
You must not waste the soap.
Nan baked a cake yesterday.

Kenneth found that the chipmunks were not very tame and that they never did get tamer.

When the lake freezes up we'll get out our skates and have a lot of fun.

James saves stamps. Dave did save stamps, but he is not saving them now.

155

bacon	paper	waken	taken	bakery
labor		awake	mistake	safety
major		awaken	mistaken	
favor				
razor				

My dad shaves with a safety razor.
Kate went to the bakery to get a cake.

Please get a pound of bacon and a bunch of grapes.
Yes, I'll get them. But is that our dinner?

Isn't Dad awake yet? He said he'd get up at
six, and now it is nearly ten!

When we have a picnic, we take paper napkins
and paper plates. If we are having cool drinks,
we take paper cups, too.

If you beat that drum, Tom, you'll awaken
everyone in the house. Then they'll get up and
chase you!

Will you tell Jane to bring back my paper.
I think she has taken it.
You are mistaken. Jane did not take your paper.

156

erase	became	parade	operate	playmate
eraser	ashamed	lemonade	separate	airplane
escape	behave		hesitate	salesman
		David	investigate	pancake

It will be fun to take a trip in an airplane.
Will you lend me your eraser, please?
Brad will spade up the flower beds.
If David will not behave, Dad will punish him.
Separate the cotton things from the silk things.

Robert, will you please stay and help me erase the blackboards.

We went to the parade Saturday. There was such a crowd that we didn't see much, but we ate a lot. We each had three bags of peanuts and three paper cups of pink lemonade.

Mr. Temple is in the hospital. The doctor may have to operate.

"Will you have a pancake?" said Kate.
James did not hesitate. "I'll take six," he said, "with blackberry jam, please."

baby	gravy	able	label	acre
lady	navy	cable	Mabel	apron
shady	Amy	table	Hazel	April
crazy	Katy	stable	cradle	favorite
lazy		unable	maple	tablespoon

| baby | babies | crazy | crazier | craziest |
| lady | ladies | shady | shadier | shadiest |

Katy, will you please fix Dad a plate of scrambled eggs and bacon? If Jane weren't lazy, she'd set the table.

Amy Moll is able to sing very well. I think she is my favorite singer. In April she will entertain the ladies at their club meeting.

Hazel thinks she can make a cake, but we think she'd better get it in a bakery.

Mabel had a baby doll. She was crazy about that doll, but she is crazier now about her kitten.

Jenny has an apron to keep her dress clean. Sally is just a baby. She has a bib.

PAUL PISTOL, DETECTIVE

Sally and David Brown and their hound pup Blacky were spending the summer with their family in a cabin near the Grand Canyon.

One day Sally said to David, "Dave, have you seen my silver pin? Did you take it?"

"I haven't got your pin." David sounded disgusted. "It's probably on one of your blouses."

"But it isn't," said Sally. "I left it on my dresser yesterday, and now it's disappeared."

"Impossible," said David.

"Please help me hunt, Dave. It's my favorite pin."

Sally and David hunted and hunted. Blacky seemed to be helping, too. He sniffed around the rugs and under the dresser, but he did not sniff out the pin.

Then David said, "Well, it seems that it did disappear. Blacky, you and I must investigate. I'll be Paul Pistol, detective. You'll be my faithful hound, Gunpowder, and you can help me.

"How about it, Gunpowder?" With a yip, Blacky said he'd be glad to help.

"Can I help?" said Sally. "It's my pin."

"Well, lady," said David, "you employed me to handle this job. Now bring me up to date about this case of the missing pin."

"I had the pin yesterday," Sally explained. "And I left it on my dresser."

"Then a robber must have sneaked in and escaped with the loot," said David.

"You're silly!" said Sally. "If a robber came in, he'd take lots of things—not just my silver pin."

"Maybe," said David, as he saw Blacky cock his ears at a scratching sound on the sill near the rip in the screen. "Men robbers, maybe. But how about animal robbers?"

"You're silly, Dave," said Sally, and then she, too, saw the little animal on the sill. "But I have swept up nut hulls in the cabin. The chipmunks can get in."

"Not chipmunks," said David. "Pack rats. They steal things and carry them away."

157

"Dave, you *are* a detective."

"Mr. Pistol, if you please," said Dave smugly. "Now let's separate and investigate the grounds."

As David and Blacky approached, a chipmunk scooted out of their way. A jay chattered, and a robin hopped away when they saw David, the detective, and his faithful hound Gunpowder.

Then David saw a little animal that was not a chipmunk, not a jay, not a robin. It scrambled out of a rotten tree and ran away. Gunpowder gave a yip and began to chase the little animal, but it scooted up a tree and disappeared.

Dave peered into the rotten tree. "Sally!" he yelled. "I've found it! I've found your pin."

Sally came running.

In the tree they saw a nest. It was a queer nest, made of twigs and leaves and bits of paper and cotton. In the middle of the nest was Sally's little silver pin.

Sally picked up her pin. "A pin's a funny thing to make a nest with. But that's a very funny nest."

"It's a pack rat's nest," said Dave. "I saw the rat scramble out of this tree and run away." Dave pointed up to the top of the tree under which Blacky was still waiting and yelping. Then he went and picked up the little dog. "We're not taking a prisoner, Gunpowder. The handcuffs will not fit that little beast."

"Mr. Pistol," said Sally, "you handled this case in a very satisfactory manner. How can I ever pay you?"

David grinned. "My fee, lady? Well, just whip up a batch of pancakes. When we've had a difficult case, we enjoy eating a bit. And we're very fond of pancakes. Aren't we, Gunpowder?"

break	great	steak	beefsteak
breaks	greater	steaks	
daybreak	greatest		
	greatly		

Sunday and yesterday and today we had meat at dinner. Sunday we had chicken, yesterday we had steak, and today we had roast veal.

Little Jimmy breaks his toys as soon as he gets them. How foolish of him! He must be a silly little boy. Now and then he breaks his sister's toys too. Then his sister gets really mad.

It's great fun, swimming in the lake on a hot day. And it's greater fun to toast in the sun on the beach.

The Smith family had to get up at daybreak to catch the plane. They had lunch on the plane—steak, string beans, hot buns with butter, and fresh peaches with cream.

When you are out shopping, will you please get me a pound of beefsteak? If you haven't too much to carry, will you bring me a box of oatmeal, too?

MABEL GETS DINNER

Mabel Oaks is just six, but she thinks she is a great help around the house.

One Sunday when Mrs. Oaks was not feeling well, Mabel's Uncle Jim came for a visit. As soon as Uncle Jim saw that Mrs. Oaks was ill, he said, "It's a shame to bother you when you're sick. I'll leave now and be back next week."

But Mabel was fond of her Uncle Jim. "Please stay," she begged. "I'll get the dinner."

"Yes, Jim," said Mr. Oaks with a wink. "You'd better stay. Mabel will get the dinner."

"I'm feeling better now," said Mrs. Oaks. "You must stay, Jim."

As soon as Uncle Jim said he'd stay, Mabel got into her apron. Then she got out the flour and the baking powder.

"We must bake a cake," said Mabel.

"Yes, dear," Mrs. Oaks agreed. "Uncle Jim has a sweet tooth."

"Several of them, in fact," said Uncle Jim with a grin.

Mrs. Oaks started mixing the cake and getting the dinner. Mabel went in and out of the kitchen getting the things to set the table. She went into the pantry and got dishes down from the shelves. Mabel did not make much noise.

"Crash!" A sudden loud noise came from the pantry. Mrs. Oaks ran to see. Mabel was standing up on a chair. At the bottom of the chair lay several plates smashed to bits.

"I dropped them," Mabel sobbed. "They just slipped out of my hands."

Mrs. Oaks helped Mabel down from the chair. "You must not feel bad," said Mrs. Oaks.

"They were your best plates," said Mabel.

"Yes," said Mrs. Oaks. "But we cannot help it now. Just sweep up the mess and finish setting the table."

When Mabel had swept up the smashed dishes she began to feel better, but she still was ashamed of dropping the plates. She did not drop the rest of the plates when she set the table.

Then Mabel said, "Shall I get a box of the little green peas out of the freezer?"

"Yes, dear," said Mrs. Oaks. "Get a box of peas. And get the steaks out of the freezer, too."

When everything was in shape, Mrs. Oaks sent Mabel to get the men in to dinner.

"Dad! Uncle Jim!" said Mabel. "We can have dinner now."

When they sat down to dinner, Mrs. Oaks said, "I'm very proud of Mabel. She helped me a great deal."

"But, Mom," said Mabel, "I dropped three of your best plates."

"Yes, Mabel dear, you did break three plates, and it was too bad, but we have to expect things such as that now and then. You helped me bake the cake and set the table and broil the steaks. You have been a big help."

"This dinner is just great," said Uncle Jim. "Mabel, when next you plan to get dinner, tell me. I'll be glad to help eat it!"

159

bare	scare	bear	there	barely
care	share	pear	where	careful
dare	spare	tear	wherever	careless
fare	square	wear	elsewhere	carelessness
hare	stare	swear	everywhere	daring
mare				scared
rare	parent		prayer	
ware	Mary		Thayer	declare
silverware	canary			compare
	contrary		secretary	prepare

Will Dad care if we take this paint?

Dan paid his fare; he gave it to the conductor.

This black stamp is very rare.

Where are the boys? Out there, under the trees.

I dare you to jump in and swim.

Gus had a great big bag of peanuts, which he shared with Paul and Mary. Then later on, when Paul and Mary had a box of candy, they let Gus have a share.

Beth had a cat and a canary. Now she has just the cat.

Sally and her parents will take a trip this summer.

Jim jumped the stream, but Mary did not dare.

Ann and Katy have to clean and polish the silverware.

Mary will prepare for a job as a secretary.

Can you draw a square?

Will you sell that brown mare, Mr. Smith?

Boys, you gave me an awful scare!

Paul ate three pears.

If Mary is careless, she will tear her dress.

Please lend me your silverware, if you can spare it.

She must not wear that dress today.

I'm not scared of that great big bear.

Be careful! You must not drop that plate. Amy was careless; she dropped the plate and smashed it.

Katy has a red handbag. She carries it everywhere with her.

There is such a big crowd that we can barely see the parade.

As we cannot get the things we need at Mr. Hill's shop, we shall have to get them elsewhere.

A BEAR STORY

Little Jerry Gates thinks it is fun to play tricks. He plays tricks on his playmates, and he plays tricks on his sister and on everyone else in his family.

Jerry's Uncle Ned is lame. He has to carry a cane. When Jerry is bigger, he will understand how Uncle Ned got lame. He was shot in the leg. Everybody in the family is proud of Uncle Ned, and little Jerry is, too, but he still enjoys teasing his uncle.

Uncle Ned has lots of medals, but he never wears them. Now and then, when Jerry behaves well, Uncle Ned lets him see his medals. Uncle Ned got the medals because he was brave.

One day Jerry got a thick brown rug and laid it on his back and said to himself, "I'll play a trick on Uncle Ned. I'll give him a scare. I'll pretend I'm a great big bear."

Uncle Ned was sitting and reading. Jerry crawled up to him. Then Jerry gave a loud growl and jumped at him.

Uncle Ned did not seem to be afraid.

"A bear!" exclaimed Uncle Ned. "I wish I had my gun; I'd shoot it. Now I'll have to catch it and kill it with my bare hands."

Uncle Ned grabbed the bear and held it. He lifted it up and began to shake it. Then he gave it a little spanking.

"Ouch, ouch! Stop!" yelled the bear.

"I think I've killed the bear. I think I'm safe now," said Uncle Ned.

"Yes, yes! You've killed the bear," said Jerry.

"Well, I declare! It's Jerry!" said Uncle Ned. "You gave me a terrible scare, Jerry. Now you'd better take that rug back where it came from."

Jerry picked up the rug and said to himself, "Uncle Ned must be a brave man. He didn't seem to be a bit scared of a bear!"

160

papa	father	what
mama	grandfather	whatever
mamma		what's

GRANDFATHER'S VISIT

It was a holiday. Amy and Tim Temple were happy because Grandfather Temple had promised to have dinner at their house.

Today Grandfather Temple was very late. "What can be keeping your father?" said Mrs. Temple. "It's nearly one o'clock. We planned to eat at twelve."

"Probably we'd better eat," said Father.

Just as they were sitting down at the table, Grandfather Temple got there.

"I had problems getting to your house today," he said, as he sank into a chair at the table. "It's a difficult trip with a camel."

Amy and Tim grinned. Then Amy said, "Grandfather, you're kidding us. You didn't take a camel. You came by bus, didn't you?"

"Yes, Grandfather," said Tim. "There isn't a camel around. Camels are in Africa and in the zoo—not traveling up and down our street."

"You think not?" said Grandfather with a grin. "Then just take a peek at your street."

Amy and Tim did.

"A camel!" yelled Amy.

"A camel!" yelled Tim. "There *is* a camel down there on the street! And there are lots of men. And a band!"

"Well!" said Grandfather. "That's just what I've been telling you. The parade held up the traffic. That's the reason my bus was late."

161

bar	card	bark	Carl	art	Charles	arch
car	hard	dark		cart	Charlie	march
far	lard	lark	arm	dart	darling	parch
jar	yard	mark	arms	part		starch
mar	scarf	park	farm	tart	marsh	carve
tar	barn	shark	harm	chart		starve
scar	darn	spark	charm	smart		
star	yarn			start		
are	barnyard		carp			
			harp			
			sharp			

AT THE LAKE

"We'll rent a boat," said Dad, "and fish."

"Let's start!" said little Jimmy, running to the boat. "I may catch a shark today."

"Let's be smart and take a lunch," said Uncle Charlie. "We'll starve if we have to eat the fish we catch."

"Not me!" said Jimmy. "I'll catch a whale. And I'll give you each part of it."

162

barber	carpet	garden	garment	army
farmer	market	sharpen		hardly
farther	target	carbon	Martha	party
partner		pardon		partly
Arthur	darkness	Martin	marble	tardy
harbor	harness	bargain		
parlor		hardware	sparkle	afar
armor	harvest	boxcar		alarm
				apart

apartment	Barbara	partnership	quantity
depart	carpenter		quality
department			

This table has a marble top.

I got these peaches at the Farmers' Market.

The boat sailed into the harbor.

Arthur can throw a dart and hit the target.

Martin is hardly ever tardy.

See the drops of rain sparkle in the sun!

Barbara is having a party next week.

162

THE PARTNERSHIP

Arthur and Martin are partners. They have
started a garden in the back yard. They will
raise strawberries and sell them.

Martin is the best farmer. He sets out the
berries. Arthur helps spade up the ground
and weed it. Arthur and Martin together will
harvest the crops.

Martin's sister Martha complains that the
boys track mud onto the parlor carpet when they
enter the house from the garden. But when the
berries are ready to market, Martha will help fix
them up in boxes to sell, and she will share
in whatever they make.

Arthur's father is a carpenter, and Martin's
father has a job in the hardware department of a
downtown shop. They help the boys, too.

"We may not have quantity," says Martin,
"but we have quality. Ours are the best
strawberries in town."

And the boys' customers agree.

163

brass	fast	can't	ask	clasp	aunt
class	last	plant	mask		
glass	mast	shan't	task	raft	
grass	past	grant			
pass	blast				
		bath		branch	
		path			

after	alas	bathtub	afternoon
master	command	grasshopper	afterward
rather			afterwards
basket			
nasty			

Aunt Martha was stung by an ant.
Let's swim out to the raft this afternoon.
Please lift up that big branch.

If you'll get a basket of strawberries when you're in town, Ellen will fix strawberry tarts.

Ted's father is planting wheat on his farm this year. Ted helps him each afternoon.

After dinner you may play out in the yard.
Please ask Ellen to make a pot of tea.
They can sharpen that saw in the hardware department.

You'd better take that boy upstairs and give him a hot bath and then get him into bed as fast as you can.

163

Please keep on the path. You must not step on the grass.

Robert did not remember to set his alarm clock. That is the reason he was late.

When Molly went to Spain last summer, she sent gifts to Betty and Jean. She sent Betty a string of glass beads with a silver clasp. She sent Jean a little pup made of brass.

Martha and Agnes had a picnic. They sat down on the grass to eat, but, alas, the ants crawled up and down their arms and legs. Martha and Agnes carried their picnic basket back to Martha's house and ate their lunch at the kitchen table. They said that they didn't miss the ants a bit.

Father will carve the roast chicken.
When you are swimming, it's fun to have a raft.
Let's plant flowers in the back yard.
Please ask Sis to bring me a glass of hot milk.
This is a very fast train.
The baby can't sleep if you make too much noise.
Please pass the butter.
The captain is in command of the ship.
Be careful. That branch may break!

You shan't play in our yard if you keep stepping on the grass and tramping on the flower beds!

I'd much rather go out and play than study, but I have to study now.

Arthur found a little snake out in the garden. He tells Martha it will not harm her. She agrees that it will not—because she will not let it get near her.

Charles, can you hear the lark singing in the park?

Barbara made a batch of apple tarts. Carl said he was starved and ate three!

164

all	tall	halt	war	dwarf	halter
ball	wall	malt	warm	quart	Walter
call	small	salt	warn	quarter	walnut
fall	squall	Walt	wart	reward	fallen
hall	stall	false	swarm		always

baseball   basketball   malted milk

All the boys are playing ball.
Call Walter and tell him I'm waiting.
Leave your umbrella in the hall.
Let's stay in the house where it's warm.
Please pass me the salt.
Ned has a wart on his hand.
Please get me a thick malted milk.
Let's play ball!
This is a small town.
Did Carl fall from that tall tree?
Richard drank nearly a quart of milk!

Walt and Charles were sailing in the harbor
when a sudden squall came up.

wash   water   swan   squash   quarrel   Washington
             wand

watch   want   swamp   squat

wasp   wander   swat

washtub   watchman   watermelon   waterproof

Wash your hands with warm water and soap.
Watch the ant drag that small twig.
What do you want?

Be careful! Take care not to fall into the
water! I must warn you that the water is deep!

What stung you, a bee or a wasp? I got into
a swarm of bees and one of them stung me.

Have you ever seen a swan? There are swans
in the pond in our zoo.

Your watch must be fast. It says six o'clock,
but it can't be six o'clock yet.

When the Robinsons went on a picnic at the lake,
they had a big watermelon. Mr. Robinson cut it up,
and they each had a quarter of it.

166

long	bog	loft	off	crossing	across
song	dog	soft		foggy	along
strong	fog		gone	softly	belong
throng	flog	broth		costly	
		cloth	boss	offer	ding-dong
honk	frog		cross	onward	coffeepot
	hog	froth	loss		tablecloth
cost	log	moth	moss	coffee	Jack Frost
frost			toss	catalog	
lost	mock	golf			

Fill up the coffeepot, and we'll all
have a cup of coffee.

Mr. Roberts belongs to the golf club
and plays golf nearly every Saturday.

Jean's dress was made of a soft cotton
cloth. She had seen the dress in a catalog
and sent away for it. The dress cost
about ten dollars.

Molly went across the Atlantic in a big
boat. She had a smooth crossing.

166

See all the moss on that tree!
Ted has gone along with Jim to play golf.
Walter spilled chicken broth on the tablecloth.
Let's sing a song.
The fog is too thick. You can't see a thing.
How much did your catcher's mitt cost?
A moth can't keep away from a flame.
Take care not to fall off that branch!

See that frog jump! A frog takes long jumps.
A frog must have very strong legs to be able to take
such long jumps.

Bill Thatcher's boss gave him a raise. Bill did
such a good job as a delivery boy that it did not
take him long to get a raise.

Speak softly! The baby is sleeping. His
parents have gone out and left him with me.

Jim wanted a hunting dog—a great big dog.
His sister Jenny wanted a small dog. Then they saw
a boxer pup and that was what they wanted. It can't
hunt, and it isn't small, but Jim and Jenny think it is just grand.

167

go	bone	joke	hole	hope	nose	goes
no	cone	poke	mole	lope	pose	hoes
so	lone	woke	pole	mope	rose	toes
ho	tone	broke	sole	pope	chose	going
	stone	choke	stole	rope	close	hoeing
hoe	shone	smoke	rode	slope	those	toeing
toe	throne	spoke	globe			
Joe	pone	stroke			rove	
	note		home		drove	
	vote				stove	
			froze			

Did I step on your toes? I beg your pardon!
The nose cone from the rocket was never found.
I need a spade and a hoe and a rake.
Our dog drove the tramp away.
Get the long, strong rope.
Betty sent Jean a note.

    Please close the gate. Those cows are just
waiting to get out and run away.

168

over	open	ago	nobody	tiptoe
Rover	token	oho	nowhere	homesick
Grover	broken			backbone
clover	chosen		closely	wishbone
	swollen			

This boy's name is Grover.
Let's go home. No, let's not go home yet.
That was just a joke.

Joe broke his leg last week. It is
painful and badly swollen.

Charles drove the car home, and Barbara
rode with him.

Toss the paper plates and cups into the
stove. That's the way to wash dishes!

Watch Rover digging that great big hole
in the back yard. Now he has hidden a bone in it!

You left the gate open, and now those cows
have got into the clover!

The latch on the gate is broken. I did
close the gate, but it came open.

169

old	hold	roll	both	host
bold	mold	troll		most
cold	sold	stroll	don't	post
fold	told		won't	
gold	scold	bolt		
		colt		

In the South the winters are not so cold.

Please don't scold me.

You must not sulk and mope.

We need a long rope.

I hope you don't catch cold.

Last winter it was so cold that the river froze up.

Give the dog his bone.

I hope Joe gets home soon.

Grover sold both the colt and the old mare.

If you want to set up this post so that it will hold, you must dig a deep hole in the ground. If you don't dig a deep hole, the post won't hold.

Grover told us to go home. He said, "Go home, both of you!"

170

also	spoken	poem	local	holy	hello
auto	frozen	older	postal	lonely	almost
banjo	golden	holder	noble	only	alone
buffalo	moment	motor	locate	mostly	hotel
piano	program	rolling			November
potato		clothing	soda	hopeful	October
tobacco		pony	sofa	hopeless	suppose
tomato		cozy	unfold		
Colorado			behold		

When you get up, please fold up your blanket.
Aunt Martha made potato pancakes.
Mr. Hill has a gold watch.
Sally fell off her pony and broke her nose.
The sun shone all day.
Don't stumble over that stone.
Don't go in there; you'll choke in the smoke.
Thanksgiving is always in November.

We had a long program. Carl played the piano.
Walter spoke a poem. Arthur played the banjo.
Martin played the sweet potato.

171

bow	blow	own	owe	below	snowball
low	flow	blown	bowl	elbow	snowflake
row	glow	flown	growth		rainbow
mow	slow	grown			rowboat
sow	grow	shown		snowy	
tow	show	thrown	owner	slowly	
	crow				
	snow				
	throw				

Last winter we had lots of snow.

Can you row this boat?

Please show me those stamps you spoke of.

Don't be so slow.

Quick, throw the ball to second base!

I hope this wind will not blow down our chimney.

See the red coals glow in the stove!

When this boy gets his growth, he will be taller than his father.

Did you hear the rooster crow? He woke me up at six o'clock.

172

shadow	bellow	arrow	swallow
window	fellow	narrow	follow
pillow	mellow	sparrow	hollow
willow	yellow		

I can hardly swallow those big pills.
We had a narrow escape.
That fellow is afraid of his own shadow!
Crows and sparrows stay with us all winter.
That old road is much too narrow.
This river flows into a big lake.
They have a weeping willow tree in the yard.
Can you shoot with a bow and arrow?
Martin rode the pony down the narrow path.
Be careful that you don't hit a window and break it.
Just hear that old cow bellow!

Butter-and-eggs is the name of a yellow flower.
It grows in moist soil.

Let's play "follow the leader." I will be
the leader, and you fellows must follow me
in every way.

173

or	cord	cork	born	scorn	sort
for	lord	fork	corn	thorn	short
nor		stork	horn	torch	snort
				scorch	north
		form			
		storm			horse

THE STORM

One April afternoon Walt and Martin went strolling down the road.

Much later Martin said, "Hear that thunder? We'd better get back." The boys started running, but the storm broke when home was still far away.

Suddenly a horn sounded, and a car stopped.

"Mr. Hall!" Walt yelled. "Are we ever glad to see you!" Soaked to the skin, the boys scrambled into the car.

"I'll bet you boys didn't remember," said Mr. Hall with a grin, "that it always takes just as long to get back as it did to get there."

Walt grinned too. "Not in a car!" he said.

174

order	northern	organ	orchard	morning	popcorn
border	normal	Norman	forward		platform
corner	formal		forty		horseback
former			stormy	important	
formerly					

Is this gift for Linda or for me?
Let's go to the orchard and get apples.
It was stormy, and there was a cold north wind.
Where is the cork to this bottle?
Which way shall we go—east, west, north, or south?
This cow has short horns.

Norman can play the organ. He will play at the club meeting in October. Forty club members will be at the meeting. Mr. and Mrs. Thatcher will sit on the platform and will wear formal dress.

This morning Barbara went out to the orchard in order to see the apple trees. She thinks there is a better apple crop this year than in former years.

It's so cold and stormy out. Let's just stay in the house and eat popcorn and play games.

175

borrow	sorry	forget	forgive	forbid
sorrow	forest	forgot	forgave	forbidden
tomorrow	horrible	forgotten	forgiven	
	horrid			

May I please borrow a cup of flour?

Tomorrow we'll visit the zoo. We'll have peanuts and popcorn, and we'll share them with the animals. The animals seldom get peanuts and popcorn when they are living in the forest.

The chipmunk gathers nuts in the forest and saves them for the winter. Sally is always afraid the chipmunk will forget where he has hidden the nuts. Then he will have to borrow nuts from the chipmunk living in the next tree.

Barbara was sorry that she forgot to bring a cake for the club's cake sale.

Martha remembered to bring a cake, but she found that she had forgotten the soda, and the cake tasted horrible. She wished that she had forgotten her cake, too.

ore	chore	fort	ford	before	story
bore	score	port	pork	therefore	glory
core	shore	sport	torn		airport
fore	snore		worn	support	moreover
more	store		shorn	report	
sore	swore		sworn		
tore			forth		
wore			porch		

Don't eat the core of your apple.

Fred ate more than we did.

Sam wore his best coat and tore it.

Will you please get three pork chops at the store?

Let's go sit on the porch.

Don't forget to shut the windows before you go out.

Ted has a blister on his heel, and it is sore.

Baseball is Carl's favorite sport.

Grandfather sat on the porch in a rocking chair.

The man wore a torn red cap.

After the sheep are shorn, they seem bare and cold.

Will you please take me to the airport tomorrow?

177

door	indoors	four	fourth	toward
floor	outdoors	pour	fourteen	towards
	doorbell	mourn		
	doorstep	court		
		course		

Hold your horses!

What sort of cheese shall I get from the store?

Please forgive me! I'm sorry I was so late.

Don't tramp mud all over the floor.

My dog's name is Sport.

Please get me a pound of salt pork.

We need four forks and four spoons.

When Uncle Dick sleeps, he always snores.

You must finish your chores before you leave.

Please tell us a story!

Don't swim too far away from the shore.

Please, may I have a bag of popcorn?

This horse runs very fast.

Ring the doorbell and wait on the doorstep.

It is fun to play outdoors in the summer.

178

I	hide	fife	bike	file	dime
I'm	ride	life	hike	mile	lime
I'd	side	wife	like	pile	rime
I've	tide	strife	Mike	tile	time
I'll	wide		spike	smile	chime
	slide		strike	while	crime
	glide			awhile	slime
	bride				
	pride				

dine	pipe	fire	bite	dive	rise
fine	ripe	hire	kite	five	wise
line	wipe	tire	quite	hive	size
mine	stripe	wire	spite	live	prize
nine			white	drive	
pine				lives	
vine				wives	
wine					
shine					
twine					

178

THE BORROWED BIKE

Mike had a bike, but James did not.
"Let me ride your bike for a while,"
begged James one morning.

"You may ride it for a while," Mike agreed,
"but bring it back at five to nine. At
nine o'clock I have to go to the store."

James got onto the bike and happily
rode away. He rode for miles, waving at
everyone. He was having such a fine time
that he did not get back till nearly ten.

Mike waited till nine fifteen and then
had to hike to the store. He was mad.

James met him at the store. "I'm sorry,"
said James. "I did not keep track of the time."

"Well you'd better next time," said Mike.
"When my dad parks too long, he has to pay
a fine. So if you ride too long, *you'll*
have to pay a fine.

"Next time," said James with a smile.
"I'll take along an alarm clock."

side	sides	sided	siding	tide	tides
like	likes	liked	liking	bike	bikes
smile	smiles	smiled	smiling	mile	miles
time	times	timed	timing	dime	dimes
dine	dines	dined	dining	mine	mines
wipe	wipes	wiped	wiping	pipe	pipes
wire	wires	wired	wiring	fife	fifes

white	whiter	whitest	kite	kites
ripe	riper	ripest	wife	wives
wise	wiser	wisest	life	lives

Sit down and stay for a while.
Please leave your bike at the back door.

It always seems that the peaches at the top
of the tree are the biggest and the ripest.

Every time Charlie goes for a drive, his car
gets a flat tire. Last week he had four or five.
As long as he has that old car with those
rotten old tires, he'll keep on having flats.
I think he'd better get a bike!

180

alike	tiny	admire	campfire	aside	divide
dislike	shiny	desire	bonfire	beside	
	ninth	entire	firecracker	besides	lively
	ninety	entirely	fireman	outside	arrive
daytime	nineteen	require		upside	
bedtime	outline	inquire	invite	inside	describe
meantime	sunshine		polite		
	valentine		satellite		recognize

Billy can add, but he cannot divide yet.
Please, may I ride your bike awhile?
Five times five is twenty-five.
Nine times five is forty-five.

Sam wants to be a fireman when he grows up.
He thinks he'll be a fine fireman because he
likes getting cats down from trees.

Sally just hates to go to bed at bedtime.
That is the time when she feels the most lively.
Ted dislikes going to bed, too.

Let's sit around the campfire and tell stories
and roast hot dogs.

181

die	bind	pint	blinds	unkind	Bible
lie	find		minded	behind	title
pie	kind	mild	kindly	blindfold	Ira
tie	mind	wild	kindness		tiger
	wind	child			tigress
	blind				china
	grind				Nina
					Inez
					final
					finally

iron	O'Brien	idle	library
lion		ivy	wildcat
lioness		ivory	necktie
violet		silent	grandchild
violent		Friday	Lima beans
quiet			

Shall we play hide and seek or blind man's bluff? Blind man's bluff is more fun. We'll blindfold Ira, and then we'll hide. He must find us if he can.

181

This kind of candy costs a dime.
Five is one ninth of forty-five.
My child, don't be so wild!
Our car has a flat tire.
I like the way Mike smiles.
The dog won't bite you. He just likes to bark.
Our flag has stars and stripes.
Please give me a quart of milk and a pint of cream.

Where we live there are no tigers. I have seen
a tiger skin made into a rug, but I have never seen
a live tiger.

At this mill they grind corn into corn meal.
There is yellow corn meal, and there is white
corn meal.

I hope tomorrow will be a fine day. I hope
the sun will shine all day.

Mrs. O'Brien got out her best china—the ivy
pattern with the gold border—and gave everyone
apple pie with cheese.

Don't forget to wind the clock or it will stop.
This is not an electric clock.

181

THE ZOO

In our town, on the North Side, there is a big park. In one part of this park they keep all kinds of animals. This is called the zoo.

One fine day last week my little sister Inez and I went to the zoo with our father to see the animals.

Our father said, "Let's go to the house where they keep the cats."

"But Dad," said Inez, "we have a cat at home. I've seen lots of cats. Let's not go to see the cats."

Father smiled and said, "When they say 'cats' at the zoo, child, they don't mean plain tame cats like our Nina. They mean animals that are like cats but are wild and much bigger.

"So let's go there, and if you don't like the great cats, we needn't stay there long."

We went into the house where they keep the great cats, and we saw the animals there.

"But these are lions and tigers and things like that!" said Inez. "So that's what they mean when they say 'cats'!"

We got there just in time to see them feed the lions and the tigers. A man went around with a big basket of raw meat, and he flung slabs of meat to the lions and the tigers. When the lions and the tigers smelled the meat, they became quite wild. The tigers growled, and the lions roared. When they got hold of the meat, they gobbled it up in no time. For a lion or a tiger, a big slab of meat is just one bite.

There were wildcats there, too, and all kinds of beasts, but I liked watching the lions and the tigers. The lion has a long mane, but the

334

lioness is more like a cat. I liked the tiger with his black and yellow stripes. But I was glad there were strong iron bars between them and us.

When we had been there a little while, Inez said, "Let's go now. I'd rather see the bears."

I said, "I like to watch the lions. May I stay a while and then meet you outside?"

"No," said Father. "I'm afraid you'd never find us if we went off without you. Let's stop at the stand and get some peanuts. Then we'll go visit the bears."

Inez clapped her hands. "The bears are the best!" she said. "I'm going to give them all my peanuts."

On the way to the bear pits, Inez kept nibbling at her peanuts. And when she got there, not a peanut was left.

Then Inez saw the bears. There were black bears and brown bears and one big white bear. They sat up and pawed the air, begging for peanuts.

"Oh, dear!" said Inez. "I'm sorry, you bears. I haven't a thing to give you."

Then Father grinned and reached in his pocket. "We can't let those poor bears starve," he said. And he handed Inez a second bag of peanuts.

"Oh, Dad!" cried Inez, as she gave him a big hug. "I like you much better than the bears. I like you the best of all."

182

by	cry	rye	Ryan	whys
my	dry	dye	Bryan	skies
shy	fry	type	Byron	styles
sky	try	style	nearby	
sly	fly		bye-bye	
spy			butterfly	
why			butterflies	

cry	cries	cried	crying	
dry	dries	dried	drying	
fry	fries	fried	frying	
try	tries	tried	trying	
fly	flies		flying	
type	types	typed	typing	typist
dye	dyes	dyed	dyeing	
die	dies	died	dying	
lie	lies	lied	lying	
tie	ties	tied	tying	

Peggy Ryan will fly home by jet.
My sister can type very fast.

183

son	one	front	Monday	grandson
ton	done	month	wonder	
won	none	monthly	wonderful	monkey
		honey		donkey
		money		does
				doesn't

MY FAVORITE ANIMAL

Some children like to see the lions and the tigers at the zoo. Others like the monkey house better.

I think the best thing at the zoo is the little gray donkey. Jane likes the black colt and the little red pigs.

My big brother says that animals such as donkeys and pigs and colts don't belong in the zoo at all. He says that wild animals belong in a zoo and farm animals belong on a farm.

I think all kinds of animals belong in the zoo. City kids like us never go to a farm. We'd never see farm animals if they weren't at the zoo.

mother	other	come	some	somewhat	comfort
brother	otherwise	coming	someone	somewhere	
godmother	another	become	somehow	something	company
stepmother			somebody	sometime	
grandmother				sometimes	

May I have another strawberry tart?

Some of you can ride; the others will have to hike.

Can someone drive a car?

COMPANY'S COMING

Dry your hands on another towel. This is Mother's best towel, and she saves it for company.

When is the company coming? Will they be here in time for dinner?

Yes, they will come for dinner. Mother will fry those fresh fish Aunt Martha gave us. Mother has baked an apple pie, too.

I can hardly wait. I wish I had something to eat now. Maybe just a bit of that warm apple pie.

You'd better not think about that pie. Mother will get after you.

185

dove	oven	above	color	among
love	cover	shovel	nothing	
glove		lovely	dozen	
shove		discover		

WHEN MY BROTHER SHOVELS SNOW

My brother just loves to shovel snow. He
wears his warm gloves, and he covers up his ears
with big fuzzy earmuffs. Then he cannot hear
a thing we say to him, and he is glad. I think he
must wear about a dozen pairs of socks so that
his feet will fit into Dad's big boots.

Then when my brother has shoveled all the snow
for us and for the Smiths next door, he comes into
the house and sits in front of the oven. We fix
popcorn and hot drinks while he thaws out.

Come to think of it, maybe my brother doesn't
like shoveling snow. Maybe he just likes what comes
afterwards—the popcorn and things.

Or maybe he likes best the money Mr. Smith
and my dad give him for shoveling their snow!

186

blood	touch	cousin	young	famous
flood	touches	couple	youngster	
	touched	double	southern	
	country	trouble		

April and May are spring months. August is
a summer month. September, October, and November
come in the fall of the year. Where does the
month of March belong? March comes between
winter and spring.

I've spent all my money for popcorn and candy.
I've eaten the popcorn, and I've eaten the candy,
and now I have nothing. I wish I had done something
else with that money.

My father and mother have three sons. I am
one of them, and the others are my brothers.

Charles has a couple of young cousins that
live in the country. When he visited them, they had
nothing but trouble. They had rain and hail and
a horrible flood in the southern part of the state.
They must have been glad when Charles left.

187

put	bull	bullet	cushion	armful
push	pull	bulletin	pudding	cupful
bush	full	bushel		handful
puss	fully	butcher		
pussy				

Bring home a bushel of apples.
Please put your things away carefully.
Don't push or crowd; there's lots of time.
Mrs. Smith, may I borrow a cupful of flour?
Will you pull down that shade, please?
This bush is full of berries.
Don't tease that bull; he is very cross.
Please bring a sofa cushion for Mother.
Let's have pudding for lunch tomorrow.

Please run over to the butcher shop and
get me four pounds of round steak.

Mary, will you please put this paper
on the bulletin board? Pull out all
the extra tacks, too, and put them in
this little tin box.

188

book	brook	good	cooky	wooden	understood
cook	crook	hood	crooked	woolen	football
hook	shook	wood	goods		
look		woods	goodness		
nook		foot	good-by		
took		wool	goody		
		stood			

Ned got three good books from the library.
That crooked little path leads to the brook.
Will you please bring in some wood for the fire?
Ellen stood on the porch and waited.
Sally took off her coat and shook the snow off it.

Let's take some milk and some oatmeal cookies
and have a picnic down by the brook. Let's take
about a bushel of those good cookies!

"It's cold out today. Let's put on our woolen
coats with the hoods and our woolen gloves, too."
"My goodness!" said Aunt Martha. "You look
as if you are going to the North Pole—not just
to a football game!"

189

room	roof	root	coop	bedroom
broom	hoof	soot	hoop	bathroom
groom		sooty	Cooper	classroom

This is a cozy nook.

The baby was pulling up flowers by the roots.

I have to saw all this wood.

The dog came out of the water and shook itself.

Bill stepped on my foot, but he did not mean to.

Please get a broom and sweep out this room.

The horse cut its hoof on the wire.

Our roof is covered with soot.

Can you roll a hoop?

My coat is made of wool.

Woolen coats are the warmest.

Just look in the book and see.

Jess is a good cook.

Joe takes wonderful care of his horse. He feeds it hay and grain. Every day he grooms it. And he sweeps out the stall so well that it is as clean as the rooms in the house.

190

fir	girl	dirt	first
sir	twirl	dirty	thirst
stir	whirl	shirt	thirsty
bird	firm	skirt	Irma
third	squirm	squirt	thirty
shirk	chirp	squirrel	thirteen
birth	birch		
birthday			

This is the first game I have won.
See the little squirrel under that tall birch.
Pam's canary sings, but mine just chirps.
Irma will be thirteen on her next birthday.

Take off that dirty shirt and let me give you a clean shirt to put on. That is the third shirt you have gotten dirty today!

I'm so thirsty. May I have a bottle of soda pop, please?

Betty is our cheer leader. See her jump up and down and twirl and whirl! Betty is a very lively girl.

344

her	serve	Earl	word	Myrtle
hers	servant	early	work	journey
herd	person	pearl	worm	
jerk	clerk	earn	world	
fern	term	learn	worse	
stern	perhaps	earnest	worst	
Bert	deserve	heard	worth	
Ernest		earth	worry	
perch		search	worship	

Earl, Bert, and Ernest are working in order to earn money for camp next summer.

On Irma's birthday her father gave her a gold ring with a pearl in it.

A LUNCH FOR THE BIRDS

"See that mother bird?" said Carl to Hazel. "There in that nest in the birch tree. She is feeding the baby birds in the nest."

"But look what she's feeding them!" said Hazel with a shudder. "She's feeding them worms. That's not what you feed a baby."

192

cur	churn	hurry	curtain	unhurt
fur	burnt	furry	furnish	return
burr	church	flurry	burden	overturn
purr	curve	curdle	surprise	
hurt	curse	hurdle	Thursday	
curl	nurse	purple	turkey	
burn	purse	turtle	purpose	
turn	burst		murder	

Hear that cat purr when you stroke its fur!
Take your purse to church with you.
Turn the pancakes before they burn.
My dog got a burr in his paw.

When Bert's Uncle Earl went on a journey,
he returned with a surprise for Bert—a turtle.

Thanksgiving Day is Thursday. Our kitchen
is in a flurry. We're going to have a big roast
turkey with stuffing, squash, sweet potatoes, pie,
and lots of other good things. My brother is in
such a hurry for Thanksgiving to come you'd think
he never had a thing to eat the rest of the year.

193

use	cute	fuel	mule	January	pure
used	excuse	perfume	music	regular	cure
useful		refuse	pupil		fury
United States			human		figure
useless		continue			
unite					

Go wash your hands; use lots of soap and water.
This scarf is made of pure silk.
Bert is good at figures but poor in spelling.
It's no use. I can't get this mule to start.

Ernest is staying home today. He hopes
he can cure his cold that way. This is Ernest's
regular January cold. His mother will send
an excuse to Ernest's teacher.

Miss Earl is Irma's music teacher. Irma
has been studying music with her since January.
Miss Earl says that Irma will soon be one of
her best pupils.

Ten dollars is a lot of money for such a
small bottle of perfume.

194

rule	June	blue	Ruth	cruel	blueberry
ruler	July	glue	true	gruel	bluebird
rude			truth	prune	bluejay
ruin			truly		

Blueberry pie is his favorite.
June, July, and August are summer months.
Ruth wore a blue dress to the party.
Mother's birthday is the thirteenth of June.
We saw a bluebird and a bluejay in the woods.
Never be rude.
The Golden Rule is a very good rule.
If you want to draw a neat line, use a ruler.
Do you like prunes? Prunes are dried plums.

So you want me to tell you a story?
Shall I tell you a fairy tale or a true story?
Or shall I tell you one of each?

If you'll get some glue, we'll try to mend
this broken box.

It is a fine day. The sky is blue and
the air is warm.

195

tune	student	due	numeral	during
tulip	Stuart	duel	numerous	
Tuesday	stupid	duke		avenue
		duty		

When Irma was learning to type, she had no
trouble typing the letters, but she made numerous
mistakes on the figures. But Irma was a good
student, and she soon learned to type figures, too.

When Molly went on her journey, she sent
Betty some tulip bulbs and a music box that
played a little tune.

THE COUNTRY COUSIN AND THE CITY COUSIN

Ruth lives on Elm Avenue in town. Myrtle
lives in the country. The mailman brings Ruth's
mail to her front door, but Myrtle gets her mail
in a mailbox beside the road.

Myrtle has a big dog named Duke. Ruth has
a canary named Jenny.

Ruth and Myrtle are cousins. During the
summer they visit each other a great deal.

196

chew	blew	crew	drew	few	new
Jew	flew	screw	grew	mew	news
		strew	threw	pew	

dew

newspaper   New York   stew

Please give me a few of those mints.

At church I always sit in the same pew.

Chew your food before you swallow it.

I'm sorry I threw away the newspaper.

Don't strew those papers all over the floor.

The wind blew down our chimney.

A butterfly flew from flower to flower.

Last year our plants grew better than this year.

Bert Thorn has a new bike.

Have you heard the news?

Don't sit on the grass; it's wet with dew.

Do you like stewed prunes?

Let's have stew for dinner. Let's not put just a few things in our stew. Let's put in everything.

dead	bread	deaf	sweat	feather	heaven
head	dread	threat	dreamt	leather	threaten
lead	tread	death	meant	weather	pleasant
read	spread	breath	dealt		weapon
	thread	health	breast		
		wealth			

ready	dreadful	heavy	ahead	sweater
already	meadow		overhead	breakfast
steady	jealous			
instead	healthy			
	wealthy			

Spread jam on the bread instead of butter.
He wore a heavy leather jacket.

Don't go out like that, without your sweater!
You'll catch your death of cold!

If the weather is pleasant, we'll have a
picnic. If the weather is dreadful, we won't.

You must have a good breakfast if you want to
be healthy. I'll get it ready.

198

be	Eve	Pete	these	secret
he	even	Peter	equal	Jesus
me	evening		evil	Negro
we	Steve		fever	theater
she	Steven		idea	frequent
				athlete

Steve is a frequent visitor at our house.
Myrtle sometimes goes to the theater in New York.
Eve was quite ill with a fever.

OCTOBER PARTY

Pete Stevens is having a party this evening.
We are all supposed to wear masks.

Fran is trying to keep it a secret, but I have an idea she is going to come to the party dressed as an evil old witch.

I can't tell you what I am wearing. It's a secret—even from me. Mom has been fixing something for me all afternoon. I just bring her things like a needle and thread and her thimble, but when I come into the room she hides whatever she is working on.

199

here   hero   mere   material   severe
here's   merely

A baseball is covered with leather.
Ruth has a severe cold.
Hazel's new skirt is made of soft woolen material.

You did not water the flowers during
the hot weather, and now they are all dead.

If you don't get up now, you'll be too
late for breakfast.

Why don't you tell me what you want,
instead of whining and crying?

A hawk flies faster than a duck. An eagle
flies fastest of all.

Here's a good book you may want to read.
The hero of the book is a fine athlete and is
the captain of the football team.

I did not mean to push and be rude. I only
meant to help you.

It is a mere ten-mile hike up the hill. I'll
just sit here in the sun until you come back.

LET'S READ

Part VI
The Commonest
Irregular Spellings
of Consonant Sounds

THE COMMONEST IRREGULAR SPELLINGS
OF CONSONANT SOUNDS

Guide to Lessons 200 through 245

In LESSONS 200-245 we take up irregular consonant spellings and some irregular vowel spellings which occur in small groups of words.

Lessons 200-202: The use of the letter *c* for the sound which is normally represented by *s* is a semi-irregular spelling, since we can set up the rule that *c* before *e*, *i*, and *y* generally represents the sound of *s*. On the other hand, there are of course many words in which this sound before *e* and *i* is represented by the letter *s*, words like *set, sit*.

The words here given contain vowel letters in various irregular values: *ice, face, spruce*. In words like *dance*, the *a* has its regular sound (as in *man*) in some parts of the country, but in other parts of the country these words have the vowel sound of *father*.

In the word *once* the letter *o* has the same irregular value as in *one (wun)*.

Lessons 203-205 take up words in which the letter *g* or the combination *dg* represents the sound that is regularly represented by *j*: words like *gem, edge*. In most of these the *g* is followed by *e*, *i*, or *y*, especially by silent *e*. On the other hand, there are a few words in which *g* before *e* or *i* has its regular value: *get, give*.

Lessons 206-213 take up words like *debt* in which there is a consonant letter that does not represent any sound. Only the words with silent *gh* are kept back for Lessons 214-218.

This work can be made easier at the start if one uses colored chalk (say, green) for the silent letters, but ordinary white chalk for the rest of the word, in first presenting the words on the blackboard.

In Lessons 214-218 we give words which contain silent *gh*, such as *caught*. The device of using colored chalk for the *gh* will help at the start. The words should be given in sets, with the same vowel sound in each set.

Lessons 219, 220: In Lesson 219 we take up the words in which the letters *gh* represent the sound of *f*. In this group we have irregular uses of the vowel letters *au* and *ou*. In Lesson 220 we take up words in which *ph* represents the sound of *f*.

Lesson 221 takes up some words in which the vowel sound of *put* is represented by peculiar spellings: *o* in *wolf* and *ou* in *would*.

Lessons 222, 223 take up a few words in which the vowel sound of *oo* (as in *moon*) is represented by irregular spellings; also a few in which the sound combination *yoo* (as in *few*) is irregularly represented. The word *to*, which we have been using right along, belongs in the former group. In a few words either sound, *oo* or *yoo*, is used in different regions or by different persons.

Lesson 224 takes up a few words which have irregular spellings for the vowel sound that is regularly represented by *i*, the vowel sound of words like *pin, bit, twig*.

Lesson 225 covers irregular spellings for *i* in unaccented syllables: *ui* in *biscuit*, *ie* in *mischief*, *u* in *minute*, *a* in *spinach*.

Lesson 226 contains words in which the vowel sound regularly represented by *ee* or *ea* (*beet*, *heat*) is represented by *ie* and by *i*, as *piece*, *police*. We take also spellings with *ei*, such as *receive*. The words *either*, *neither* have the *ee* sound in most American pronunciations; in others, especially in England, these words have the vowel sound of *ice*, *bite*.

Needless to say, the teacher or parent should omit words that are unfamiliar to the child and add any that may be familiar to him, provided they contain no irregular spellings not yet taught the child.

The word *people*, entirely odd in its spelling but of course very common, is included here, because it contains the *ee* sound.

Lesson 227: The vowel sound of words like *net*, *pen*, *red*, which is regularly represented by the letter *e*, is in some words represented by irregular letters and combinations. In Lesson 197 we took up the use of *ea* for *e*, as in *head*. We have been using the words *says* and *said*, in which this vowel sound is represented by *ay* and *ai*. Other irregular spellings of the *e* vowel are also given in this lesson.

The words *again* and *against* are in some regions pronounced with the *ai* vowel; for this pronunciation the spelling is regular.

Lessons 228-231: In Lesson 228 we take up some remaining irregular spellings of vowel sounds. Among the words here given, *island* and *aisle* have silent *s*. The spellings are grouped as follows: The *ai*-sound: (Lesson 228) *reins*, *obey*, *they*, *weigh*. The *oa*-sound: (Lesson 229) *soul*, *shoulder*, *sew*. The *aw*-sound: (Lesson 229) *broad*. The sound of *i* in *bite*: (Lesson 230) *eye*, *buy*, *guy*, *guide*, *island*, *aisle*. The sound of *a* in *car*: (Lesson 231) *heart*, *hearth*, *guard*.

Lesson 232: The regular value of the combination *ng* is the sound which these letters represent in words like *sing*, *singer*, *ring*. In Lesson 232 we take up words in which these letters represent this sound followed by the sound of *g*; words like *finger*. Contrast the sounds of the words *singer* and *finger*.

Lessons 233, 234: In Lesson 233 we take up words like *onion*, in which the letter *i* represents the sound of *y*. In some words, such as *serious* (in Lesson 234), an *i* sound is often spoken before the *y* sound: "seeryus" or "seeriyus."

In some words the letter *u* represents the sound of *w* or of *oo* followed by *w*; of these we take only one, however: the word *language* "langgwij." (Of course *u* also has the sound of *w* in words with the *qu* combination, which we have previously studied.)

Lessons 235-242 take up a type of spelling that plays a big part in the reading of adults but appears in only a few words of the child's vocabulary. This is the use of irregular letter combinations for the sounds that are regularly represented by *sh*, *ch*, and *j*, and the use of *s* (sometimes *g* or *z*) to represent the consonant sound which comes at the end of the word *rouge*, the "zh" sound.

The word *garage* (in Lesson 239) is in some places pronounced with a final *j* sound, "garadge." Where this pronunciation is used, the word illustrates the use of *g* for *j*.

Lessons 240-242 deal with the "ch" sound as represented by *t* in certain combinations: *question, fortune, picture*, and other words in *-ture* listed here. Closely related is the *d* for "j" sound in *soldier* which is presented in Lesson 242.

Lessons 243-245 contain a final miscellany of irregularities.

Lesson 243 takes up words such as *exact* and *example*, which have *x* for "gz."

Lesson 244 takes up letters which may be silent, such as the second *o* in *chocolate*, the *r* in *February*, the *d* in *handkerchief* and *Wednesday*, the *h* in *forehead*; and such words as *tongue* ("tung"), *grandma* ("gramma"), *grandpa* ("grampa").

Lesson 245 deals with variant pronunciations in *direct* (*di-* with "short" or "long" *i*), and *envelope* (also frequent pronunciation "onvelope"), and others.

200

cent	cinder	December	necessary	grocer
center	certain	decide		grocery
central	certainly			groceries
cell	circus			saucer
cedar	Cecil			
city				
cities				

Those potatoes will be burned to a cinder!
Why did you decide to leave this city?
It will cost seven cents to send this letter.
It certainly gets cold in December.
The circus is coming to town. Let's all go!
Cecil, will you give the cat a saucer of milk?
Did the prisoner escape from his cell?

When you go to the grocery store, will you
please get a dozen lemons?
I am certain that it will not be necessary
for you to go as far as Central Avenue. I think
the grocer on Cedar Street will have all
the groceries on that order.

201

face	ice	icy	peace	palace
lace	lice	nicely	peaceful	surface
pace	mice	advice	fleece	service
race	nice			notice
brace	rice	scarce	choice	office
Grace	price	force	voice	officer
place	slice			Alice
space	spice		spruce	lettuce
trace	twice		reduce	practice
bracelet	icebox			

What is the price of this bracelet?
Pete likes books about space travel.

EACH TO HIS TASTE

Our cat thinks that mice are a choice snack.
When mice are scarce, she is willing to settle
for a bird or a lizard.

Birds think that worms are quite nice. They
like bugs, too.

Cats are fond of birds, but birds are not fond
of cats.

202

chance	lance	since	accident
dance	glance	prince	succeed
dancer	France	once	
	fence	ounce	except
	hence	bounce	exciting
		pounce	

princess	pencil	absence	distance
principal	Francis	difference	entrance
fancy	Frances	Florence	
Nancy	San Francisco	sentence	

If you do not have a pen, you may use a pencil.
I wish we had a fence around our yard.
Frances is a wonderful dancer.
We have a good chance of winning the game.

This ball bounces very well. It bounced way
up onto the roof of Florence's house.

Nancy has been trying to reduce since December,
but she hasn't lost an ounce. She ate so much candy
during the holidays that she gained ten pounds.

gem	gentle	general		
George	gentleman	generous		
giant	gentlemen	German		
		Germany		

age	rage	change	range	angel
cage	sage	danger	ranger	arrange
page	wage	manger	strange	arrangement
	stage		stranger	engage
				exchange
				dangerous

large	lounge	urge	magic	engine	pigeon
charge	huge		vegetable	engineer	
	bulge			imagine	

Can you read all the words on this page?

This boy is tall for his age.

Can you give me change for a dollar?

Our dog is very gentle.

We are having engine trouble in our car.

204

bandage	garbage	passage	carriage	orange
cabbage	manage	postage	marriage	passenger
cottage	manager	sausage		messenger
courage	message	savage	college	
damage	package	village		
		voyage		

My dog is gentle, but yours is savage.
You'd better put a bandage on that cut.
They lived in the village in a small cottage.
The storm did a lot of damage.
I wonder what is in that package.
Will you please carry out the garbage?
There are lots of tame pigeons around here.
Mr. Hill is the manager of the store.

When you go to the store, can you manage
to carry home a dozen of those big oranges?
If you can, we'll have sliced oranges and
pancakes and pork sausages for breakfast tomorrow.

Dad sent a message that the trains are
delayed and the passengers will be late.

205

ridge	badge	edge	budge	drudge	judgment
bridge	gadget	hedge	fudge	grudge	
Bridget	Madge	ledge	judge	smudge	
fidget		wedge	nudge		
midget	lodge				
	dodge				

THE SPY

"Look at that strange man," said Madge.
"That huge man with the big, black beard.
He must be a spy."

"Perhaps he is," said Bridget. "See that
bulge in the pocket of his coat? He must be
dangerous. We'd better get the FBI to
follow him."

"You silly girls are always imagining things,"
said George. "That bearded gentleman is a giant—
but not a dangerous one. I saw him yesterday on
the stage at the Palace Theater. He does magic
tricks. In that bulging pocket he probably has
eggs and vegetables—and maybe even a pigeon."

206

knee	knew	knelt	knot	doorknob
kneel	know	knife	knock	jackknife
knit	known	knives	knob	
knitted		knack		

George sliced the apple with his pocket knife.
Did you hear someone knock at the door?
Little Jimmy was sitting on his father's knee.
Mrs. Thatcher wore a blue knitted dress.
Put the knives beside the plates.
Come on in! Just turn the doorknob.
Jerry is learning to tie knots.

Do you know where Madge is? I wish
I knew, but I don't. She has a knack
of slipping away without my knowing it.

Paul's sister Tess is knitting him a sweater.
It already comes down to his knees, and it isn't
even finished! The last sweater Tess knitted
for Paul was so big he didn't grow into it for
three years. He will have to grow fast
to catch up with this one!

207

gnash   sign
gnat
gnaw

NO GNATS ALLOWED

"I'd like sitting out here on the lawn,"
said Beth, "if it weren't for those nasty gnats."

"And I'd like lying in this hammock," said
Nancy, "if those gnats didn't keep gnawing on me.
They just sit out here in the trees gnashing
their teeth until I get here. Then they say,
'Here comes Nancy. Time for dinner!'"

"How can we get rid of them?" Beth wondered.
"They just love insect poison. They gulp it down
like soda pop."

"And they are too small to swat," said Nancy.

Just then Richard came along and heard the
girls complaining. "Put up a sign," he told them.
"Say NO GNATS ALLOWED."

"It wouldn't do a bit of good," said Nancy.
"I bet those stupid gnats can't even read."

208

wren	wrap	wring	write	sword
wrench	wrapped	wringer	writing	answer
wreck	wrist	wrung	wrote	whole
wreath		wrong	written	
			writer	
			typewriter	
			handwriting	

When Mom had a broken wrist, Sis did the washing, wrung it out, and hung it up.

SALLY'S WRITING

Sally's dad let her use his typewriter to answer the letter from her grandmother.

"Your handwriting is so bad," he told Sally, "that your grandmother won't know what you have written. She will spend all day trying to figure it out."

"My writing isn't that bad," said Sally. "My teacher can read it. She finds every word that is spelled wrong. I sometimes wish she had more trouble reading my handwriting."

209

lamb	dumb	crumb	climb	debt
limb	numb	thumb	comb	doubt

Mary had a little lamb.

Little Jimmy just hates to comb his hair.
His mother has to hold him down with one hand and
comb his hair with the other. He is almost as bad
about washing his face. And as for a bath—he
and our cat feel the same way about that.

Must you climb out on that limb, Jack?
We may have to call the Fire Department to get
you down from there. That's what we had to do
last week when our cat climbed that same tree.

George owes Pete five cents. George will
pay his debt to Pete, no doubt, if Pete can find
him.

Yesterday Barbara smashed her thumb in
the car door. Today her thumb feels numb.

May I have another slice of cake?
Just a tiny bit. I know I've already had three
slices, but I'd still like just one more crumb.

210

talk	talked	chalk	sidewalk	folks
talks	talker	walk		yolk

calf	calves	calm	almond	calmly
half	halves	palm	alms	

George raised a calf to show at the fair.
My hands are numb from the cold.
The teacher writes on the blackboard with chalk.
Let me see the palm of your hand.

The grocer wrapped up the package of almond
cookies, but the delivery boy took it to the wrong house.

When you write a letter, you must sign
your name at the end.

All of us learn to write, and some of us
learn to use a typewriter.

Can a cat climb a tree? Yes, cats are very good
at climbing.

Grace and Linda stood on the sidewalk and
talked until Jim said, "You folks will be
late to class." Then they stopped talking and ran.

210

A person that can't talk is called "dumb."

Sometimes we say "dumb" when we mean "foolish."

A wren is a very small bird.

Throw some crumbs to the birds.

Press down the tack with your thumb.

Can you climb this tree?

I don't doubt what you say.

He'll wreck his car if he keeps driving so fast.

Let's take a walk.

The yellow part of an egg is called the "yolk."

How are your folks?

Look at that cute, funny calf!

Let's make a wreath of these flowers.

A rat gnawed a hole in the wall.

THE MONKEY WRENCH

"Where is my wrench?" asked Dad.

"I never use it," said Mother, "and I haven't even seen it lately."

"Is this it?" said Sally. "I've been using it to crack almonds. But it isn't very good for that. You may have it, Dad."

hour	ah	scheme	ache	John	Thomas
honest	oh	school	headache	Johnny	Thomson
honesty	hurrah	schoolboy		Johnson	Thompson
honestly	ghost	schoolroom			
honor		schoolhouse			
		schoolmaster			

On my honor, I waited half an hour.
Have you ever seen a palm tree?
Mrs. Thompson leads the band at school.
John is an honest boy and very good in school.
Mr. Johnson had a terrible headache.

Next year there will be a new schoolhouse,
and Mr. Thomas will be the new schoolmaster.

JOHNNY'S SCHEME

Johnny had a scheme for scaring Anna.
He dressed up in a sheet. "Anna won't know me,"
he said. "She'll think I am a ghost."
When Anna saw him, she said, "Hello, Johnny.
Why are you wearing such a funny outfit?
Is all your clothing at the cleaners?"

212

often	fasten	castle	gristle	mustn't
soften	hasten	bustle	whistle	
	listen	hustle	whistler	
	Christmas			

Don't jostle me.

Are you often tardy to school?

Please lend me your knife.

We mustn't bother Dad when he is working.

Bridget fell and hurt her knees.

Let's put a Christmas wreath on the door.

If you don't hustle, you'll be late.

Drive carefully; don't wreck the car.

If you heat wax, it will soften.

Please run upstairs and get mother a warm wrap.

You didn't listen to a word I said!

I can't sing, but I can whistle.

Fasten your coat; it's cold out.

Let's make a castle in the sand.

When we have roast beef, we give Pal the bones and the gristle.

autumn	clothes	scene	scissors
column		scent	science
		muscle	

We can't always have new clothes.

John writes a column for the school paper.

Can you whistle a tune?

George likes books about science.

In autumn the trees shed their leaves.

Just listen to that kitten purr!

Please bring me a pair of scissors.

Dogs have a very keen scent.

Those football players have strong muscles.

Listen to what the teacher says!

Dick was whistling as he walked in the woods.

We must remember not to talk too much.

The bird dog stood still the moment he got the scent of the game.

The snow falling on the trees made a lovely scene. But the children did not notice it. "Hurrah!" they yelled. "We can get out our sleds!"

WHEN SALLY AND BILL RAN THE RANCH

Sally almost snatched the letter away from the mailman and ran with it to her mother. "It's from Aunt Ellen, Mom," she said. "Please read it out loud."

"Very well," Mrs. Thomas agreed. "But first let's open it."

As she was getting a paper knife from the desk, Bill came in. "A letter from Aunt Ellen? Maybe she and Uncle Jim are coming to visit us."

"I doubt it," said Mrs. Thomas, putting on her glasses. "They have that ranch now, you know. They can't just leave it to run itself while they go gadding off to the city."

At last Mrs. Thomas was ready to read the letter. "Dear Ruth and Al and Sally and Bill," she read aloud, "I know it has been a long time since you heard from us out Colorado way. We have been up to our ears in ranch work. Ever since Clem left us, we haven't been able to get another hired hand. It's a small ranch, but we need more help—"

"Mom," said Bill.

But Mrs. Thomas did not seem to hear him and went on reading. "The weather has been cool here for June—"

"Mom!" said Bill once more. Mrs. Thomas looked up.

"Mom, why can't I work for Aunt Ellen and Uncle Jim this summer? Why can't I be their hired hand?"

Mrs. Thomas smiled, "But, Billy, you've never even been on a ranch. And you're too young and too small to be a hired hand."

"Oh, no, he isn't, Mom," said Sally. "Not if he has me to help him with the work. We can each be half a hired hand. Put us both together, and they'll have a whole hired hand to help them on the ranch."

"That's a great idea," said Bill. "How about it, Mom?"

"We'll see," said Mrs. Thomas, and she went on reading the rest of the letter to herself. But later Bill and Sally saw her talking quietly to their father. Then she sat down at the desk and started to write.

"Mom," Bill asked, "are you telling Aunt Ellen and Uncle Jim about our good idea.?"

"Maybe they won't think it's so good," said Mrs. Thomas with a smile. "And besides, Uncle Jim has never even met you. But I'll write to them."

When Mrs. Thomas had finished the letter, she put an air-mail stamp on it. "You two cow hands can gallop over to the mailbox and mail this letter. But don't feel bad if nothing comes of it. Aunt Ellen and Uncle Jim may not want you bothering them."

Each day Bill and Sally rushed to meet the mailman. At last a letter did arrive. This letter was addressed to Sally and Bill.

"We'll be glad to have you visit us," the letter said. "And of course you can be a great help to us on the ranch. Let us know when you will get here. We are quite a distance from town, and we shall have to arrange to drive in and pick you up. We are looking forward to seeing you."

"Yip-ee!" yelled Bill. "Got to polish up my cowboy boots!" and he went racing away to hunt for the boot polish while Sally went upstairs to start packing.

At last they were on their way! And at last the plane had landed in Colorado. Shivering in the early morning cold, Sally and Bill walked down the ramp. They were trying to get a glimpse of Aunt Ellen and Uncle Jim behind the gates.

"There they are!" shouted Bill. Aunt Ellen they recognized, and they knew that the tall man beside her must be Uncle Jim. He looked, Bill decided, just the way a rancher is supposed to look. He wore blue jeans, a faded blue shirt, a leather jacket, and cowboy boots. On his head he had a battered Stetson.

"My goodness!" exclaimed Aunt Ellen as she hugged them. "How you children have grown."

Uncle Jim stretched out a big hand to each of them. "Welcome to

Colorado," he said. "We're glad to have a couple of fresh hands on the place. Hop into the old pickup."

Driving over the mountain pass on their way to the ranch, Sally kept sniffing the air. "What a lot of pine trees!" she exclaimed. "And how good they smell. It smells like Christmas all year round, doesn't it?"

"Just wait till we get back to the ranch," Uncle Jim promised. "Then you'll smell something even better. Your Aunt Ellen's hot cakes!"

In another hour they were sitting in the big ranch house kitchen eating hot cakes and enjoying the heat of the big iron stove.

When they all had finished breakfast, Uncle Jim pushed back his chair. "Well, I'd better go out now and milk the cows. I'm so late with my milking this morning those cows will think I've forgotten about them."

"Can I help?" asked Bill.

"Come along," said Uncle Jim, taking his hat from the hook. "You can both come if you want to."

"Yes, dear," said Aunt Ellen to Sally. "You run along too. We'll leave the breakfast dishes for a little while. This is my bread-baking day."

Sally and Bill followed Uncle Jim out to the barn. "We milk only four cows now," Uncle Jim explained as he milked. "That gives us some milk for our own use and some cream to sell. Most of our stock is beef cattle. They aren't here now. We drive them out to the range each spring and let them graze all summer."

"Won't we even see them?" asked Bill.

"Oh, yes. I'll have to ride out to the range to take a look at them next week. You kids can each take a horse and come along."

"Riding the range!" yelled Billy. "Oh, boy!"

At Bill's shout the surprised cow jumped and kicked at the milk bucket. Uncle Jim grabbed the bucket just in time to save some of the milk.

"No harm, Bill," said Uncle Jim with a grin. "And this finishes our milking." He opened the barn door, and the cows went out toward the woods at the back of the ranch. "We'll bring those cows in again this evening to be milked."

Then Uncle Jim said, "Grab a bucket," and he led Bill and Sally to a small shed. "This is the milk house. Just set down the buckets here. We'll separate later." Then, picking up one of the buckets of milk, Uncle Jim led the way to the barnyard. As they entered the yard, a calf came running towards them.

"Oh, the darling little thing," cried Sally and tried to hug the calf. But it pushed past her to Uncle Jim. The moment the calf reached the bucket, it stuck its head into it and began gulping down the milk greedily.

"He's got milk all over his head up to his ears," said Sally. "Now I know what they mean by a white-faced calf."

"Well, this one is a white-faced calf even when he isn't all covered with milk," said Uncle Jim as he pulled the empty bucket away from the calf. "Come along now and I'll show you the horses you can ride next week."

Surrounded by a rail fence were three horses. Uncle Jim went inside the yard. "You kids stay out there," he said as he closed the gate. He patted the brown horse. "You can ride this little brown mare,

Sally," he said. "And you can ride that white one, Bill. But stay away from this fellow." He pointed to a spotted horse. "He's a wild one. I got him yesterday, and I'm just trying to break him."

Sally and Bill patted the nose of the white horse, who had come over to the fence, and when they looked up, Uncle Jim was on the spotted horse. The horse was rearing and jumping and trying in every way to throw Uncle Jim off his back.

"Look at that horse buck!" yelled Bill. "Ride him, Uncle Jim!" Then before Sally and Bill knew what had happened, Uncle Jim was lying on the ground next to one of the fence posts, with his leg bent in an odd way.

Sally and Bill opened the gate and rushed to him. He tried to get up but lay back with a groan. "Better get your Aunt Ellen," he said. "I'm hurt."

From the kitchen window Aunt Ellen had seen the accident and was already on her way. When she looked at Uncle Jim's leg she shook her head. "We'll have to get you to the hospital, Jim. Bill, will you and Sally give me a hand?" Together they helped Uncle Jim into the pickup.

"We'll probably be gone quite awhile," Aunt Ellen told Bill and Sally. "It's seventy-five miles each way. And we can't take you along. There isn't any extra room in the pickup with Uncle Jim's leg like that. Can you children get along here alone?"

"We'll be just fine," said Sally.

"Don't worry about a thing," said Bill. "We'll take care of the ranch for you."

But Aunt Ellen did look worried, as she drove away so fast that the chickens ran clucking from in front of the pickup.

"Well, we're on our own now," said Bill importantly. "It's all up to us."

(To be continued)

214

caught	ought	straight
taught	fought	straighten
daughter	sought	
slaughter	bought	
naughty	brought	
	thought	

Bob's big sister taught him to ice-skate.

I caught the cat and brought it back to the house.

My father bought me a new cap.

Please make your bed and straighten your room.

You ought to help your brother chop that wood.

I cannot draw a straight line.

Frank is not naughty very often.

I've never seen such a long train as this.

I thought you'd never get here!

Mrs. Means has three daughters: Mabel, Helen, and Grace.

The cat and the dog fought with each other so much that we thought they hated each other. But when the cat got lost, the dog was sad and lonely.

215

high	fight	bright	highness	higher
sigh	light	fright	brightness	highest
thigh	might	flight	lightness	highly
	night	knight		
	right	slight		
	sight	frighten		
	tight	tighten		

highway	flashlight	delight	height
lightning	moonlight	tonight	heights
midnight	sunlight	overnight	
		mighty	

That ghost did not frighten Anna.
What is the height of that mountain?
This coat is getting too tight for you.
Thomas came in tonight on a jet flight.
It is getting dark. Please turn on the light.

This moonlight is so bright tonight
that we won't need our flashlights.

Johnny has a cut on his knee. It is just
a slight cut, but we'd better bandage it.

216

bough   plough

A squirrel sat on the highest bough of the tree.

We had a smooth flight last night all the way.
We flew quite high most of the time.

Write down on this card your name, your
height, and your age.

Andy Johnson's father has a farm. Each
spring Mr. Johnson ploughs the ground and
plants wheat and corn and often some other
crops. Andy helps his father on the farm.
He helps with the ploughing, the sowing, and
the harvesting.

Dad is going to cut the big dead bough from
the elm tree. It sticks out onto the highway and
does not look nice. He says we can help him saw
off the branch when he gets home from work tonight.
It seems to me like a mighty big job for this
evening. I think we'd better start cutting that
bough early some morning. I'd rather work by
sunlight than by moonlight or flashlight.

217

dough	though	thorough
doughnut	although	thoroughly

Tomorrow you must clean your room thoroughly.

Mother has made the bread dough and will let it rise overnight. Tomorrow she will bake bread. Probably she will bake a small loaf of bread for little Nancy.

A BIG HELP

"Let's visit Aunt Martha today," said George. "I know she'll be glad to see us."

"What makes you think so?" asked Linda.

"Because she's going to make doughnuts today. She'll be glad to have us help her," said George.

"Help her eat them, you mean!" said Linda. "Well, I like doughnuts too. I think it's a fine idea to visit Aunt Martha today, although I doubt that she needs us. Her own kids can do a thorough job of eating up those doughnuts."

218

through   throughout

NANCY WONDERS ABOUT SCHOOL

Little Nancy was going to start school
in the autumn. All through the summer she talked
about it and wondered how it would be.

"Will it be fun?" she asked Madge.

"Well, yes," said Madge. "You will have fun
at school. You will have to work, though."

Nancy thought about that for a while.
Then she said, "What kind of work? Sweeping?
I'd better take along my little broom."

"No," said Madge with a smile. "You won't
have to sweep out the schoolroom. Each night
someone sweeps the school throughout."

"Cooking?" asked Nancy. "I can make fudge."

"No cooking," said Madge. "Someone else
fixes the hot lunches. We seldom have fudge."

"Then how will I work?" asked Nancy.

"School work," Madge told her. "And that
is something no one else can ever do for you."

219

rough   cough   laugh

tough   trough   laughter

enough

You must not be rough with the kitten.

Tough meat is good for your teeth.

Have you had enough to eat?

Poor Florence has a bad cough.

See the greedy pigs crowd up to the trough!

Tim told us a good joke, and we all laughed.

It looks as if it might rain.

I'll have to stop and tighten my skates.

When you're through eating, we can play ball.

We did not see them, but we heard their laughter.

The car drove away, and soon it was out of sight.

My coat is made of rough, thick cloth.

Is the ice thick enough for skating?

Lead the horse to the watering trough.

I don't care if you laugh at me.

When you have read all through this book,
I'll give you another.

220

Phil	phone	photo	orphan	paragraph
Philip	telephone	photograph	elephant	geography
Ralph		photographer	hyphen	
Joseph		telegraph		

John likes to read books on geography and travel.
When we telegraph we send a "wire."
Someone wants to speak to you on the telephone.
If you can't come, Joseph, please phone me.
Here is a photograph of Aunt May and Uncle Phil.
Please let me see that photo.
Arthur Johnson's father is a photographer.
These children are orphans.

Nancy wants a pet, but her parents will not
get it for her. They say they do not have room
in their apartment for a baby elephant.

If a word begins on one line of print, and the
end of the word comes on the next line, we use a
hyphen.

Phil's teacher asked him to write a paragraph
about elephants.

woman could should would
wolf couldn't shouldn't wouldn't
wolves

I would do it if I could.
If I could help you, I should be very glad.
Sam's mother is a very good woman.
Would you mind if I opened the window?
Should this door be left open?
I know I shouldn't eat this candy.
Could you explain this, please?

A wolf is a wild animal. Wolves look like
big dogs. Wolves are bigger than foxes.

MADGE'S ZOO

Madge picked up the stray kitten and hugged
it. "Couldn't we keep it, Mother?" she begged.
"It's small. It wouldn't be much trouble."

"Oh, Madge," said her mother. "If you had
your way, you would take in every animal you
see—even wolves and camels and elephants."

"Yes," said Madge, "I'd like a young camel.
But right now I'll settle for this small kitten."

222

do	shoe	move	remove
two	canoe	movie	improve
who	lose	prove	movement
whom	loser		improvement
whose			approve
who's			

Who is at the door? Who's there?
Whom did you see at two o'clock?
I can't prove you're wrong.
You must try to improve your handwriting.
Let's get the canoe and go out on the lake.
I can't move this great big table.

THE CHECKERS GAME

"You may not be a good checkers player,
but I must say you are a good loser," said Mike.
"I'd much rather be a good winner," said George.

WHOSE SHOES?

"If you remove your shoes in the theater, you
may lose them. Or you might get someone else's."
"That might be a great improvement."

223

soup	wound	fruit	beautiful	view	suit
soupy	youth	juice	beauty	review	nuisance
group	Lou	juicy			
	Louis				

Fruit is better for you than candy.

The view from this hill is beautiful.

Let's review Lesson Six.

Tom has a new suit and a new pair of shoes.

Does that suit you?

These are certainly juicy apples!

Louis drinks orange juice every morning.

Don't make a nuisance of yourself.

Will you please help me serve the soup?

A large group of boys went on the hike.

Don't let the ice cream get soft and soupy.

George's father spent his youth on a farm.

Isn't my new bike a beauty? Yes,
it's a beautiful bike.

Oh! I have been wounded! I sat down
on a tack.

224

build	busy	pretty	hymn	sieve	women
built	busily		Sylvia		
building	business		sympathy	physical	
guilt			mystery		
guilty			system		
			bicycle		
			tricycle		

Let's build a house with these blocks.
Jane is as busy as a bee.
Sylvia likes to read mystery stories.
Who built this house?
Father has business in town today.
Where are those women going?
That is a very pretty flower.

When a dog feels guilty he puts his tail
between his legs.

I want to strain this soup; please hand me
the sieve.

Little Jimmy tried to hide his guilt, but
there was blackberry jam all over his face.

biscuit   mischief   minute   spinach
mischievous

When Mother wants to give us all a treat, she bakes a batch of biscuits.

OUR BROTHER JIMMY

Little Jimmy is full of mischief. He is never still for a minute except when he is sleeping. Grandmother says that Jimmy is the most mischievous child she has ever seen.

Just around Christmas, though, Jimmy acts like an angel. He brushes his teeth and washes his neck and eats his spinach. We think we have a different child in the family—not our mischievous little brother Jimmy. This year Jimmy is hoping to get a bicycle. Dad has already bought him a bicycle and has hidden it up in the attic. When Jimmy wants to know what is in the attic, we tell him it is none of his business. Jimmy is making it his business, though, to get into that attic.

226

field		niece	either	people	gasoline
brief		piece	neither		magazine
chief		apiece	seize	key	automobile
shield		fierce	ceiling		Louise
yield		priest	deceive		police
thief	thieves		receive		policeman
grief	grieve				ski
belief	believe				
airfield					

A thief is a person who steals things.

What are you going to sow in this field?

If you deceive people, no one will believe you.

You children may have two apples apiece.

Our pup tries to be very fierce, but he is so tiny that no one is afraid of him.

The thieves tried to seize the store owner and steal the cash, but the owner would not yield. The chief of police happened to drive past the store in his automobile and after a brief chase caught the thieves.

WHEN SALLY AND BILL RAN THE RANCH

"Oh, dear," said Sally as they watched the pickup out of sight. "I hope Uncle Jim's leg will be all right."

"Isn't it lucky they have us to take care of the ranch while they're gone?" said Bill.

"They'd be luckier," Sally said, "if they had someone else. Well, we can at least do the dishes. Grab a dish towel, Billy."

As Sally was filling a dishpan with hot water, Bill started to pick up a clean dish towel lying on the kitchen table. "Sis, look what's under this towel. Aunt Ellen's bread dough!"

Sally looked under the towel at the dough in the bread pans. "She didn't have time to bake it. And now it's rising some more."

"What can we do with it?" asked Bill.

"Let's cover it up," said Sally. "We just won't bother it."

So Bill got another towel from the drawer, and they started the dishes.

They were not quite through with the pots and pans when they heard a sound at the back door.

"Meow!"

Bill opened the door. In walked a big gray cat. It glanced at Bill; then it went over to Sally. She reached down and petted it. "Hello, cat. Come on in and visit."

"Meow," said the cat. It walked over to the icebox. Then it came back to Sally.

"What do you want?" Sally asked. But the cat just purred and wound itself around her legs so that she could hardly move.

After a while the cat gave a disgusted "Meow," and walked over to the door. Bill let it out.

When the dishes had been washed and dried and put away, Sally said, "We'll have to do something about that milk out in the milk house. If we leave it there, it may sour."

"Uncle Jim said we'd separate later. What was he talking about?"

"He meant we'd have to separate the milk from the cream. But we don't know how. So why don't we just put the milk in bottles and let the cream come to the top. Are there some clean bottles?"

A search of the service porch turned up two clean half-gallon milk bottles, two one-gallon jugs, and a case of empty pop bottles. Sally filled all these, but when she was through there still was a pail full of milk.

"Well, let's just stuff these bottles into the icebox. Then we'll give that pail of milk to the calf. It must be almost his lunch time."

"I'll feed the calf," said Bill. "That's man's work," and he picked up the pail.

"All right," Sally agreed. "But I'll watch." She opened the barnyard door for him to go through.

The moment the calf saw the milk pail, it made a rush at Bill. "Take it easy," said Bill, and he tipped the pail a bit for the calf to drink, just as he had seen Uncle Jim do it. Greedily the calf drank milk till the pail was nearly empty. Then suddenly it drew back and butted the pail.

Down went Bill with the milk pail on top of him!

Sally could not help laughing, but Bill did not think it was very funny. "Lucky that milk pail wasn't full," she said. Then she spoke to the calf. "You have no manners. No manners at all." But the calf did not seem to care.

While Billy was cleaning up and changing his clothes, Sally washed the milk pail. Then she decided to take a peek at the bread dough.

"Oh, dear!" she said and covered it quickly.

When Bill came in, he lifted the towel and looked, too. "That dough's coming over the top of the pan and onto the kitchen table."

"What shall we do with all that dough?" moaned Sally. "There's getting to be more and more. Soon it will be all over the kitchen and we'll have to wade through it."

"Well, bake it then," said Bill crossly.

"I can't. It doesn't fit into the pans any more. It won't even fit into the oven."

Scowling, Billy stared straight down at one of the pans of bread. Then he punched it with his fist.

"Billy!" cried Sally. "What are you doing?"

But Bill did not say a word. He just stared at the bread dough, which was sinking back into the pan. He punched the next pan of dough, and it did the same. Then he punched down each pan of dough.

When he was through, Bill covered the pans and strutted around the kitchen. "You just have to know how to handle that stuff."

Just then they heard another sound at the door—several sounds in fact: one loud "Meow" and three squeaky little mews.

"The cat's come back," said Sally, opening the door. Into the kitchen marched the big gray cat. But this time she was followed by three kittens!

"Oh, the darling little things!" cried Sally, scooping up one of the kittens.

Bill sat down on the floor and picked up two of them. Putting one kitten on each knee, he said, "I like this little yellow one. And this little black one."

"Mine's trying to purr, but I think it doesn't know how yet."

"My little black one is purring," said Bill. "The yellow one has its motor running too, but I think it needs new spark plugs."

"Mrs. Cat," said Sally, "that was nice of you to bring your family to visit."

The big gray cat walked over to the icebox and turned to Sally. "Meow," she said.

"Say!" said Bill. "That cat didn't just bring her kittens to visit. She brought them to dinner. She's showing us that she has more than one mouth to feed."

Sally jumped up. "I'm sorry, kitty." She got a big mixing bowl and three small bowls and filled all of them with milk from the icebox. As soon as she set down the big bowl, the mother cat began drinking the milk. Sally and Bill set down a kitten in front of each small bowl. Then the children sat down on the floor and watched the cats eat. As soon as each cat had had enough, it stepped back, sat down, and began to wash its face and paws.

"You cats are very neat," Sally approved. "Not a bit like that calf!"

But Bill did not seem to want to hear about the calf. "The cats have eaten now," he said. "How about us? It's afternoon already."

"I can cook some eggs," Sally offered. She opened the icebox. "But there aren't any."

"We'll find some," Bill told her. "I saw a whole crowd of hens around here."

"Yes, they're all over the place," said Sally. "Lets follow them. Then we'll see where they keep their eggs."

They watched the hens for a long time, but the hens just seemed to be pecking at gravel instead of being on their way to lay eggs.

Then Bill said, "There goes one!" They followed the hen into a shed. And there on a shelf sat another hen on a nest made of straw. As they came closer they could even get a glimpse of some brown eggs beneath her.

Bill walked up to the hen bravely. "Come on, old fellow. Let's have those eggs."

The big red hen ruffled up her feathers as Bill came near. When he reached for the eggs, she suddenly jabbed at him with her beak.

"He stabbed me!" cried Billy, jumping back and sucking his hand.

"No wonder," said Sally. "That isn't the way you talk to a hen. You don't call a hen 'old fellow'!"

"Well, I never spoke to a hen before," said Billy. "You talk to him if you're so smart."

Sally walked up to the hen, speaking softly. "Nice, pretty, charming, good, kind hen," she crooned, reaching for one of the eggs. But the moment Sally's hand got near, the hen gave a loud squawk, flapped her wings, and flew at Sally!

Sally screamed and jumped back. The hen settled back onto her nest.

"Say!" said Bill. "That's the way to do it. You make her jump off the nest once more, and then I'll grab the eggs."

"Not me!" said Sally.

"Well, there's another hen over there on a nest. Want to try that one?"

"No," said Sally. "That one's crouched on its nest, too, just waiting to spring at us. I really don't care for eggs."

"Well, I'm starved," said Bill. "We'll probably have to go out in the woods and live on nuts and berries."

"Oh, I just remembered. Those cows are out in the woods," said Sally. "Uncle Jim said they'd have to be brought in this evening. It's late afternoon now. We'd better go hunt for them."

"All right," Bill agreed. "It's quite a hike out to the woods. Let's get started."

When they got to the woods, Sally and Bill did not see the cows. "We'll have to call them," said Bill.

"What shall we call them?" asked Sally. "I don't know their names."

"I don't think they know their own names," said Bill. "They didn't look very smart. We'll just whistle for them the way people do when they call a dog."

So they whistled and whistled, and they said, "Here, cows. Come on, cows!" But no cows appeared, although they walked around and around in the woods calling them.

After a while Sally said, "Do you know the way back? I can't see the house from here."

"I thought you'd know the way," said Bill. "Everything looks alike to me here. I'm lost."

"Oh, dear," Sally groaned. "We may never get out of here. And it's starting to get dark."

"Oh, it's dark on account of all the trees," said Bill. "If we just keep walking, we're bound to get somewhere."

"That's right," said Sally. "Deeper into the woods. I don't care if we never find those old cows. I just want to get home."

It seemed as if they had walked for miles when suddenly Billy said, "I saw something move up ahead."

"Wild animals!" cried Sally. "A bear! Run for your life!"

"No," said Billy. "Come back. This looks more like a cow. In fact, it is a cow."

Soon they could see all the cows walking along one after the other. They seemed to know just where they were going, although they seemed to be in no hurry to get there.

"Let's follow the cows," said Bill. "Maybe they know the way home."

So Sally and Bill followed the cows. Whenever the cows stopped to nibble bits of grass, Sally and Bill stopped too.

"Does that grass taste good?" Bill asked a cow. "I'm so starved I'm about ready to try it."

At last they came to the edge of the woods. There was the house! They ran towards it.

The pickup stood in the driveway. In a chair on the porch sat Uncle Jim, his leg in a cast. "Here they are!" he called.

"Thank goodness!" said Aunt Ellen, bustling out of the kitchen. "We were wondering what had happened to you, after you took such good care of everything. I see that you did the dishes and punched down the bread dough—"

"We fed the calf and the cats, too," said Bill.

"After the mother cat mentioned it," Sally added.

"And you even went out to the woods and brought home the cows," said Uncle Jim.

Sally and Bill burst into laughter. "We didn't bring the cows home," said Bill. "If those cows hadn't known the way, we'd still be wandering around in the woods. The cows brought *us* home."

"Yes, Uncle Jim," said Sally. "When you have people like us on your ranch, isn't it lucky you have smart animals?"

227

any	anybody	again	guess	friend	Leonard
many	anyhow	against	guest	friendly	leopard
	anyone	said		friendship	
	anything	says	bury	unfriendly	
	anyway				
	anywhere				

Have you any money with you?
I can't find my cap anywhere.
Please tell me that story again.
I do not know anything about it.
In the dark, Tim bumped his head against the table.
Guess what I've got for you! Can't you guess?
Be kind and friendly to your guests.
We buried the dead bird under a tree.
Phil invited all his friends to his party.
My dog seized the bone and ran away.

We went to the zoo and saw Leonard the leopard.
He did not seem very friendly. I asked him if he
had eaten anybody lately. He seemed to nod, but
he did not say how many people he'd eaten.

228

reins	hey	weigh	eight
reindeer	they	sleigh	eighth
vein	grey	neighbor	eighty
	prey	neighborhood	eighteen
reign	obey		freight
			weight

John has a big grey cat.

What a long freight train!

There was Santa with his reindeer and sleigh!

Jane weighs much more than she did last year. She is not just growing and gaining weight as she should. Jane eats too many sweets. Yesterday she had eight almond cookies.

People who drive cars must watch the lights and obey the traffic laws.

Charlie has lived in the house next door to us for eighteen years. He is our neighbor.

When you drive a horse, you hold the reins in your hands. If you pull at the reins, the horse will stop.

229

soul   sew   broad
shoulder   abroad
                broadcast

THE SECRET

"Can you keep a secret?" said Joan to Betty. "Promise not to tell a soul?"

"I guess so," Betty agreed.

"Well, do you remember the talk I gave in front of the class when i got back from my trip abroad?" Joan asked.

"I remember. Miss Dean said it was such a good talk she wished more people could hear it."

"Well, that's my secret," said Joan. "I'm going to give the talk again. And this time I'll use the speaker in the office and broadcast it to the whole school."

"What a secret!" said Betty with a laugh. "You are going to broadcast your secret!"

Joan thought for a minute. "Come to think of it," she said, "that is a silly kind of a secret."

230

eye	buy	guide	island	aisle
eyebrow	guy		isle	

Susan got a cinder in her eye.
An isle is a small island.
A guide took us around the island.
Stand in the aisle, next to your desk.
Frances has brown eyes and black eyebrows.
Father sent me out to buy a newspaper.
Did you see the play called *Guys and Dolls?*
Alice and her folks live on an island.

Annie received many beautiful birthday gifts. Her father gave her a bicycle. From her mother she received a leather sewing kit. And her sister Mabel gave her a little purse made of reindeer hide. Annie says she is planning to have another birthday soon—along about next month.

When little Jimmy goes to a toy store, he wants to buy everything he sees. When Liz goes to a dress shop, she wants to buy everything she sees. Madge looks at everything, but she never buys a thing. She saves all her money.

231

heart	guard
hearth	lifeguard
sweetheart	

A JOB FOR CHARLIE

Bob's big brother Charlie is looking for a summer job while he is home from college.

"He has his heart set on being a lifeguard at the Twin Lakes Pool," Bob told Leonard. "He says that's a good way to get a beautiful coat of tan and get paid for it besides."

"Sounds like nice work," said Leonard. "I'd like to be a guard if I were older—and if I knew how to swim."

"Oh, Charlie can't swim either. But he thinks it would be a fine chance to learn—just sitting around at the pool all summer with nothing else to do."

"Somehow I have a feeling that Charlie won't get that job," said Leonard. "If he does, it isn't going to be very safe swimming at Twin Lakes."

232

finger	anger	hunger	jingle	angle
longer	angry	hungry	single	dangle
longest	stronger	English	tingle	jangle
	younger	England	shingle	tangle

Be careful; don't cut your finger.

Are you hungry?

Just hear the bells jingle!

The kitten got hold of the string and tangled it.

When a dog is angry, it does not wag its tail.

This month Tommy has not been tardy a single time.

Last summer Miss Smith took a trip to England.

In England and in the United States most people speak English.

Milly is two years younger than Nell and three years younger than Frances. She is the youngest of the three girls.

If you just dangle the bait in the water, maybe a hungry fish will grab it.

Max is stronger than Kenneth. But of course Kenneth is much younger than Max.

onion	junior	Daniel	Julia	convenience
million	senior		Celia	convenient
companion	behavior	William	California	
Italian	familiar		Virginia	
	peculiar		Pennsylvania	

Put plenty of onions in the stew.

Celia lives only two blocks from the school. This is very convenient.

William is a senior in high school. His brother Daniel is a junior.

California, Virginia, and Pennsylvania are all names of states. Virginia is also a girl's name, but few girls are named California or Pennsylvania.

JULIA'S LEMONADE STAND

William's little sister Julia is selling lemonade today. "I'll make a lot of money," she said.

"How much do you expect to make?" William asked.

"About a million dollars," she told him.

William laughed. "Not a chance!" he said. "You are drinking all the lemonade yourself!"

234

India	champion	obedient	curious	language
Columbia	Indian		furious	
Philadelphia	guardian	Muriel	glorious	
	Indiana		serious	
period		radio		

Are you joking or are you serious?
Isn't it a beautiful day? Such glorious weather!
Put a period at the end of the sentence.

Celia wants to visit her favorite aunt in Philadelphia. Though Philadelphia is quite far from Indiana, where Celia lives, Celia is going to visit her aunt next summer.

My dad was late for his train, and he was simply furious.

Is your dog obedient? Does he come when you call him?
Yes, my dog comes when I call him—if he feels like it. If he doesn't feel like it, he makes believe he doesn't understand my language.

235

sure	insure	issue	Russia
surely	insurance		Russian
sugar			

There will be a new issue of stamps next month.

Russia is a large country. And it is simply full of Russians!

Jane likes everything very sweet. She puts sugar on her oatmeal, more sugar on her apple pie, and I even saw her put sugar on her roast beef once! She claims, though, that she thought it was salt.

WAKE UP TO MUSIC

"Are you sure you can get there by seven o'clock? Seven is mighty early."

"Yes, I can surely get there. I'll set my clock radio, and it will wake me up to music."

"I used to do that, too. But the music always lulled me back to sleep. Now I use a loud alarm clock, too. That is my wake-up insurance."

236

ocean	special	commercial	ancient	precious
	specially	financial	sufficient	gracious
		social		
		official		appreciate
		physician		

Let's sing, "Columbia, the Gem of the Ocean."
William likes to read stories about ancient times.
When Aunt Martha is surprised, she says, "Gracious me!"

If you should travel to England or France, you would cross the Atlantic Ocean. You might cross this ocean by ship. That would take several days. Or you might cross it by jet plane in just a few hours.

Sally's big sister Julia is taking a commercial course in high school. When she has had sufficient training, she wants to be secretary to a physician.

When Helen's mother wants to give Helen a special treat, she makes rice pudding.

anxious	machine	mustache	Chicago
anxiously	machinery		Michigan

My grandfather has a grey mustache.
Chicago is a city on the shore of Lake Michigan.

My mother was very anxious because my sister Celia did not get home on time.

THE LITTLE PINK TYPEWRITER

For years and years, it seemed, Sally had wanted a typewriter. Last Christmas she had asked for a typewriter, but none appeared under the tree.

At last, when Sally was in the sixth grade, she received a typewriter as a Christmas gift from her grandmother. It was a beautiful little pink machine with a tan carrying case.

"This is just what I've always needed," cried Sally. "Now all the school papers I write will look just like a printed book. They will be neat, beautifully arranged, and all the periods will be in the right places."

Sally's older sister Julia laughed. "You are expecting quite a bit of that little typewriter," she said. "I've taken typing for nearly two years, and I still have problems."

Sally used the typewriter a great deal. First she wrote letters to all her cousins who lived in Michigan. Then as soon as school started again in January, she began to type all her school papers.

One day Julia looked over Sally's shoulder and said, "You have a word misspelled."

"Oh, this bad little typewriter!" said Sally crossly. "It misspells words all the time. I fight and fight with it. And the periods don't go into the right places either."

Julia laughed. "Maybe that's the fault of the typist—not the typewriter. Did you ever think of that?"

"Well, yes," Sally admitted. "But I had hoped I'd get a typewriter which could spell better than I can."

(To be continued)

238

nation	motion	action	mention	patient
station	notion		attention	impatient

In school you have to pay attention.
"Don't mention it" means "Don't talk about it."
"Our nation" means all the people in our country.
My dog can do tricks when he takes a notion.

When anyone thanks you, it's polite to answer, "You're welcome!" or else "Don't mention it!"

When Ned pitches he always first makes a funny motion with his arms.

Virginia and William had to wait at the railroad station in Chicago. Virginia was patient and read a book. But William was impatient and paced the floor.

At the last club meeting Daniel made a motion to have a Christmas party. Someone seconded the motion, and all the members of the club went into action to get ready for the party.

George likes movies with plenty of action. That is why he likes westerns.

measure	usual	occasion	garage	decision
pleasure	usually	occasionally	rouge	division
treasure	unusual			

Edna got too much rouge on her cheeks.

How wide is this table? Please measure it.

It's a great pleasure to see you.

Today we are having a bigger breakfast than usual.

Usually we don't have such a big breakfast.

Occasionally we go out for dinner.

This is a very unusual book.

Can you do long division?

When you bake, you should measure the flour carefully.

Have you read *Treasure Island?* It is a very exciting book about a search for buried treasure.

Julia is going to her first dance. She cannot make a decision about what to wear for this great occasion.

We shall have to stop at a garage to have the car repaired.

240

picture	mixture	nature	furniture
lecture		natural	adventure
manufacture	creature	naturally	temperature
	feature		signature
			literature

| pasture | future | century |

Put your signature at the end of the letter.
It is natural for children to play.
Stew is a mixture of meat and vegetables.
A toad is a funny creature, isn't it?

In the future I hope you will always be able to read easily and naturally.

Nature study is the study of plants and animals; of soil and stones; of wind and weather; of sun, moon, and stars.

Francis and Charlie arrived home late from the show because it was a double feature. Charlie liked the adventure film because he likes anything exciting. Francis liked the feature about life in the eighteenth century.

241

question	statue	actual	fortune
		actually	fortunate
		mutual	
		situation	

STILL MORE ABOUT THE TYPEWRITER

Sally kept right on typing all her school papers. "I get better grades," she told Julia.

"That's because the teacher doesn't have to struggle with your horrible handwriting," Julia told her.

"Actually it's because I can see my own mistakes better when they are typed," said Sally.

Then one day when Sally was typing, she noticed a strange thing.

"Oh, dear," she said. "I must have been working this good little machine so hard that I've tired it out. Now it's too weak to work."

Impatiently she waited for Julia to come home so that she could question her about the typewriter's peculiar behavior.

(To be continued)

242

soldier   cordial   education   gradual
             cordially   gradually
                                       graduate
                                       graduation
                                       individual
                                       schedule

RICHARD'S EDUCATION

Miss Johnson gives each pupil in her class a great deal of individual attention. Some days, though, Richard wishes she would not notice him.

Yesterday Richard was in a bad situation. He could not answer Miss Johnson's question. Actually he did not know the answer because he had not studied the lesson.

In one way, however, Richard was fortunate. Miss Johnson did not give a test that day.

Now Richard has put himself on a schedule to study at home a certain length of time each day. "Oh!" he sighs. "It is hard to get an education."

exact	example	examine
exactly		examination

THE TYPEWRITER AGAIN

When Julia got home she examined the little pink typewriter. Then she typed a line or two.

"See!" said Sally. "That poor little machine is so weak and worn out you can hardly read a word it writes. All the letters are too light."

Julia laughed. "There's nothing wrong with your typewriter that a new ribbon won't cure. I know you can't get along without that typewriter. So you go to the store tomorrow and buy a ribbon. Then I'll show you how to put it on."

Next day Sally bought a ribbon. Impatiently she waited for Julia to get home, but Julia had a job after school and was late.

Sally opened up the little tin box and examined the ribbon. "I guess anyone can put on a typewriter ribbon," she said. "I won't wait for Julia to get home."

(To be continued)

chocolate	guarantee	grandma
February	tongue	grandpa
forehead		handkerchief
pumpkin		Wednesday

THE TYPEWRITER (CONTINUED)

Though Sally worked at it through most of Wednesday afternoon, she could not get the ribbon onto the typewriter. There seemed to be any number of different ways to wind the ribbon, and all kinds of little slots and gadgets into which the ribbon was supposed to fit.

Sally wiped the ink off her hands with her handkerchief. Then she wiped her forehead, getting ink all over her face.

"Maybe I'd better send the typewriter back to Grandma," she said to herself. "Perhaps the guarantee covers ribbon changes." But she kept right on struggling, while the little pink typewriter seemed to stick out its little pink tongue at her and dare her to make him wear that ribbon.

(To be continued)

direct   perfect   envelope   route   Asia   syrup
directly   perfectly
direction   diamond

THE LAST WORD ABOUT THE TYPEWRITER

When Julia finally got home, she found Sally bent over the typewriter, muttering and scowling furiously. There were ink smudges on her fingers, her chin, and her forehead. And she seemed to be all wound up in typewriter ribbon!

"What are you doing, Sis, all tied up like a Christmas package?" Julia inquired.

"Oh, this mean little typewriter!" Sally complained. "I just can't get the ribbon on."

"I'll help you," said Julia. And in a few minutes she had the ribbon on the typewriter.

"Well!" said Sally. "At least we taught that little typewriter who's the boss."

"We did?" asked Julia with a smile.

"Sure," said Sally. "We taught him who's boss. And I guess it isn't me!"

THE PICTURE COUNTRY

Florence lived with her father and mother in a big apartment building in the city. The street where they lived was busy and noisy because of the trucks and cars driving past all day and all night. When Florence went downstairs, she was not allowed to go into the street because she might get run over. Florence and her playmates had to play indoors or in the hall or on the sidewalk, and even the sidewalk was crowded most of the time with people who were going this way and that. So there was not much for children to do. When Florence stayed upstairs at home, she was lonely, for she had no brothers or sisters.

Sometimes she tagged after her mother and bothered her, and then her mother would say, "Oh, Florence! I'm busy! Go and find something to do." But later her mother would pat her and say, "Well, I suppose you do get bored. I wish you could live in the country, as I did."

And she would turn to Florence and tell her about the way children live in the open country, where there is lots of space to play in and there are many things to do.

Then when Florence was just six years old, a strange thing happened.

One summer day the doorbell rang. Florence opened the door. There stood an old man with a long gray beard. He carried several big boxes and bundles slung over his back, and hanging round his neck he had an open tray with all kinds of things in it: pins and needles and ribbons and combs and little mirrors. He was going from house to house selling these things. When Florence's mother went to the door, the old man asked her if she wanted to buy some of his things.

He began lifting things up from the tray to show them, and telling about the other things he had in his boxes and bundles.

"I'm very sorry," said Florence's mother, "but I haven't any extra money that I can spend on things like these. I am sure your things are very nice, and I thank you for letting me see some of them, but I really can't afford to buy any."

The old man smiled and thanked her and started down the hall toward the stairs that went up to the next floor of the building. He walked very slowly.

"Oh, Mother," said Florence, "that man is very tired. Look at the way he walks. Maybe he would like to come in and rest."

Florence's mother patted her on the head and said, "That's right, child. It's a very hot day, and he has a heavy load. Run and ask him to come in and rest and have a cup of tea."

Florence ran down the hall after the old man. When she had caught up to him, she said, "Please, sir, won't you come in and rest? My mother wants you to have a cup of tea."

The old man said, "Thank you, dear," and went back with Florence. He put down all his boxes and bundles and his tray. Florence's mother invited him to sit in the big chair by the window, and then she made a cup of tea for him. While the old man rested and drank the tea, he talked with Florence's mother. They talked about the city and the country and how hard it is for children to live in the city, where there is so little room to play. Florence listened because she liked the old man. From time to time he looked at Florence and smiled. His beard and mustache covered his mouth, but the twinkle in his bright blue eyes showed that he was smiling.

When the old man got up to go, he opened one of his boxes and said, "This young lady, your daughter Florence, has been very kind to me. I wish I could give her a present. I can't do that, but I have a picture here that will please her. I will lend it to her for one year. Hang it up on the wall. It will give her a great deal of pleasure. A year from now I will come back and get it."

Then the old man got out a big picture in a wooden frame. The picture showed a great stretch of land with a lake or perhaps the ocean showing at one side. On the lake or the ocean there was a big steamship, and there were several little sailboats with men and women and boys and girls in them. At the edge of the water there were people fishing, and there was a landing place with some people just getting into a little launch to go for a ride. On the land you could see many things, too. There was a track with a railroad train steaming along, and you could see people sitting in the train, at the windows. The train was just coming to a station, and there were people waiting at the station—men and women and boys and girls. Beyond the tracks there was a big farm with men plowing and a woman tending to a herd of cows and children playing under the trees in an orchard. Another thing you could see in the picture was a road with motor cars and horses and wagons on it. In another place there were some soldiers marching along, with guns on their shoulders and flags flying. The top of the picture showed the blue sky with white clouds on it and a flock of birds flying and a balloon going up in the air.

Florence and her mother thanked the old man for letting them have the picture.

Then, when Florence opened the door for him to go out, he leaned down and said in a low voice to Florence, "Child, when you are lonely or have nothing to do, you can walk into the picture and let all kinds of things happen. You needn't be afraid, because nothing really happens. Whenever you are alone in the room, you can walk right out into the picture. Good-by, my child!"

When Florence's father came home that evening, Florence and her mother told him about the old man. Florence's father hung the picture up on the wall above the sofa and opposite the window.

"It's not a very beautiful picture," he said. "There are too many things in it. But the colors are bright, and it will entertain Florence to look at all the different things and people."

The next day Florence's father was away, as usual, at work. Then in the morning, Florence's mother had to go out marketing, and Florence was left alone in the apartment. She stood looking at the picture, and then after a while she remembered what the old man had said to her. The picture was up on the wall, higher than Florence's head.

"It doesn't seem natural that I could walk into it," she thought. "I wonder how I can step through the frame."

She stepped toward the picture and then she got the answer to her question. The picture seemed to get bigger and bigger and to reach right down to the floor, as if the sofa were not there at all, and Florence found herself stepping onto the soft grass at the edge of the orchard.

There she was, under the trees, with the children that were playing in the orchard! The first one to notice her was a girl about her own age.

"Hello!" said the girl to Florence. "What's your name?"

"Florence Smith," said Florence. "What's your name?"

At that moment Florence had a feeling that she wanted this girl's name to be Mary Ryan. Mary Ryan was the name of one of the girls she played with in her real life at home.

245

"My name's Mary Ryan," said the girl.

And so Florence played with the children and had a great deal of fun. And whenever Florence had a feeling that she wanted something to be a certain way, then that was the way it would be. One boy climbed way up to the top of a tree, and Florence thought, "He might fall down now, but I don't want him to get hurt. Anyway, he wouldn't get hurt, because the whole thing isn't real."

Then suddenly the boy lost his hold and came crashing through the branches and tumbling down onto the grass right in front of Florence. He got up and laughed and said, "It didn't hurt me at all. I just had a good tumble."

After a while Florence said to Mary, "Let's go for a ride on the train. The train will take us to the shore."

The railway station seemed to be miles away, down in a valley. But Florence and Mary walked just a little while. They went around some big bushes, and there right before them was the station. They went inside the station to the ticket window, and Florence asked the man for two tickets to go all the way to the shore.

The man said, "Two dollars, please," and there in Florence's hand were two one-dollar bills!

So she paid for the tickets, and she and Mary went out on the platform. Soon the train came in.

"All aboard!" cried the conductor, and Florence and Mary climbed into a coach and found two seats by a window. Then the train started, and the girls looked out of the window. They enjoyed watching the country and the people at the stations. When a man came through the train selling popcorn, all Florence had to do was to reach into the pocket of her dress, and there was a dime to buy popcorn.

At last the train came to a station at the shore. Florence and Mary got out and ran to the landing place. Two men dressed in sailor suits were just getting ready to take a party of children out sailing.

"I am sure they will invite us to go along," thought Florence.

Then one of the sailors turned around and said, "Come on, little girls. There's just room for two more in the boat."

Florence and Mary got into the boat. Then the sailors hoisted the sail and pushed away from the shore. As the boat sped through the water, the spray flew in the children's faces. How fast they went! They sailed far out to sea, and then they turned around and sailed back. When they got back to the landing place, Florence thought it must be nearly lunch time.

"I must go home now," she said to Mary.

Then she ran along the beach and thought, "Now I am coming to the end of the picture; I'll just step out of it and into our room."

She took a step or two, and there she was, back in the room, standing with her back to the picture. But now the picture was up over her head, on the wall. Her mother was in the room, getting ready for lunch.

"Well, Florence," said Mother, "where have you been all this time? Downstairs playing with Mary?"

Florence did not quite know how to answer her mother's question.

"Why, Mother," she said, "it seems to me as if I've been in that picture the old man lent us—as if I had been playing there, with those children."

Her mother smiled and said, "That's natural enough," and asked no more questions.

After that Florence was never lonely. Whenever she was alone at home, she walked into the picture and let all kinds of things happen. Mostly she played or walked around and looked at things.

Sometimes strange or frightening things happened. Florence could wish them to stop or she could let them go on. Once the soldiers came marching along the road. When the children got in their way, the soldiers caught them and took them off to prison. Florence let it happen because she wanted to see what the prison was like, and she knew that the things that happened were not real anyway. Besides, she knew that if she did not like the way things were going in the picture, she could always step right back into the room, and the picture would be just hanging up there on the wall.

No matter how long Florence stayed away in the picture, her mother never seemed to be worried or anxious. Her mother seemed to understand about the picture and to think that Florence's trips were quite natural.

That autumn Florence began going to school. She did not have so much time now to walk into the picture. Still, on Saturdays and Sundays and holidays she often went there and had all kinds of exciting times.

Toward the end of the school year, in spring, Florence began to bring home books from school, because by this time she could read quite well. Then one day her father bought her a story book. Florence liked the stories in this book. The next Saturday and Sunday when she was alone, she spent the time reading in her book and did not once walk into the picture. After the end of the school year, when she was at home much more, she spent more time reading than she did in the picture.

Then one day the doorbell rang, and there was the old man with his boxes and bundles and his tray.

"Oh, how do you do, sir! Do come in and have a cup of tea," said Florence. "I want to tell you what wonderful times I've had walking into the picture and playing there."

The old man smiled at Florence with his blue eyes and said, "I am glad, child, that you liked the picture. But I know you haven't been going into it so much lately. All the picture was good for was to entertain you till you learned to read. Now you can read about much more wonderful things than just the few things that are in this picture. In the future you will want books to keep you company when you are alone. You will not need the picture any more. So now I am going to take it and lend it to some other child who has not yet learned how to read books."

Florence's mother helped the old man take the picture down from the wall. The old man opened one of the boxes that he carried and put the picture into it. Then Florence's mother made some tea. While they drank tea, Florence listened to what the old man and her mother were saying. She did not understand all of what they said, but she knew that they were talking about books and reading.

When the old man got up to go, Florence went with him to the door. He looked down at her with his bright blue eyes and said, "If you should need me, I'll come to see you again. But I don't think it will be necessary, because you need never again feel bored and unhappy when you are alone.

"Now you know how to read."

ABCDEFGHIJKLMNOPQRSTUVWXYZABCDEFGHIJKLMNOPQRSTUVWXYZABCDEFGHIJKLMNOP

BCDEFGHIJKLMNOPQRSTUVWXYZABCDEFGHI

LET'S READ
Index

JKLMNOPQRSTUVWXYZABCDEFGHIJKLMNOPQRSTUVWXYZABCDEFGHIJKLMNOPQUSTUVWX

Index TO ALL WORDS INCLUDED IN WORD LISTS

The following is an alphabetical listing of all words included in the word lists of *Let's Read*. Inflected forms (plurals, past tenses, etc.) used in the exercises are not listed here unless these forms were introduced in the word lists.

Numbers refer to lessons, not to pages.

beck, 68
become, 184
bed, 27
bedroom, 189
beds, 100
bedtime, 180
bee, 72
beech, 73
beechnut, 73
beef, 73
beefsteak, 158
been, 115
beer, 74
beet, 72
before, 176
beg, 28
began, 127
beggar, 132
begged, 108
begin, 127
begun, 127
behave, 156
behavior, 233
behind, 181
behold, 170
being, 122
belch, 60
belief, 226
believe, 226
bell, 64
bellow, 172
bells, 100
belong, 166
below, 171
belt, 49
Ben, 26
bench, 60
bend, 46

beneath, 127
benefit, 128
Ben's, 102
bent, 47
berry, 146
Bert, 191
beside, 180
besides, 180
Bess, 63
Bess's, 105
best, 48
bet, 25
Beth, 61
better, 131
Betty, 145
between, 127
bib, 13
Bible, 181
bibs, 100
bicycle, 224
bid, 11
biff, 62
big, 9
bigger, 131
biggest, 120
bike, 178, 179
bikes, 179
bilk, 49
bill, 64
billboard, 117
Billy, 145
bin, 10
bind, 181
birch, 190
bird, 190
birth, 190
birthday, 190
biscuit, 225

bit, 12
bite, 178
bitten, 138
bitter, 131
blab, 43, 44
black, 67
blackberry, 146
blackboard, 117
blackness, 121
blacksmith, 67, 117
Blacky, 145
blade, 152
blame, 152, 153
blamed, 153
blames, 153
blaming, 153
blank, 56
blanket, 121
blast, 163
blat, 43
blaze, 152
blazer, 154
bleach, 76
bleak, 76
bleat, 75
bled, 43, 44
bleed, 72
blend, 53
bless, 63
blessing, 122
blew, 196
blimp, 53
blimps, 54
blind, 181
blindfold, 181
blinds, 181
blink, 56
bliss, 63

blister, 129
blob, 43, 44
block, 68
blond, 53
blood, 186
bloom, 80
blossom, 144
blot, 43, 44
blotch, 69
blouse, 95
blow, 171
blown, 171
blue, 194
blueberry, 194
bluebird, 194
bluejay, 194
bluff, 62
blunt, 53
blunts, 54
blush, 58
boar, 87
board, 87
boast, 86
boat, 86
Bob, 32
Bobby, 145
bobcat, 32
body, 146
bog, 166
boil, 94
boiled, 106
bold, 169
bolt, 169
bond, 46
bone, 167
bonfire, 180
bonnet, 121
boo, 79

buzz, 65
buzzed, 106
buzzes, 104
buzzing, 122
by, 182
bye-bye, 182
Byron, 182

cab, 7
cabbage, 205
cabin, 141
cabinet, 128
cable, 157
cackle, 135, 136
cackled, 136
cackler, 136
cackles, 136
cackling, 136
cad, 3
cage, 203
cake, 152
Cal, 8
calf, 210
California, 233
call, 164
calm, 210
calmly, 210
calves, 210
cam, 6
came, 152
camel, 137
camera, 130
camp, 50
camped, 110
campfire, 180
camps, 51
can, 1
canal, 123

canary, 159
candle, 135
candy, 145
cane, 152, 153
caned, 153
canes, 153
caning, 153
cannon, 139
canoe, 222
can't, 163
canvas, 119
canyon, 139
cap, 4
cape, 152, 153
capes, 153
capital, 137
caps, 51
captain, 142
car, 161
carbon, 162
card, 161
care, 159
careful, 159
careless, 159
carelessness, 159
Carl, 161
carp, 161
carpenter, 162
carpet, 162
carriage, 204
carried, 148
carries, 148
carry, 148
cart, 161
carve, 161
case, 152, 153
cases, 153
cash, 58

castle, 212
cat, 2
catalog, 166
catch, 69
catcher, 130
catching, 122
catfish, 58, 117
cats, 51
cat's, 52
cattle, 135
caught, 214
cause, 99
cave, 152, 153
caves, 153
caw, 91
Cecil, 200
cedar, 200
ceiling, 226
Celia, 233
cell, 200
cent, 200
center, 200
central, 200
century, 240
certain, 200
certainly, 200
Chad, 59
chain, 82
chair, 84
chairman, 140
chalk, 210
champ, 59
champion, 234
chance, 202
change, 203
chap, 59
chapter, 130
charge, 203

Charles, 161
Charlie, 161
charm, 161
chart, 161
chase, 152, 153
chased, 153
chases, 153
chasing, 153
chat, 59
chatter, 131
cheap, 77
cheat, 75
check, 68
checkers, 130
cheek, 73
cheer, 74
cheered, 106
cheerful, 137
cheers, 100
cheese, 99
cherries, 146
cherry, 146
chess, 63
chest, 59
Chet, 59
chew, 196
Chicago, 237
chick, 67
chicken, 138
chid, 59
chief, 226
child, 181
children, 138
chill, 64
chilly, 147
chime, 178
chimney, 150
chin, 59

dove, 185
down, 90
downstairs, 100, 117
downtown, 90
dozen, 185
drab, 40, 42
drag, 40, 42
dragged, 108
drain, 82
dram, 40, 42
drank, 56
drape, 152
draw, 91
drawing, 122
drawn, 91
dray, 85
dread, 197
dreadful, 197
dream, 77
dreamt, 197
drench, 60
dress, 63
dresser, 130
drew, 196
dried, 182
dries, 182
drift, 53
drifts, 54
drill, 64
drink, 56
drinking, 122
drip, 40, 42
drive, 178
driven, 138
drizzle, 135
drool, 79
droop, 79
drop, 40, 42

drove, 167
drown, 90
drowsy, 147
drub, 40, 42
drudge, 205
drug, 40, 42
drum, 40, 42
drummed, 108
drums, 100
drunk, 56
dry, 182
drying, 182
dub, 22
duck, 68
duckling, 122
duct, 50
dud, 24
due, 195
duel, 195
dug, 21
duke, 195
dull, 64
dumb, 209
dump, 50
dun, 17
dung, 55
during, 195
dusk, 48
dust, 48
dusts, 51
dusty, 147
Dutch, 69
duty, 195
dwarf, 164
dwell, 64
dye, 182
dyed, 182
dyeing, 182

dyes, 182
dying, 182

each, 76
eager, 129
eagle, 135
ear, 78
Earl, 191
early, 191
earmuff, 117
earn, 191
earnest, 191
ears, 100
earth, 191
easier, 148
easiest, 148
easily, 148
easiness, 148
east, 77
Easter, 129
eastern, 133
easy, 148
eat, 75
eaten, 138
eating, 122
ebb, 65
Ed, 27
edge, 205
education, 242
Edward, 132
egg, 65
eggs, 100
eggshell, 117
eight, 228
eighteen, 228
eighth, 228
eighty, 228
either, 226

elbow, 171
elect, 127
electric, 128
elephant, 220
eleven, 138
elf, 49
elk, 49
ell, 64
Ellen, 138
elm, 49
else, 95
elsewhere, 159
elves, 101
employ, 126
empty, 147
end, 46
ending, 122
engage, 203
engine, 203
engineer, 203
England, 232
English, 232
enjoy, 126
enough, 219
enter, 129
entertain, 134
entire, 180
entirely, 180
entrance, 202
envelope, 245
equal, 198
erase, 156
eraser, 156
Ernest, 191
errand, 140
error, 132
escape, 156
etch, 69

flay, 85
flea, 75
fled, 43, 44
flee, 72
fleece, 201
fleet, 72
flesh, 58
flew, 196
flex, 71
flick, 67
flicker, 130
flies, 182
flight, 215
fling, 55
flip, 43, 44
flip-flop, 43
flit, 43, 44
flitch, 69
float, 86
flock, 68
flog, 43, 166
flood, 186
floor, 177
flop, 43, 44
Florence, 202
flour, 89
flow, 171
flower, 129
flown, 171
fluff, 62
flung, 55
flunk, 56
flurry, 192
flush, 58
flutter, 131
flux, 71
fly, 182
flying, 182

foal, 86
foam, 86
fob, 32
fog, 166
foggy, 166
foil, 94
foist, 94
fold, 169
folks, 210
follow, 172
fond, 46
food, 80
fool, 79
foolish, 120
foot, 188
football, 188
fop, 33
for, 173
forbid, 175
forbidden, 175
force, 201
ford, 176
fore, 176
forehead, 244
forest, 175
forgave, 175
forget, 175
forgive, 175
forgiven, 175
forgot, 175
forgotten, 175
fork, 173
form, 173
formal, 174
former, 174
formerly, 174
fort, 176
forth, 176

fortunate, 241
fortune, 241
forty, 174
forward, 174
fought, 214
foul, 88
found, 88
fount, 88
fountain, 142
four, 177
fourteen, 177
fourth, 177
fowl, 90
fox, 71
frail, 83
frame, 152
Fran, 40, 42
France, 202
Frances, 202
Francis, 202
frank, 56
Frank, 56
Frankie, 150
fray, 85
freak, 76
Fred, 40, 42
free, 72
freed, 72
freedom, 144
freeze, 96
freight, 228
French, 60
frequent, 198
fresh, 58
fret, 40, 42
Friday, 181
fried, 182
friend, 227

friendly, 227
friendship, 227
fries, 182
fright, 215
frighten, 215
frill, 64
frisk, 53
frisks, 54
frock, 68
frog, 166
from, 40, 42
front, 183
frost, 166
froth, 166
frown, 90
froze, 167
frozen, 170
fruit, 223
frump, 53
frumps, 54
fry, 182
frying, 182
fudge, 205
fuel, 193
full, 187
fully, 187
fumble, 135
fun, 17
fund, 46
funk, 56
funny, 147
fur, 192
furious, 234
furnish, 192
furniture, 240
furry, 192
fury, 193
fuss, 63

Kate, 152
Katy, 157
keel, 73
keen, 73
keep, 73
keg, 28
kelp, 49
Ken, 26
Kenneth, 120
kept, 50
ketch, 69
kettle, 135
key, 226
kick, 67
kid, 11
kill, 64
killed, 106
kilt, 49
Kim, 14
kin, 10
kind, 181
kindle, 135
kindly, 181
kindness, 181
king, 55
kingdom, 144
Kip, 15
kiss, 63
kissed, 110
kisses, 104
kit, 12
kitchen, 138
kite, 178, 179
kites, 179
kitten, 138
kitty, 146
knack, 206
knee, 206

kneel, 206
knelt, 206
knew, 206
knife, 206
knight, 215
knit, 206
knitted, 206
knives, 206
knob, 206
knock, 206
knot, 206
know, 206
known, 206

lab, 7
label, 157
labor, 155
lace, 201
lack, 67
lad, 3
ladder, 131
ladies, 157
lady, 157
lag, 5
laid, 82
lain, 82
lair, 84
lake, 152, 153
lakes, 153
lamb, 209
lame, 152
lamp, 50
lamps, 51
lance, 202
land, 46
landed, 110
lane, 152, 153
lanes, 153

language, 234
lank, 56
lantern, 133
lap, 4
lapse, 95
lard, 161
large, 203
lark, 161
lash, 58
lass, 63
last, 163
latch, 69
late, 152, 154
later, 154
latest, 154
lathe, 152, 153
lather, 130
lathes, 153
Latin, 141
laugh, 219
laughter, 219
launch, 92
laundry, 146
law, 91
lawn, 91
laws, 100
lawyer, 129
lax, 71
lay, 85
layer, 129
lazy, 157
lea, 75
lead (*lēd*), 76
lead (*led*), 197
leader, 129
leaf, 77
leak, 76
lean, 75

leap, 77
learn, 191
lease, 95
leash, 77
least, 77
leather, 197
leave, 97
leaves, 101
leaving, 122
lecture, 240
led, 27
ledge, 205
lee, 72
leech, 73
leek, 73
leer, 74
left, 50
leg, 28
legs, 100
Lem, 29
lemon, 139
lemonade, 156
Len, 26
lend, 46
length, 61
lent, 47
Leonard, 227
leopard, 227
Les, 29
less, 63
lesson, 139
lest, 48
let, 25
lets, 51
let's, 52
letter, 131
letting, 122
lettuce, 201

pearl, 191
peat, 75
peck, 68
peculiar, 233
pedal, 137
peek, 73
peel, 73
peep, 73
peer, 74
peeve, 97
peg, 28
Peggy, 145
pelt, 49
pen, 26
pencil, 202
pend, 46
pennies, 146
Pennsylvania, 233
penny, 146
pent, 47
people, 226
pep, 29
pepper, 131
perch, 191
perfect, 245
perfectly, 245
perfume, 193
perhaps, 191
period, 234
person, 191
pest, 48
pet, 25
petal, 137
Pete, 198
Peter, 198
pets, 51
petted, 109
pew, 196

Phil, 220
Philadelphia, 234
Philip, 220
phone, 220
photo, 220
photograph, 220
photographer, 220
physical, 224
physician, 236
piano, 170
pick, 67
pickle, 135
pickup, 67
picnic, 118
picture, 240
pie, 181
piece, 226
pig, 9
pigeon, 203
piggy, 146
pigpen, 26
pile, 178
pill, 64
pillow, 172
pin, 10
pinch, 60
pinched, 110
pine, 178
ping, 55
pink, 56
pint, 181
pip, 15
pipe, 178, 179
pipes, 179
pistol, 137
pit, 12
pitch, 69
pitcher, 130

pitching, 122
pity, 145
place, 201
plain, 82
plan, 43, 44
plane, 152, 153
planed, 153
planes, 153
planing, 153
plank, 56
plant, 163
plat, 43, 44
plate, 152
platform, 174
platter, 131
play, 85
played, 106
player, 129
playground, 88, 117
playing, 122
playmate, 156
plaything, 85, 117
pleasant, 197
please, 99
pleased, 107
pleasure, 239
plenty, 145
plod, 43
plot, 43, 44
plough, 216
plow, 90
pluck, 68
plug, 43, 44
plum, 43, 44
plump, 53
plums, 100
plus, 43, 44
plush, 58

poach, 86
pock, 68
pocket, 121
pod, 34
poem, 170
point, 94
pointer, 129
poison, 139
poke, 167
pole, 167
police, 226
policeman, 226
polish, 120
polite, 180
Polly, 145
pond, 46
pone, 167
pony, 170
poof, 80
pool, 79
poor, 81
pop, 33
popcorn, 174
pope, 167
popgun, 32
poplar, 132
porch, 176
pork, 176
port, 176
pose, 167
possible, 136
possibly, 145
post, 169
postage, 204
postal, 170
pot, 31
potato, 170
pots, 51

rust, 48
rusty, 147
rut, 20
Ruth, 194
Ryan, 182
rye, 182

sack, 67
sad, 3
sadden, 138
sadness, 121
safe, 152, 154
safer, 154
safest, 154
safety, 155
sag, 5
sage, 203
said, 115, 227
sail, 83
sailboat, 86, 117
sailed, 106
sailor, 132
sails, 100
saint, 82
sake, 152
Sal, 8
salad, 119
salary, 149
sale, 152, 153
sales, 153
salesman, 156
Sally, 145
salt, 164
Sam, 6
same, 152
sample, 135
San Francisco, 202

sand, 46
sandbox, 71
sandwich, 60, 118
sandy, 147
Sandy, 145
sang, 55
sank, 56
Santa Claus, 128
sap, 4
sash, 58
sat, 2
satellite, 180
satin, 141
satisfactory, 149
Saturday, 151
saucer, 200
sausage, 204
savage, 204
save, 152, 153
saved, 153
saver, 154
saves, 153
saving, 153
saw, 91
Sawyer, 129
say, 85
says, 115, 227
scab, 37, 39
scale, 152, 153
scaled, 153
scales, 153
scaling, 153
scamp, 53
scamps, 54
scan, 37, 39
scant, 53
scar, 161
scarce, 201

scare, 159
scared, 159
scarf, 161
scat, 37, 39
scatter, 131
scene, 213
scent, 213
schedule, 242
scheme, 211
school, 211
schoolboy, 211
schoolhouse, 211
schoolmaster, 211
schoolroom, 211
science, 213
scissors, 213
scold, 169
scoop, 79
scoot, 79
scooter, 129
scorch, 173
score, 176
scorn, 173
Scot, 37, 39
Scotch, 69
scour, 89
scout, 88
scow, 90
scowl, 90
scram, 41, 42
scramble, 135
scrap, 41, 42
scrape, 152
scraper, 154
scratch, 69
scratched, 110
scrawl, 91
scream, 77

screech, 73
screen, 73
screw, 196
scrip, 41, 42
scrub, 41, 42
scrubbing, 122
scruff, 62
scuff, 62
scum, 37, 39
sea, 75
seal, 76
seam, 77
search, 191
season, 139
seat, 75
second, 140
secret, 198
secretary, 159
sect, 50
see, 72
seed, 72
seeing, 122
seek, 73
seem, 73
seen, 73
seep, 73
seesaw, 91, 118
seize, 226
seldom, 144
self, 49
selfish, 120
sell, 64
semester, 134
send, 46
senior, 233
sense, 95
sent, 47
sentence, 202

stammer, 131
stamp, 53
stamps, 54
Stan, 38, 39
stand, 53
standard, 132
stank, 56
star, 161
starch, 161
stare, 159
start, 161
starve, 161
stash, 58
state, 152
station, 238
statue, 241
stay, 85
staying, 122
steady, 197
steak, 158
steaks, 158
steal, 76
steam, 77
steamboat, 86, 117
steamer, 129
steamship, 117
steel, 73
steep, 73
steeper, 129
steer, 74
stem, 38, 39
step, 38, 39
stepmother, 184
stern, 191
Stetson, 139
Steve, 198
Steven, 198
stew, 196

stick, 67
sticker, 130
sticky, 147
stiff, 62
stiffer, 130
still, 64
stillness, 121
sting, 55
stink, 56
stint, 53
stints, 54
stir, 190
stitch, 69
stock, 68
stocking, 122
stole, 167
stone, 167
stood, 188
stool, 79
stoop, 79
stop, 38, 39
stopper, 131
stopping, 122
store, 176
stork, 173
storm, 173
stormy, 174
story, 176
stout, 88
stove, 167
straight, 214
straighten, 214
strain, 82
strand, 53
strange, 203
stranger, 203
strap, 41, 42
straw, 91

strawberry, 146
stray, 85
streak, 76
stream, 77
street, 72
strength, 61
stress, 63
stretch, 69
strew, 196
strict, 53
strife, 178
strike, 178
string, 55
strip, 41, 42
stripe, 178
stroke, 167
stroll, 169
strong, 166
stronger, 232
strop, 41, 42
struck, 68
struggle, 135
strum, 41, 42
strung, 55
strut, 41, 42
Stuart, 195
stub, 38, 39
stubbed, 108
stuck, 68
stud, 38, 39
student, 195
studied, 148
studies, 148
study, 148
stuff, 62
stumble, 135
stump, 53
stumps, 54

stun, 38, 39
stung, 55
stunk, 56
stunt, 53
stupid, 195
stutter, 131
style, 182
styles, 182
sub, 22
succeed, 202
such, 60
suck, 68
sudden, 138
suddenly, 145
suffer, 130
sufficient, 236
sugar, 235
suit, 223
sulk, 49
sulks, 51
sum, 23
summer, 131
summon, 139
sun, 17
sunbeam, 77
Sunday, 151
sunflower, 134
sung, 55
sunk, 56
sunlight, 215
sunny, 147
sunset, 25, 117
sunshine, 180
sup, 19
supper, 131
support, 176
suppose, 170
sups, 51

who's, 222
whose, 222
why, 182
whys, 182
wick, 67
wicked, 120
wide, 178
width, 61
wife, 178, 179
wig, 9
wiggle, 135
wild, 181
wildcat, 181
will, 64
William, 233
Willie, 150
willing, 122
willow, 172
Willy, 150
Wilma, 119
wilt, 49
win, 10
winch, 60
wind (wind), 46
wind (wind), 181
windmill, 64, 117
window, 172
windy, 147
wine, 178
wing, 55
wink, 56
winked, 110
winner, 131
Winnie, 150
winter, 129
wipe, 178, 179
wiped, 179
wipes, 179

wiping, 179
wire, 178, 179
wired, 179
wires, 179
wiring, 179
Wisconsin, 141
wisdom, 144
wise, 178, 179
wiser, 179
wisest, 179
wish, 58
wishbone, 168
wished, 110
wishes, 104
wisp, 48
wit, 12
witch, 69
with, 98
withdraw, 126
wither, 130
within, 126
without, 98, 126
wives, 178, 179
wizard, 132
woke, 167
wolf, 221
wolves, 221
woman, 221
women, 224
won, 183
wonder, 183
wonderful, 183
won't, 169
woo, 79
wood, 188
wooden, 188
woods, 188
woof, 80

wool, 188
woolen, 188
word, 191
wore, 176
work, 191
world, 191
worm, 191
worn, 176
worry, 191
worse, 191
worship, 191
worst, 191
worth, 191
wot, 31
would, 221
wouldn't, 221
wound (wound), 88
wound (woond), 223
wrap, 208
wrapped, 208
wreath, 208
wreck, 208
wren, 208
wrench, 208
wring, 208
wringer, 208
wrist, 208
write, 208
writer, 208
writing, 208
written, 208
wrong, 208
wrote, 208
wrung, 208

yam, 6
yank, 56
yap, 4

yard, 161
yarn, 161
year, 78
yeast, 77
yell, 64
yellow, 172
yelp, 49
yen, 26
yes, 29
yesterday, 151
yet, 25
yield, 226
yip, 15
yolk, 210
yon, 36
yonder, 129
you, 116
you'd, 116
you'll, 116
young, 186
younger, 232
youngster, 186
your, 116
you're, 116
yours, 116
yourself, 116
yourselves, 116
youth, 223
you've, 116
yum, 23

Zeb, 30
zest, 48
zing, 55
zip, 15
zoo, 79
zoom, 80

Leonard Bloomfield served on the staffs of the universities of Wisconsin, Illinois, Ohio State, and Chicago. He was Sterling Professor of Linguistics at Yale at the time of his death in 1949. Among his many significant writings, three stand out as basic to modern linguistic science, "A Set of Postulates for the Science of Language" (*Language,* II.3, 1926); *Language* (New York, 1933); and "Linguistic Aspects of Science" (*International Encyclopedia of Unified Science,* I.4, Chicago, 1939).

Clarence Barnhart is best known as the co-editor of the *Thorndike-Barnhart Dictionary Series* (Chicago, 1952-1971) and of the *World Book Dictionary* (New York, 1936, 1976) and *The Dictionary of New English since 1963* (New York, 1973).

This book was designed by William A. Bostick. The cover was designed by Don Ross. Photon Baskerville is used for both text and display type. The type is a slightly altered version of a face originally cut by John Baskerville around 1750. The type was set photographically by the Photon machine and printed by offset on S.D. Warren's '66 Antique finish text paper. The book is bound in DuPont's Tyvek cover material over boards. Manufactured in the United States of America.